THE COOL MILLENNIUM

by . . . Gerald Sykes

Prentice-Hall, Inc.
Englewood Cliffs, New Jersey

The Cool Millennium
by Gerald Sykes

Library of Congress Catalog Card Number: 67-16392

Printed in the United States of America

T17197

Prentice-Hall International, Inc., London
Prentice-Hall of Australia, Pty. Ltd., Sydney
Prentice-Hall of Canada, Ltd., Toronto
Prentice-Hall of India Private Ltd., New Delhi
Prentice-Hall of Japan, Inc., Tokyo

To Trofimov, Lopakhin and Nellie

CONTENTS

	Notice	viii
1	OVERTURE: UNOFFICIAL AMERICAN AID TO FRANCE	1
2	ON FINDING ANCIENT ENEMIES IN A MODERN BED	18
3	FEAR OF THE MARKETPLACE	35
4	THE OVERSTUFFED VOID	53
5	AZTEC INTO AZTECH	62
6	HEALTH (PARTICIPATION)	71
7	SICKNESS (WITHDRAWAL)	83
8	THE RAINCOAT MIND	94
9	AGAINST THE WEATHER	106
10	SACRED, REMOVAL OF THE	114
11	OTHER STUDENTS, OTHER QUESTIONS	124
12	SALVATION BY CHECKBOOK (USA)	135
13	SALVATION BY ART (FRANCE)	145
14	SALVATION BY TEAMWORK (BRITAIN)	161
15	SALVATION BY IDEOLOGY (SOVIET UNION)	179
16	THE NEW RULING CLASS	195
17	TERROR AND PLAYING IT COOL	208
18	WHAT CAN BE DONE FOR THIS WOMAN?	220
19	THE GRIEVANCES OF WEALTH	235
20	THE DEATH OF CHAOS	246
	Bibliography	263
	Notes	265
	Index	275

Notice

This book was written for students, exceptional students. The three persons to whom it is dedicated bear the disguised names of former students of mine. The first chapter was addressed to scholars on a specific occasion. Since they were all specialists who had trouble following one another's language, it was made especially easy for almost anyone to understand. Thereafter the book is for and about students, and describes the world they must face. Non-students are advised against reading it. The situation it presents has already encircled them, and is beyond their control.

OVERTURE:
UNOFFICIAL AMERICAN
AID TO FRANCE

1

In an opera house the overture is usually played while the audience is still opening stoles, collapsing tall hats, peering under red plush chairs, rattling programs or apologetically looking for seats. Torch-bearing ushers move like barely audible fireflies. There is a ceremonial scent of flowers.

A book cannot hope for so resplendent a hush of expectation. But a book can have an overture, and the overture can score a rather melancholy French horn against some tart American jazz. It can indicate some of the themes to follow. It can—

There is no more time, however, to describe it. It has already begun to play. Listen.

Man rushes first to be saved *by* technology, and then to be saved *from* it. We Americans are front-runners in both races. The United States led the world away from small wheatfields and toward big ones, away from outhouses and toward toilets, away from the virgin forest and toward the pulp mill, away from scarcity and toward abundance, away from few loaves of bread that were nutritious and toward many loaves of bread that are not, away from the peasant and toward the factory worker, away from the child of nature and toward the quiz kid. Now a few Americans want to go, not in the other direction, but toward an intelligent use of their new advantages that permits them to find abundance in their personal lives, lives that have not been processed out of genuineness or fulfillment. It seems like a reasonable wish. Actually, it is a presumptuous wish, which may never be granted, even to the most intelligent. The snags in the zipper of progress are not so easily unsnarled.

The effect of advanced technology on human beings is better observed in the United States than anywhere else, because Americans have been exposed to it more nakedly, more eagerly, more rewardedly than anyone else. This effect becomes clear when relatively traditionless Americans are compared with the citizens of a highly traditional country, the French. Some years of residence in France have permitted me to observe a few of the differences. Also, I have recently read a French book on the subject, *The Technological Society* by Jacques Ellul. The difference between Monsieur Ellul's approach and my own will perhaps dramatize a fundamental difference between our countries on an important question. The question is this: what happens to people when they are highly technicized, spared much of the drudgery of the past and given opportunities that their ancestors never dreamed of? What has already happened to the Americans? What may happen to the French?

My answer, in brief, is that most people relish their opportunities and do not ask difficult questions about them. The vast majority are as pleased and as thoughtless as a child with a candy bar. A few of them, however, look for ways to be saved from their savior. And then they, too, are offered a new salvation by the many. And most of the specially gifted few accept it. And this American drama may very well be restaged in France.

Ellul's book formulates a social philosophy of our present technological civilization. Its thesis is that modern technology is, or soon will be (unless we consciously prevent it), quite autonomous. Its discernible direction can rarely be reconciled with human values. It gives every impression of having already gotten out of hand. Men have become the slaves of what was supposed to be their servant. This thesis, which was dramatized in Aldous Huxley's *Brave New World* many years before Ellul's book appeared, and since then has become the stock in trade of a great deal of science fiction, has been put by Ellul into the abstractly portentous language that sociologists seem to prefer. In the original French, many pages of it appear to be lecture notes rather than a *written* text, since they lack any verbs at all.

Ellul disregards the effect of technology on specific human beings. "It is not possible for me to treat the individual sphere," he writes, and when he so much as glances at it he writes the most superficial part of his book, the latter part. By training, by temperament, above all by experience—or lack of it—he is better equipped to construct a *Grand Guignol* horror story of new social developments that we Americans know at firsthand. His book is almost a melodramatic tale of "no exit" from irresistible mechanization. The truth, as actually lived by Americans, is more horrible, more interesting and more resistible. A few Americans are already resisting it. Their resistance may fail, but it exists, and this symposium, which would never have taken place anywhere else, is part of its existence. Americans have not been protected against improved technique by traditional culture. They have been uprooted, in a manner that has not yet been put into the language of ideology, by the real revolution of our time, and they have had to develop insights and resources that are quite new. There are no new ethical dilemmas in the Ellul book. There are many of them in every American's life.

One of the new ethical dilemmas is this: the American can now have more power than he or his ancestors ever had before (not abstract power such as presidents wield, but the concrete kind that most people prefer) power to cure disease, to make love with impunity, to live longer, to be rich, to travel, to acquire more knowledge, to transform oneself from provincial to world citizen, at least in information. But if the American obtains this new power—and it is all but impossible for him, if he has talent, to avoid obtaining it—a social demand will be put upon him. He will be required (all quite impersonally of course: no pact between Faust and Mephistopheles, or anything medieval like that) to use symbols—verbal symbols, words—in a way that his society desires. His society is committed to turnover, to production and to consumption in ever-increasing amounts. And words are more important now to turnover than things. Merchandising is of greater value to the economy than manufacture, which can be turned over to robots or semi-robots. Craftsmanship has become vestigial.

The gifted American, then, must learn how to merchan-

dise his talents. His talents must be bought, or else he will
"starve"—that is, get enough to eat perhaps but share none of
the prestige or excitement of the new society. Today we do not
live Platonically off slave labor, or Benedictinely on a feudal
farm or Jeffersonianly next door to wilderness; we live "Madi-
sonianly" by the sale of our wits. And our wits must be pack-
aged attractively—even in universities—or they go unnoticed.
Our wits express themselves in symbols, but the symbols must
seem real if anyone is to pay real dollars for them. If this means
that symbols must be aimed at customers, at the worst and
weakest in customers so that a steady stream of real dollars
may be obtained (and it does mean just this, with mathematical
precision), we begin to understand an inherent ethical catch in
the new technical order, its obligation to rely on the *misuse of
symbols*.

     This catch is most obvious in politics and commerce, but
it also exists in art and science. In academic life it usually takes
discreet forms: excessive specialization, excessive avoidance of
value-judgments, and similar devices of shrewd hedging and
unnoticed secession from the concerns of other men. These
evasions of responsibility become inevitable as soon as morality
becomes social, not personal. In a highly technicized society,
morality becomes more and more social and less and less personal.
It is easier to fool society than one's inner voice, so long as that
anachronism remains audible.

     The trend of an impersonal, "autonomous" technology,
such as Monsieur Ellul describes, is to reward those who can
successfully lie to others, at least for a while, and also to themselves. Monsieur Ellul fails to mention this development in the
technological society, no doubt because in his protected innocence
he was spared any personal experience of it. In the United States
such innocence would be impossible. In the United States the
man of action has more unchallenged power than his kind has
had since the beginning of civilization. There is no prestigious
priesthood or sacred text, even secular, to dispute him. He can
only be corrected by facts, never by tradition or by criticism.
If he makes a costly mistake that can be avoided in the future by
getting criticism, he puts a critic on his payroll. He knows that
he needs men of thought because he gets his power now, not

through action, as in the old redhanded days of blood and guts, but through words, which he uses in any way he legally can. To use them effectively, he needs the cooperation of men of thought. He has discovered that things cannot be sold without the enhancement of ideas and the ornaments of culture. He therefore rewards men of thought when they cooperate with him, and fails to reward them when they do not. In nearly every case they cooperate, not because of coercion but because their lives, and those of their families, become more enjoyable when they do. They are admitted to the many benefits of the new prosperity—a second car, for example, or a first wine cellar. Few of the few men of thought are immune to such privileges. Indeed, it would be unhistorical to expect them to cling to their traditional poverty in an age which has made abundance part of its style of life. If he were alive today, Socrates would be expected to be at ease in the new Hilton Hotel in Athens.

The anthropological terms "men of thought" and "men of action" are used here to describe the present struggle for power. The men of action have it, but they need the assistance of the men of thought. The men of thought resemble the Toltecs who, archaeologists tell us, created the civilization of Mexico which was taken away from them by a cruder, more military, more commercial tribe called the Aztecs. The word Toltec meant master craftsman. The Toltecs originated Mexican architecture, painting, featherwork, music, medicine, literature, astronomy and a subtle philosophy that the Aztecs debased into barbarous witchcraft. If we add a modernizing "h" to Toltec, we get "Toltech," embodied by such men of thought as the poet, the physicist, the philosopher. If we add a modernizing "h" to Aztec, we get "Aztech," or such men of action as storekeepers, statesmen, chiefs of staff. The Aztechs have achieved unprecedented control over nature through the application of scientific methods they did not create. Like the old Aztecs, the new Aztechs took over ideas and skills that had been patiently produced over centuries by men of greater imagination but less practical capacity for leadership. Like the old Toltecs, the new Toltechs—the scientists and artists of our own day—must submit to the authority of a more primitive kind of man who happened to be on hand when thought to which he had contributed nothing produced a bonanza. His less sophisticated but more reliable skills are needed for organization, distribution and regularity.

The man of action, or Aztech, does not have to face delicate ethical dilemmas. He has his troubles, many more and much subtler than the man of thought, or Toltech, is willing to admit or even to contemplate. It is significant that social novels dealing sympathetically with "titans" or tycoons are no longer produced by good novelists, who on the whole have turned as narcissistic as good poets, because they are similarly preoccupied with a quest for identity in a time of drastic alienation. But the Aztech, though neglected as a subject for works of art, is not concerned with finding who he is, or with lamenting a time that has given him more undisputed power than his tribe ever had before. He has no delicate ethical dilemmas because he has also been given, by men of thought, a philosophy called pragmatism, This solves most of his dilemmas for him, not as Charles Sanders Peirce or William James might have expected, but on the side of an expediency that is to his taste.

He has encountered so few obstacles to his acquisition of power that he understandably holds contemporary men of thought in low esteem, except when they may help create such things as a rival to Sputnik, a theology to shore up the church, or paintings that offer social prestige, sound investment and tax deduction. The new prosperity, made possible in part by the thought of Toltech economists, such as John Maynard Keynes, has been so vast, so fast, so irrational—that is, dependent on mass purchasing that has been stimulated by appeals to subliminal factors—that newly rich Aztechs no longer turn to intellectual Toltechs for philosophic guidance. Thought no longer intimidates them. Nor do they hold any clergy in awe. They have cut themselves free from the forms of salvation that they inherited from their parents and their teachers, salvation religious or salvation secular, salvation by faith or salvation by good works. They respect all these earlier forms of salvation, but they save their real enthusiasm for a new salvation, one that they invented themselves.

The new salvation is the product of a new tempo, the extraordinary speed with which successful men of action must now operate. They want to do good works, especially good works that may bring favorable publicity or stabilize the economy that made them rich. But they lack time to go properly into the nature of the good works, so they engage experts to tell them which works are good and most advisable to support. And when they receive the best advice possible, they sign a check and feel better. It is the quickest and easiest form of salvation: no immersions, no conversions, no sermons. You merely put your name in the right place, and you enter the newest extension of heaven. If you don't happen to be a millionaire, you can also be saved. Smaller sums will also do the job.

Every nation has its own road to salvation. The new American road is salvation by checkbook. An earlier religious book has been superseded by the ingenuity of our time. Occasionally the new salvation leads to a mistake, but ordinarily it pays off. One of its better known mistakes took place in the Bay of Pigs in Cuba. The landings by anti-Castro Cubans in the Bay of Pigs were made possible by the signing of checks. They originated in the belief that something could be got for relatively little. Long-standing habits of easily bought success entered that decision. New habits of overhasty reliance on counselors also entered into it. Some foreigners offered to restore the Caribbean to its beautiful old submissiveness. Why not let them do it? Salvation by checkbook was offered us, and we grabbed it.

Not often does it work out so badly. Usually everyone is made happy; fund raisers, donors and beneficiaries. It permits the donors to go back to work right away, and they have to go back right away to make sure that they have lost nothing while they were out doing a good deed. More important, a pattern of incessant action is maintained, without the bother of painful thought. The Aztech does not have to face the swarm of doubts that might incapacitate him if he gave them the chance, doubts that might in an earlier time have led him in his middle years into a monastic life of expiation.

Lest the non-Americans in my audience derive too much satirical satisfaction from this latest Yankee contribution to religious thought, let me hasten to say that this kind of salvation may soon become international. It is like those appealing gadgets that almost simultaneously appear everywhere, once the need for them is felt. The speed of the impersonal technology that we are discussing here seems to have created a need for this one. Other countries cannot be expected to adopt this gadget literally; their customs and their tax laws are different. But they can be expected to adopt the state of mind that accompanies salvation by checkbook.

The United States is unofficially offering France, quite aside from its official economic aid, the new state of mind that goes along with salvation by checkbook. The evidence indicates that France will accept the new state of mind, and adapt it to its own purposes in its own way. I do not suggest that French wealth will suddenly become generous. I suggest that France is going to be Aztechized. It has already made considerable progress in that direction.

Offhand, France would seem the last country on earth that would accept so material, so vulgar a form of salvation. France is one of the few nations where the man of thought may still influence the course of public action. When I am in Paris I can read excellent men of letters on events in Europe, Africa or Asia, not the mass-dominated newspapermen whom I have to read at home. There I am among the most literary people in the world, trained to think well and write well. The French Minister of Cultural Affairs is a world-famous writer who gives intellectual advice to a President who has written history books with style. In his own person and in his ability to be at home both in the world of thought and the world of action, the Minister of Cultural Affairs dramatizes a new and necessary development in *la condition humaine,* a phrase that we have all borrowed from one of his novels. On the streets of Paris I pass children who seem to me to be getting the best education in the world, as an introduction to the most closely reasoned way of life that I have found anywhere. I pass craftsmen who love their work, their food, their wine, their talk, their women as my technicized compatriots can rarely be expected to do. The Toltech faith in craftsmanship and its attendant enthusiasms has not yet died in France.

But it is already under attack. Making things has become less important than selling them in such key industries as the *couture,* perfume, films, automobiles. The impersonal march of technique which Ellul describes so well has already changed the external appearance of France, both in the traffic jams of the cities and the electrification of the farms. Now it moves toward its next major objective, which is internal and is reached through the word. Technique operates by constantly improving its efficiency. Having altered things and places, it now seeks to alter, perhaps in more senses than one, man himself. How will this affect the French? What happens to faith in literature when it encounters faith in advertising? Is faith in literature a dead faith, a faith in inertia, an attempt to live off the spiritual capital of the great past without replacing it with real confrontation of self and society?

These questions lead to another: if the technological revolution should someday take essentially the same directions in France that it has already taken in the United States, what developments may be expected among the French people? Without attempting to answer that question, I shall list some of the outstanding effects of that revolution upon the American people and leave it to you to speculate on whether or not the effect on the French will be at all similar once they have been more fully technicized. Notice, please, that I do not say "Americanized" but "technicized." Each nation must adjust itself to the new blessings and the new drawbacks in its own way. Man wants first to be saved *by* technology, and then he wants to be saved *from* it.

Here are some of the outstanding effects, at least as I have observed them, of the technological revolution upon Americans. First let me speak of that little-known and much misunderstood class, the American intellectuals, the eggheads. Most of them no longer fear the technological revolution; they laugh at it. Since the war they have been permitted to forget the nightsweats that Fascisti, Bolsheviki and Nazis once induced in them. They have also learned to regard the hydrogen bomb as an unintentional blessing that actually protects the man of thought from persecution, so long as no one dares use it. The bomb has created many new industrial, military and educational needs for his skills. Moreover, he profits by the vivid presence in everyone's mind of death, which has long been his subtle ally in his transactions with the mighty. He has therefore regained some of his lost prestige. He has also acquired more money. He

can merge with the joyful millions, the happy victims of alienation, who are only too willing to suffer its hidden impoverish-
ments so long as it sends its manifest riches their way. He has
forgotten all about the *trahison des clercs* that Julien Benda
once described. He does not mind what Marshall McLuhan calls
"the servile role of the confidential clerk to the tycoon," so long
as he gets what he can from the new windfall. (Actually, he is
not always so abject, but this may do for a group portrait of
the opportunists in his class.)

When the windfall reaches France, will French intellectuals behave in the same way? Some of you will say no, and
others will say it would be unrealistic to expect them to behave
otherwise, and French intellectuals have already joined the
moratorium on truth, or misuse of symbols, that is a precondition
of learned affluence. To demand more of intellectuals as a class
would be to forget the stern logic of Spinoza, who reminded
us in the last line of his *Ethics* that all great things are as difficult as they are rare.

But let us look more closely at the effect of the technological revolution not on intellectuals, but on ordinary human
beings. In the United States the demand for greater efficiency
has produced, even in the man in the street, a capacity for
abstractive, technical thought because only by developing this
capacity can he share in the new wealth. Skilled labor might be
redefined as labor that knows how to shut out everything that
does not apply to the job in hand. Unskilled labor is that performed by a man whose mind wanders. The professional attention that long ago enabled the physician to see only the disease,
not the patient (until psychosomatics asked him to reverse the
process), has now been duplicated by every garage mechanic
or TV tube-fitter who wants to stay on the payroll. Don't bore
the mechanic with how you happened to smash your car. Don't
ask the TV man what he thinks of your favorite program. Both
of them have been trained to think only one thing: how to make
the job seem bigger than it is, so that they can charge you more
for it. No film director prepares his actors more purposively
than corporations prepare technicians.

This technical mode of thought is necessary to survival,
and it creates a mental vacuum. The technicized mind is drained

of folklore, of human interest, of lazy give-and-take, of everything that does not contribute to doing the job and, more especially, since the job becomes more and more foolproof, to getting the most out of it. The technician has to think fast. Time, as Ben Franklin said, is money.

But the vacuum that his work creates in the technician's mind has to be filled. Other specialists think up things to put into his empty mind so that he may buy their products, support their party or do whatever else they wish of him. This propaganda maneuver is executed so expertly that the mind of the public is now an *overstuffed void*. Most of its stuffing is put there by interested persons for reasons of their own, but one tenant of the popular imagination seems to be a free improvisation of the public fancy, a theological improvisation, a typical religious by-product of our age which might be called *the new supernatural*.

The new supernatural, which the new public mind has created on its own, is not an unmoved mover, not a messiah, not something mental. It *is* an expression of a new public awe and thus qualifies as a religious creation. Our awe has shifted from animals, from figures in paradise, from our own kind to the solid, practical creations of our hands. We have found a new supernatural in our own ingenious manufacture, or more exactly in the godlike powers that we unexpectedly and quite unconsciously have conferred upon it. Our technology, which started out as no more than a way to improve our material condition, has lately grown so much better, so profitable, so *marvelous* that it has produced technolatry on a level so profound that now it can afford to laugh at itself, as it does daily in the funnies and in science fiction.

Personally, I am inclined to believe that the French people will never be quite as technolatrous as we Americans. They have too many roots in history. There is a skepticism in their training that will prevent them from attaching excessive importance to mechanical improvements—except for a lunatic fringe which after all exists everywhere. We can only wait and see. In the United States children usually yield the new supernatural their only real awe, their only real reverence, and seldom shake off their primary allegiance to mechanized marvels.

Whether this will also happen to French children I cannot say, but I am sure it is an important part of contemporary religious life, as it is actually lived. Early worship of power repeats the Aztec debasement of Toltec subtlety into barbarous idolatry. It accompanies the new salvation.

A technical god sets up standards of perfection that mere flesh and blood cannot satisfy. Its first standard is that of eternal youthfulness, the closest human approximation to continuing immaculateness of form and fullness of vigor. Except for those committed to traditional standards of good and evil, sin becomes any capacity for growing old, infirm, or unphotogenic. Guilt still besets us all, but its post-technological form might be illustrated by what a woman feels when she can no longer hide the normal effects of age and childbearing. The new "other-directed" merchants, with the persuasive mass media at their command, take full advantage of her pangs of remorse, and of any other dupes who let themselves be ad-bullied into conformity with the criteria of mechanical perfection. The new salvation offers many opportunities to the new men of power, who with few governmental restrictions exploit it to the limit of their ingenuity. The effect of this upon artists is to make them secede, whenever it is possible, into wavelengths of sensibility where none but the lonelyhearts can follow them. The effect upon scholars is to make them secede linguistically into specialties where popular ignorance cannot disturb them.

The new men of power develop a *raincoat mind,* an almost instantaneous ability to shed any experience that does not seem profitable to them. They recondition their reflexes with a shrewd awareness of the uneconomic, the inefficient, the wasteful. They develop what Harry Stack Sullivan called "selective inattention," a refinement of Freud's censor. They tune out most of their daily experience, but especially that which, if they heard it, would disqualify them for effective competition. Self-induced deafness becomes such a source of additional power to them that it is imitated, in self-defense, by others who are professionally committed to open minds. Many artists and scientists follow the lead of businessmen when they discover that it has also become a disadvantage to them to remain vulnerable to experience. The now notorious effect of this upon the arts

and sciences is to make them prudent careers, rather than bold
voyages into the unknown.

To say that "the intellectual suddenly holds the whip
hand in society," as McLuhan believes, is to ignore the most
obvious fact about most intellectuals, who are only too happy to
play Toltech jackal to the Aztech lion. It also ignores the fact
that every new technical advance must in the nature of things
bring a new ethical dilemma for the intellectual, since power is
real and thought symbolic. Men who want power will misuse
their symbolic capabilities to get it. Men determined to make
the most of their symbolic capabilities will not settle for power,
and will take only as much of it as they need to keep alive and
able to function. They will *not* make their minds impermeable to
experience, however painful it may be.

As for ordinary citizens, an example of the power of
the raincoat mind is the American people's attitude toward the
war in Viet Nam which, except for the next of kin of lost soldiers,
they have been able to shut out with the skill required of those
who must do the rough chores of mankind. Were the French able
to shut out Algeria with equal skill? It is a question that interests me, since I spent two years in Algeria, but I cannot answer it.

What happens to highly technicized people with minds
skillfully waterproofed against experience? They obtain more
power than others. They know what they want, and how to get
it. They also get the prestige of success, and they grow extremely
competent in holding on to power, once they have it. They
persuade most others that everything that does not contribute
to success, and to an accompanying sense of spiritual progress,
is decadent. Their technical skill is not content to remain technical; it develops religious pretensions, and attempts to convert
others to its kind of salvation. Its pragmatic faith is more con-
vincing today to most people throughout the world than older
faiths of religious revelation or social teamwork or political
ideology—in spite of all outcries to the contrary. It creates more
awe, and it produces more results. It offers more to both the
big man and the little man. It also offers more to the man of
thought if he is willing to join, as he usually is, the "happy victims" of progress. The technical millennium seems to have no
serious opposition, and may well dominate the next thousand

years. It offers people more power, more safety, more comfort than they ever had before. They only need to follow the line of least resistance.

It has, of course, its unfortunate side effects. Let me recall a few of the most elementary kind. A materialistic way of life has had the paradoxical effect of estranging people from matter. We have grown more expert in controlling matter, and more inexpert in relating ourselves to it, whether it is animal, vegetable or mineral. "We have all forgotten what horses are," said Gertrude Stein. City dwellers weep when a documentary film reminds them that there are still trees and stones and running water. When they move to the country, their minds remain amid the concerns of the city—and have to—for reasons of survival. Sculptors with a special feeling for stone or wood or metal erect huge pieces of them, with a minimum of reworking, to remind us of what they look like. Chastened, we put up their oversimple work in public places. Dancers return to the earliest forms of bodily movement, painters to the simple enjoyment of color and prehistoric shapes. The neat commercial packaging of matter is making our sense of it vestigial. We are like a child who gets too many gifts and no longer plays with them.

Improved medical technology is making people themselves vestigial, at least in their capacity to relate to one another and make the most of the gift of life. Because we now lose so few of our kind in childbirth, there are so many of us that we usually think of others, and sometimes even of ourselves, in the abstract. All our humane perspectives have come to us from less populous times. Unless we can train our minds to think both statistically, in the new mode, and personally, in the old mode, our opportunities slip away from us, unrealized, and we lament them with curses. A great deal of our new art is vengeful bluster, or "masculine protest." The more tender-minded sigh for the day of small communities. Ecclesiastical authorities begin to change their minds about birth control. Physicists and biologists work out ingenious ways to reduce the gross amount of too-solid flesh that surrounds us.

In the reproduction of our kind we develop a new attitude toward the emotions that for centuries accompanied it. Tenderness is wilting before the demands of efficiency. Sex has become "the one green thing" in a world of steel and calculation, and therefore more desperate, more fearful of impotence. Hence in popular entertainment almost every song is a lovesong that expresses exaggerated altruism, and boys and girls treat it as a mere convention of the day, not wholly unlike the poetic conventions of the Troubadours and the Elizabethans. A romantic cover is needed against the psychoanalytic frankness that youth picks up very young. A quick grasp of motives is now required, even by the unlettered, as part of their technical preparation.

Women suffer more obviously than men from this change in the mores, which has attracted much attention from writers, but their justified feminine protests against technology are usually quieted with gifts made possible by its ever greater efficiency and ingenuity. The effect on children is to snap them out of childish bemusement as soon as possible, and into a juvenile sharpness that can win applause and promise advancement. They must make good soon; slow maturation is suspect. Scholarships go to talents that are readily negotiable in "the academic marketplace," rather than to more complex and more interesting minds that would take longer to ripen. Richness of gift becomes vestigial.

In the halls of learning, the raincoat mind operates as effectively as it does in the Stock Exchange or in Congress. When a colleague says something that might require a reconsideration of a scholar's ideas, the scholar often simply does not listen. Such conditions have always existed, but in the past they were subject to criticism. Now they are regarded as the best way to get ahead in a specialty, mere common sense. In such circumstances thought risks becoming vestigial.

In the arts the rewards of the new prosperity go to those who can make the prosperous believe that they are still having a full life, in spite of all they have shut out to "get where they are." This mythology is usually provided them by easy-to-read best sellers which subtly reassure them that all is well, the applecart still intact. However, an anti-prosperity novel or a "far-out" avant-garde painting may at times unexpectedly perform this needed act of symbolic restitution. Such a turn of events will cause rejoicing among the more adventurous pub-

lishers and dealers; but after he has become used to his new
share of the wealth it seldom makes the artist himself happy.
The avant-garde now nourishes so many hucksters and para-
sites that he has lost the faith in the avant-garde that formerly
compensated him for the public's lack of understanding. He no
longer believes, as his predecessors once did, that his vision will
be shared some day by succeeding generations. On the contrary,
he usually believes, as his professional statements make clear,
that there is now so much bad art in the overstuffed void of the
public's mind, and so much evidence that it will be followed by
still worse, that only a few can ever be expected to understand
the good art of our day. The advance guard is now in retreat.
Faith in it must be replaced by an undiscovered new faith that
will take the artist and the scientist into a new loneliness, grim-
mer than he ever knew before.

Originally there were no men of thought, only men of
action, hunters. It was after the comparatively recent discovery
of agriculture that primitive cultures began to produce a few
men of thought whom we now call *shamans* (a Siberian word)
or medicine men. Out of their talents, which were fostered by
settlement on one parcel of fertile soil (as opposed to the restless
nomadry of the hunters) and by a considerable increase in time
for reflection—out of their talents, which once consisted chiefly
of magical tricks to impress the slow minds of hunters, grew in
time the historical forms of religion, philosophy, art and science
as we now know them.

Men of thought have been the advance agents of
humanity's later evolution. They have won much prestige and
some power through their ability to awaken awe with such
marvels as astronomical predictions, guilt-fixing and guilt-
removing, dream interpretation, prophetic zeal, priestly austerity,
magical words, sounds and images and finally scientific discoveries. These latter have grown into popular inventions so
foolproof and so easily made that as a reward, all men of thought
have lost their previous ability, except in success stories written
for children, to awaken awe. They have been demoted to the
rank of servants of the very mechanisms, metal or mental, that
they themselves made possible. In the present struggle for power
they are no match for those who devote all of their time to it.

Both the man of action and the man of thought have received many advantages from our improved control of nature, but the man of thought has characteristically been the first to feel the *dis*advantages. His quicker imagination does not mean superiority, moral or social; it merely means earlier, thinner-skinned exposure to impending realities, and it calls for his kind of social action, which is to serve as lonely forerunner into the unknown. He cannot properly communicate his discoveries, however, unless he reestablishes a dialogue with the slower but steadier leaders of men, who must adapt his discoveries to the still slower masses who follow them. At present, on the whole, he avoids such dialogue, prefers to speak only to his own kind, and despairs of healing his alienation from society. The men of action are no less guilty of serious mistakes when they insist, as they almost always do, that the man of thought uncritically support their programs and provide words that will get others to support them too. Two kinds of arrogance, one intellectual and the other managerial, have been encouraged by windfalls to guide the legacy of progress towards a court of bankruptcy. To be optimistic is to be irresponsible—or deliberately dishonest. Hope is not impossible, but only after real self-confrontation. Man must now face his full complexity.

This is a situation, I think, that exists today in the United States. Will it also exist in France? If and when it crosses the Atlantic, how will it be changed? Whatever you answers, I think you will agree that discussions of technology must henceforth get along without schematic forecasts, shun the future tense and speak instead of what is happening here and now. If man is to be saved from technology, he will begin by looking at what it has already done to him.

ON FINDING
ANCIENT ENEMIES
IN A MODERN BED

2

One day after class two students came to my desk. Although they had other names, I privately thought of them as two characters in Chekhov's play *The Cherry Orchard*. The lean, melancholy, thin-haired, steel-spectacled one was "Trofimov," who is called a "permanent student" in the play, and drifts from one disaster to another. The plump, vigorous one, always well-groomed in a fashionable dark suit, was "Lopakhin," the up-and-coming businessman who finally acquires the orchard and has it chopped down to make way for a real estate development.

Trofimov said to me in a rush of dismay: "I know what my term paper will be about now! I'll call it *The Rat Race*. No, *The Chromium Maze*. You convinced me today. We're just as helpless as rats in one of those electronic labyrinths that psychologists build to see what will drive them insane. The same thing is being done to us. No, we do it to ourselves!"

Lopakhin told me with apparent enthusiasm: "I liked what you said today. You're right, there will be greater opportunities than ever from now on. Turnover! That's the word. If I had time to do a second paper for you, I'd write about the new plateau of prosperity."

My lecture had been called "The Takeover of Turnover." I had suggested that anyone who dared to set up other standards than those which aided production and consumption would probably be ignored. Even works of art and science were now judged by their contribution to turnover. Misunderstood genius had no value until it was "understood" and sold. And it was a waste of breath to decry so vast a communal trend. It was

18

more intelligent to try to understand it impersonally, without emotion; to examine its effect on others and on yourself; to study its weak spots; to study its strengths; to find ways of living with it; to compel the respect of its adherents (who were invariably less competent than they seemed because a public front claimed so much of their energy) by your own new achievements of suppleness and honesty. The test of your human resources was your group's inhumanity.

Neither Trofimov nor Lopakhin had listened. Both had simply reacted with Pavlovian predictability. A teacher could sympathize with the unreflecting despair of one and the unreflecting hope of the other; he could also wish for something better, less canine.

Yet neither of these students, of whom the reader will be hearing more, was stupid. Through what he called "the bulldog" in him, Lopakhin was able to maintain a C average in a course that must have antagonized him from the start because it attacked all his agreed-upons. Sometimes he wrote a paper that was worthy of a B. To my surprise he took a second course with me, despite his barely concealed distaste for the first, and most likely because he thought he should learn from his opponents—and how to refute them. (He planned to become a lawyer.) When I met him he was twenty years old. When he got his bachelor's degree he was twenty-one, and looked at least five years older. Determination had already underscored the premature lines between set mouth and extra-dark jowls. He could afford to expose himself to my ideas, which he sometimes indirectly, as if discussing someone else, described as "screwball," because he felt so secure in his own. He also needed some credits in the department to which I belonged.

Trofimov might have been an A student from the start, if he had not believed that life was unduly unjust to him because he had more sensibility than anyone else in sight. He did have talent, as his published work made clear, but it was giving him a hard time. During his first course with me he screamed so often and so hysterically, especially when I touched on the present trials of the artist (when he actually wept), that I remembered an offhand revelation, made to me in my office, that he had once been in a mental institution. He was twenty-four years old, and so fearful of "the marketplace" (a favorite expression of his) that he had still not taken his A.B. Yet when he wrote term papers or answers to exams he was a delight to read. All his better energies had been conscripted by the written word. With real intelligence he had read the authors whom I asked him to discuss, and analyzed them far better than anyone else in the class. I am not sure I understand him even now.

I learned a few facts about both of these students when they became involved with the same girl (actually, she was twenty-seven, and should be called a woman, though she looked younger) and she angrily discussed them with me. That happened toward the end of the second course and will come out in due time.

There are more Lopakhins than Trofimovs in college, many more. There are more Lopakhins outside of college, many more. The biological evolution of man—which, incidentally, a prominent biologist (René Dubos) assures us, will most likely remain what it is, since birth control will sharply curtail selection—presents the world with many more plump, practical optimists than lean, impractical pessimists. Doubt appears to be a biological luxury which the race can rarely afford.

The very preponderance of Lopakhin gives Trofimov important things to say, *if* he can acquire the far sterner disciplines required by a private view. Majority rule always leads to significant oversights, which only an oppressed minority can feel and formulate. The majority rules and forgets; a minority bows and remembers. In time the day of Lopakhin will yield again to the day of Trofimov, if he can convert his bitter personal animus into impersonal moral perception, or as we now say, if he can "grow up." In an age of anaesthetized surrender it is a big if.

Nevertheless higher education, if it is to be useful, must now put its emphasis on the negative, rather than on the positive aspects of our new prosperity. Education will be self-congratulatory and pointless unless it concerns itself, before anything else, with depersonalization, alienation and despair. About a thousand years off schedule, the millennium has arrived, and its social abundance, contrary to all expectations, prevents private abundance. Students everywhere, not only in the United States but in all countries, have greater opportunities and greater disappointments. Even the Lopakhins conceal many important defeats behind their carefully successful exteriors.

The disappointments receive little or no official recognition, but they are an open scandal, so real that they currently transform a once silent generation (and not only its soreheads) into a loud and at times a violent one. There is every reason to believe that the disappointments will grow more acute with time, and so will the riots. When the intellectual wealth of the past is spread before students, it does not necessarily awaken their admiration or their desire to add patiently to it; more often it awakens their fear that they are caught in a hopeless situation that makes them unable to give their own best to the commonweal. This fear is plainly visible in students today, and not only in the obviously defeated Trofimovs, but in the mechanical exuberance of the Lopakhins.

Because the pressure on *all* individuals (especially those who expose themselves to thought) increases steadily, it is not too much to say that soon universities will be judged by how rigorously they prepare the student in his search for a viable identity. Most of the job will still fall on him, but their traditional moral responsibility is to arm him with a personal culture that can be of aid in his war with a social culture that is now, as a prominent sociologist tells us, "against" him. If universities surrender to the *Zeitgeist* (as nearly all of them now plainly do, and indeed must do) they will relinquish their venerable prestige and be downgraded as surely as the clerical, legal and medical professions have been, whenever they have dodged their moral responsibility.

Not long ago the American student had almost as many illusions on Commencement Day as on the day he entered college as a freshman. For four years, education had spared him the worst about the world and himself. He went forth into "real life" with a faith that he and his classmates would soon clear up the difficulties that had been vexing his elders far too long.

Valedictorians rarely express such faith today, even in the land of opportunity. The occasion calls for an assertion of hope, and hope surges in sturdy muscles and flowing hormones; but the hope that comes out is more traditional than genuine.

The brighter student knows he cannot permit himself the unreflecting exuberance that satisfied his more naïve parents, even in the Depression years when they should have known better. Students of today realize they are in for trouble, and have been living with it since birth. The threat of destruction or something possibly worse hangs over them. The questions they ask are sober, almost apprehensive, as well as implicitly critical of their teachers. If an excess of animal spirits impels them to pranks, they give an impression of desperation or ostentation, rather than of simple fun.

In 1965 a poster appeared in New York subways, a plea against dropouts: "I quit school when I were sixteen." Someone wrote under it: "I went to college and I don't know who I am."

A new attitude has developed among all students whom I have encountered, because they are in the midst of a cultural revolution that has not yet been described in a way that helps them cope with it. They do not understand it; nor, they have reason to believe, do their teachers. It makes them feel that they live, not in the free world that most of their books and all of their newspapers still assume, but in a necessitous world that has fallen in on them without warning. Their situation seems at first incredible and unacceptable, but still they long to have it described in detail, as if it were happening to somebody else.

The new prosperity has so pleasantly and excitingly transformed the surface of their lives that they have not questioned it, as they would have questioned it had it been painful or dull. They take its many benefits—easy, generous loans and cheap travel abroad are examples of them—without asking what the catch to them is, until the catch catches up with them. The thicker their skins, the longer this takes.

When they complain of the world that has been passed on to them, are they merely spoiled? Do they have legitimate reasons for their rising cry of unpreparedness? What lies behind their compulsive "coolness"? What *should* their teachers be telling them?

The best approach to these questions, in my opinion, is through history—not recent history, however; they lie buried under that, and need a better perspective. They need an understanding of history that goes so far back in time that it requires the patient reconstruction of imaginative scholars: prehistory. More than any other period, prehistory illuminates our own neoprimitive times. Fortunately there has been valuable new research in it.

The new research rests upon the scholarly calculation that human beings, after hundreds of thousands of years as hunters, turned to agriculture not long before recorded history, and soon afterwards produced a more complex and a more humane social order. Life on collective farms permitted the release of a few specially gifted men (and women) from the demands of family and tribe. A new sorcerer-priest class came into being whom historians now call shamans and shamanesses. They were the first human beings with enough sloth at their command to respond to the world with some of the wonder it deserved. Through slowly discovered techniques of ecstasy and insight, these medicine men, usually healthy but sometimes not, usually honest but sometimes not, guided more prosaic beings into reluctant encounters with the sacred, the ghoulish, the dionysian, the prophetic, the unearthly. In time their wonder led to the arts and sciences as we now know them; but not before shamans had learned from their familiars the foxes how to withstand the constant murderous hostility of their natural antagonists, the redhanded hunters and warriors whom they slowly forced, through a superior hold on science, religion and magic, to share their power.

This brief glance at prehistory is needed for an understanding of the student's problems of today. Many scholars are now convinced that the bloody dialogue between these congenital enemies, the rude men of action and the men of rudimentary thought, produced civilization and the works of art by which our experts, safe in their museums, now measure civilizations. The killer king on a black Etruscan vase, cozy behind shatterproof glass, was born in the mind of a black-and-blue priest whose overthoughtful skull had been laid open by an angry royal stick.

The student is still caught between the misunderstandings of the men of action and the men of thought.

Wonder, extended by self-imposed austerities, opened the eyes of the shamans to fundamental questions—about mistletoe and woodpeckers, Venus and heartbeat—which still are being asked in our own time by men who no longer fast for forty days and forty nights. Wonder liberated our first seers from the necessary but narrowing concerns of their more brutal companions with enemies, children, beasts and crops. So began a cleavage between men of thought and men of action that continues to tease the classifying ingenuity of psychologists and sociologists.

The past century has witnessed the birth by book of many opposing types with which the student is familiar: the Dionysian and the Apollonian (Nietzsche); the tough-minded and the tender-minded (William James); the Prometheans and the Epimetheans (Spitteler); the extraverts and the introverts (Jung); the anals and the orals (Freud); the redskins and the palefaces (Lawrence); the viscerotonics, the somatotonics, the cerebrotonics (Sheldon); the towards-others, the against-others, the away-from-others (Horney); the tradition-directed, the inner-directed, the other-directed (Riesman). And now the present book, in an attempt to build a psychosocial bridge that is sure to be disregarded by specialists on either side of a chasm, comes on with still more types, the Aztechs and the Toltechs, drawn both from prehistory and from our own time, who look as though their dialogue will dominate the future.

Of the original Toltecs (Nahuatl for "master craftsmen"), an early Spanish chronicler wrote:

> Whatever they turned their hands to was delicate and elegant, such as the houses they made very beautifully, highly decorated within, of a certain kind of stone very green with lime, and those so adorned had a lime highly polished which was a sight to be seen, and stones also, fashioned and stuck together, that seemed like a kind of mosaic; with justice were they later called exquisite and noteworthy, because they possessed such beauty of workmanship and labor. . . .
> They were the inventors of the art of featherwork . . . the Toltecs had much experience in the qualities and virtues of herbs . . . they were also physicians and the best in the art . . . they knew all the mechanical skills . . . they were painters, stone workers, carpenters, bricklayers, masons, workers in feather and ceramics, spinners and weavers. . . .
> They were so skilled in astronomy . . . that they were the

The *palacio* of Cortés in Cuernavaca, cobblestones set in concrete, on a plateau that controls "a deepish, verdure-choked *barranca*"—the jawbreaker phrase came back from a guidebook when I entered the Indian-fighter's rough palace. Inside, however, I saw something my guide had failed to mention: a time-clock. It was hidden under a stairway, this mechanical spy, which had been imported of course from my own hated land. I had once had to punch just such a clock, when I worked on Tenth Avenue in New York. And now, as submissively as gringos, the Indio employes of the palace had to insert their timesheets into an unbribable machine which recorded, with a telltale ring, the exact hour of their arrival and the exact hour of their departure.

Efficiency had struck south of the border, in the land of *mañana*. Obsolescence was overtaking a thousand old jokes about peons sleeping off *pulque* under sombreros. Even Mexicans could not be lazy any more. The Protestant ethic had crossed the Rio Grande. Pepsi was replacing *pulque*. No refuge existed anywhere from the grey cog that turned, ever more exactingly, in the brain of an anonymous, impersonal, no doubt underpaid computer clerk. Before my eyes Aztecs were being converted into Aztechs, more bleachingly than four centuries before they had been converted, under the fierce gaze of the Conquistador, into Catholics.

What is more, their tan faces did not look unhappy. No, they looked fuller and more self-satisfied, with new gold teeth in their mouths and machine-chopped garments on their backs: first signs of progress. The despotism of the clock had already entered its benevolent phase. These victims of time-theft preferred their condition. Their historic passage from tribal solidarity to modern aloneness was being conducted with a mini-mum of pain—for a while.

They gave me a selfish satisfaction. Their gay, obsidian roller coaster, as blind as their unforgotten god Itzcoliuhqui, was just dipping into the Hilarity Hall I had known since infancy. Once again an American was reminded, as he had already been reminded in Europe, Africa, Asia and behind the Iron Curtain, that *he* was the senior citizen of our day and *his* revolution undercut all the others. These happy Aztechs would soon be imitating all the unhappy Aztechs I knew at home. I could

first to take count of and order the days of the year. . . .
also invented the art of interpreting dreams . . . they knew the
of the heavens and had given them names and knew their influ
and qualities. . . .

These Toltecs were good men and drawn to virtue . . .
were tall, larger in body than those who live now. . . . They
sang well, and while they sang or danced they used drums and
brels of wood . . . they played, composed and arranged cu
songs out of their heads; they were very devout and great orat(

Of the Aztecs, after noting that they sacrificed m
enemies ostensibly to make sure that the sun would rise ag
a modern archaeologist writes that they did this "simply f
political motives. To take their religious explanations of
seriously is to fall into a trap of state propaganda. Their l
formulae are shown up by one fact. The Aztec nobles were n(
themselves impatient to achieve the solar glory in whose n;
they were slaughtering humanity. Their lust for life equaled tl
desire for power. If they had really believed that the one ain
existence was to give up their lives, sacrifice would not h,
been limited to supposedly inferior beings, slaves and prisor
but would have been a privilege of the "elite." In fact, everyth
points to the conclusion that the Aztec lords, though brought
in the doctrine of Quetzalcoatl which taught men that in
perfection and spiritual sacrifice were supreme goals, had co
to think of ritual slaughter only as a political necessity."

The difference between the Toltechs and Aztechs is r
so black and white. Both the modern men of thought and t
modern men of action are incomplete in themselves, and ne
an education they will get chiefly from their opposite numbe
The nature of the extraordinary new wealth that they sha;
however, makes it possible for them to avoid the humiliatio
of the humanizing dialogue that might save both from the
characteristic vices. One of the most difficult of personal dram;
the fusion of thought and action, is being declined.

I became interested in the Toltecs and the Aztecs, ar
subsequently in the Toltechs and the Aztechs, during a trip
Mexico. It was in Cuernavaca, some fifty miles south of Mexi(
City, that I began to open my eyes to what was happening i
the country. Later I began to see how it affected other countrie

forechart every moment of their fever and their chills. Cholesterol and Cuba would dominate their nightmares. Soon they would be buying huge anthologies on alienation. Their progressively-educated children would need "help." They were dropping their neolithic mystery, and joining the rest of the world, or at least the world that I knew.

What do these Mexicans have to do with the plight of the American student? They introduce him to his own historical antecedents, to the kind of people who went before him. They begin a relaxed, interdisciplinary meander through the forgotten days of his fathers: a meander that will surely provoke a smile in the halls of learning, and end in an unprofessional pratfall between academic stools of known hue and respectable order. Nevertheless the meander must be made. Reality pays no heed to the cry of specialists; it gets more complex every day.

Some revisions of history disturb the present as well as the past. Darwin's apes brought few cheers from Victoria's men. (Or Buchanan's.) And recent research, with new archaeological mud on its shoes, although it clarifies not only prehistory but our own time and in all likelihood lights up the future as well, has met with similar resistance. Evolution, though accepted now in theory when it confines itself to African monkeys or Tennessee courtrooms, is still not enjoyed as a factor in our own lives. We still like to think we were born yesterday. It makes us feel younger.

Since modern shamans find it more difficult than their prototypes to achieve a passable balance of power with their modern antagonists and complain loudly that intellectual weapons they themselves created have been turned against them (nuclear fission, dialectical materialism, togetherness), they might logically be expected to look now and then to their prototypes for strategic hints in an unequal combat. On the whole, however, modern shamans avoid such instruction. The following statement will suggest why. It was taken down, by a scientific expedition to the Arctic, in the 1920's, from the words of an Eskimo shaman. It was plainly his prescription for the survival not only of his own kind but of the antagonists, whom he expected to serve as spiritual guide, despite their hostility to him. He said, "The only true wisdom lies far from mankind, out in the great loneliness, and it can only be reached through suffering. Privation and suffering alone can open the mind of a man to all that is hidden from others."

This idea, one of the oldest of all ideas, has been denounced by some good, modern minds as dangerous and revived by others as helpful. (It almost never appeals to students.) The debate will receive some attention in the present volume, which seeks above all to understand the complex, new relationship between contemporary men of action and contemporary men of thought, or as it calls them, the Aztechs and the Toltechs.

They might have been called the Horizontals and the Verticals, to indicate the direction in which each modern tribe seems naturally to move—earthward toward social adjustment or skyward toward individual fulfillment. Is self-completing Verticality, committed to sacred traditions of craft and honor, due for destruction by the leveling habits of the Horizontals? Yes, this book finds, in almost every case, and as effectively as the Aztecs destroyed or drove off the Toltecs. Will modern Toltechs learn anything from a book addressed specifically to them about their life or their death? No, it is most unlikely. Why write the book then? Because it is the most intimate (and far-reaching) question of our time. It touches each of us "where we live." And awareness of it might mean, for some students, nothing less than survival.

After all the proper qualifications have been entered to please all the proper literalists (there are no pure types, we are using metaphors, and all that), it is not too much to say that the Aztechs and the Toltechs, who symbolize the present struggle for power more completely than any other types, are engaged in a conflict that is more pertinent to an understanding of modern history than the conflict between the Americans, the Russians, the Europeans (if they ever unite) and the Chinese. The Aztech-Toltech struggle concerns men and women not as they are encountered in headlines, but as they live from day to day in their personal quest of power, love and meaning. The Aztech-Toltech struggle rips newspapers away from readers who use realism to escape reality.

The unpleasant word "power" has been mentioned. It provides the first major engagement in the Aztech-Toltech war.

When we look at it closely, we see that the nature of power has changed radically in our own time, and our literature has not been able to keep up with the change. Our Toltechs, who do most of our reading, rarely understand power itself as well as theories about power. They conceptualize, they moralize or they cynicize; they seldom merely look. They and their mistakenly despised comrades, the Aztechs with a high Toltech component (who must also decide whether they will accept an all-Aztech faith that at present sweeps everything before it, or painfully create a new faith of their own, out there in "the great loneliness" that appalls our centrally heated temperate zone), prefer to be trapped in the snares of new Aztech prosperity, created from *their* ideas, rather than face the problem of power without a shield of theory.

All of us know that power splits people into two classes, those who have it and those who do not. Under any government a child sees the difference between an automobile and a mule. Few of us know, however, or are willing to admit, that power splits people themselves. Still fewer *want* to understand the peculiarly self-divisive effect of our new technical power. The well-informed reader has been hearing more each year of the "mind-body split" and the "puritan syndrome," but remains convinced, as complacently as Oedipus, that *it* can't happen to him and certainly could not have happened to him already. (He spends so much time at the beach, and he has gotten over so many sexual tabus—how can he possibly be guilty of puritan errors?) Understanding of the new over-cortical skills now demanded for success may be necessary to health, as the medical evidence shows, but the successful shun such knowledge through superstition (it might make them fail, they think) and the failures cling repetitiously to their narcotic grievances against fate.

A theory-free look at power reveals a startling fact. If you really put your mind to it, it is far easier to get than you thought. (Once again I am speaking not of the abstract power of presidents, but the concrete power most of us prefer.) You merely have to be determined, to accept humiliations and disappointments, to have "drive." Talent, according to vocational guidance experts, may handicap you seriously, especially if multiple; but drawing a bead on the main chance can do you no harm. Talent may be complicated by an anachronistic sense of sacred obligation to make the most of it. Functional freedom from all such nonsense, preferably concealed by tireless reiteration of the most laudable motives, is calculated to win power.

Such purity of aim, however, is rare. Except for a few driven monomaniacs (like the penniless immigrant who found that many Americans chewed gum and also had constipation, and made a fortune by combining chicle and laxative in a package called Ex-Lax), we prefer to rail at our impotence. We call our laments religion, ethics or poetry. They are not. They are trace amounts of dead religion, dead ethics, dead poetry. If they are ever to be revitalized, it will be by resourceful Toltechs who can at the same time robustly make the vertical most of their talents and humbly learn from their enemies how to be as practical as Aztechs. These Toltechs will not expect so rare a double victory to be handed them, even in a hard-cover book.

Every gifted student is potentially a Toltech. Daily he wakes up, however, to read prose in his morning paper—at best toneless, at worst brainless—that washes out the verbal discrimination he began to acquire the night before from a Shakespeare tragedy or a Yeats self-reproach. He is fed many more facts than he can possibly digest. He is assured by book ads and soft drink commercials that he will never experience the anxieties and defeats of his parents, because he "thinks young," and is getting an education. He hears lectures, in crowded, half-awake classrooms, by men who have no time to give him information in the old, slow tutorial way that sought the right moment and the right phrase to speak to his particular needs. He hears many tendentious ideas, and is never informed of the purposive action they seek to implant in him. He is a cultural orphan, cut off with a library card, whom everyone congratulates on his good fortune.

The first lesson he is taught is that knowledge is power. He learns this directly from his teachers, and indirectly from the airwaves and from his classmates, who are eager to cash in their newly acquired knowledge. They believe that it will turn quickly into power—job, car, wife, house, promotion. He knows, however, already, if he is reasonably in touch with the better literature of his day which is invariably pessimistic on this point above all, that the comforting old Baconian inducement to study is under attack. The job, he has read, will mean disguised enslavement; the car, time payments; the wife, dishes to wash; the house, mortgages; promotion, a coronary. The knowledge that brings power today, he has been assured by able writers (far abler than the yea-sayers) does not bring liberation as well. Instead, it usually leads to quiet desperation, ulcerative colitis, sexual impotence, chronic alcoholism and premature demise.

Of course, if he is comfortably all-Aztech he will dismiss such predictions as sour grapes. He will read duller authors, on the best seller list, who sustain him in a blessed unawareness that after all feeds his family, contributes to the community chest, makes his nation apparently strong. If he has Toltech complications—a livelier imagination and a more obviously egocentric way of satisfying it—he will avoid group-approved commitments as skillfully as he can. If he has character, he may resolutely find a vocation and a love that satisfy him. Or he may drift into a way of life that perversely gratifies a desire for revenge against the society that placed him in his dilemma. Statistically the latter seems more likely.

The intricate effect of advanced technology on human beings has been neglected as a study, especially in those places where the effect is most evident. To the strong, who would have to pay for it, such a study would seem an unjustified concession to the weak, whom it might encourage to complain. Why should a tycoon endow a chair to investigate why he is unable to cover, in the horseman's stark sense, his wife? It was a relatively unindustrialized country, the land of the pastoral Moldau, that produced the nasty word "robot." We dislike the thought that progress can lead to regress, wealth to impoverishment, education to servitude. (We also dislike hearing from virologists that polio epidemics were caused by better plumbing.) So dismal a conclusion, if proved, would demand a complete reconsideration of everything, in miserably Arctic loneliness. There is not enough time for it. If you look at them with a prepared eye, things are going along all right as they are.

Anyway, has this "conclusion" been proved? Is it a sober summation of the evidence, or is it a Toltech distortion?

Bright students will find that the question appears like a specter in any course they may take from sociology to psychology, from histology to torts, from mechanical engineering to modern verse. The very grimness of the question has encouraged their more gifted extramural teachers, the best contemporary authors they read, to unashamed verticality and metaphysical erection. The most robust thought of our time has asked: have we been alienated from ourselves by what seemed our best legacy, the legacy of progress? Our best art and science come from men who continually face the most terrifying negatives and find strength in them.

A typically "modern" word has just been used (and also a few pages back), the word "alienated." What does it mean? First of all, it had opposite meanings for the Mandaeans in the time of Christ (it is not modern at all) and for the Christians in the Middle Ages. To the Gnostic sect it meant a wise sense of men's forlornness in a universe so meaningless that they can only be saved by an "alien god." To the Christians it meant painful estrangement from a benevolent God through the sin of doing, not His Will, but one's own. Calvin later added a note of irredeemable fall to this interpretation, to put hellfire in his sermons. To Rousseau alienation was primarily estrangement from nature, brought about by bad, urban institutions; to Marx it was primarily the workers' estrangement from the products of their labor through capitalist exploitation; to Kierkegaard it was primarily estrangement from oneself through fear of loneliness and acceptance of group tyranny. This latter meaning comes closest to the sense in which "alienated" is used here.

Thus it is near to another word that has also appeared here, "depersonalization," which means loss of identity through acceptance of mass standards. These standards now call, as every window-shopper knows, for buying your own "personalized" stationery or notepaper with your name printed on it. Some acidulous critics feel, however, that if you do buy the notepaper, or wear a signet ring, or put your initials on your car, or try to get your name in the newspaper, you have lost your "authenticity," that is, your capacity to be a genuine human being without falling back on the many "status symbols" that eager shopkeepers are only too glad to sell you. Such critics are "technophobes," or technology-fearers of "Luddite" disposition (which means they they take after an English halfwit who in the early nineteenth century smashed the most celebrated stocking frames in history and gave dozens of sociologists employment). Opposed to the technophobes are the "technolaters," or technology-worshippers, who seek electronic underwear, prefer girls who wear pancake makeup of the hue of canned chicken, and have already ordered their wrist radios from Dick Tracy. So much for definitions just now. Let us return to the alienated intellectual who is not worried.

Why should he worry? More easily than any of his predecessors he has found ways to escape an unfriendly environment. After all, when he has acquired total maladjustment in a world without blueprints, and grown hoarse crying in the wilderness, he can now fly away from it all, if he has a retiring disposition, and find some not too demanding job on a restful periphery, far from the timeclock's threatening bell.

If however he is gregarious or ambitious, he can laugh at his predicament. In a very short time, aided by several lucky breaks in recent history, the man of thought has unexpectedly acquired, whenever he is not transparently trivial, a new exemption from social pressures. He has received, to his own surprise, the opportunity to be not a terrified victim but an amused victim. He too can share in the various new windfalls, and at the same time act ironically superior to them. The few concessions that he must make to the men of actions, the few lapses from one hundred percent integrity, can be smiled off as relatively unimportant. Far more important is the fact that men of thought are no longer menaced by archaic hatreds that, when revived barbarously in our own century, seemed to foretell their extinction—at least by 1984. Now they have forgotten all that. They do not have to be tragedians any more, or anti-mass prophets either. They can play *Hamlet* for laughs, and treat the mass-man as sure to bear a guilty, snobbish son who will buy pictures, finance concerts or provide foundation grants. For the first time ever they have escaped from injustice, terror, "the great loneliness" and responsibility.

In effect they have thus stopped trying to "lick" their antagonists, but instead have "jined" them. With a shout of relief that mimicks the Ninth Symphony, they have merged with the millions of "happy victims." They see now that the struggle for power, which to their tribe meant also a struggle for meaning, was changed some time ago, without appropriate ideological notification to them, into a struggle for comfort. They have learned a few elementary lessons that were obvious all along to fact-loving, gut-minded Aztechs. At last they see through the fallacies of Marx, Veblen and other economic moralists who could not possibly foretell what full-scale production would do in time to overintellectual theories about proletarians and engineers. They find themselves enjoying their presence in the same ultra-modern bed, on a Beautyrest mattress and under an electric blanket with their ancient enemies—and with every prospect of staying there for a long time to come. How they got there, and why a few others would not climb in with them, is our story.

FEAR OF THE MARKETPLACE

3

Lopakhin looked forward eagerly to the day when he would enter the business world. The fact was, he had never left it; his father owned a store in Queens, "with everything from doughnuts to haircurlers," and he worked there as a salesclerk whenever his studies permitted.

Trofimov feared the day when he would have to go, as he put it, "out into the marketplace." Perhaps he had picked up the rather literary phrase from his father, who taught English in a high school. Surely he was extending his studies as long as possible, for he disliked any marketplace, even the relatively mild academic one that he mentioned satirically now and then. "I don't want to teach!" he told me with scorn for those who did. He seemed in somewhat the same situation as Hamlet, who prolonged his studies at Wittenberg to avoid going home to face the rottenness in Denmark. He was also like certain students I met in Yugoslavia when I lectured there. They avoid taking any degree at all as long as possible, but draw pay from the government, and sometimes reach twenty-six or twenty-seven before they are shipped off to remote provinces, as grade-school teachers, to redeem the state's investment in them.

Hamlet went home to a clean-cut tragedy. The Ghost's injunction led him into action and death. Trofimov complained that his life, despite the *succès d'estime* of his stories, was meaningless. No poet seems likely to read a tragic significance into it. His epitaph will probably be composed in the private language of the Loony Left. He was glad that the draft did not want him for military service, but he regarded civilian life as an only

35

slightly better form of rodent torture. Sometimes, he said, he didn't want to get out of bed at all, and I wondered now and then if he was still wearing his pajamas under a jacket and slacks that looked as if they might also have been slept in. Yet his paper on *The Chromium Maze* proved to be excellent, and more than anyone else he helped me to understand why it was *after* President Clark Kerr had frankly told the students at Berkeley that they were going straight from the "multiversity" to the factory that the famous riots occurred. They too disliked the prospect of a life without meaning or more exactly, a life which seemed to offer no prospect of giving it meaning.

Trofimov has talent, but the odds are he won't make much of it. Most likely he will remain "beat," he has not shown a capacity to align his energy and put it at the service of his complex ideas. In two years he has once again been in and out of a mental hospital. He looks as if he will continue to collect grievances and stay locked in neurotic protest. If he had a stronger instinct for money he might break free from his illness, or seem to for a while, by making a splash with a commercialization of his protest. But a "sacred" sense of obligation appears to prevent him from being able to "betray" his "deepest self" to "the enemy." (The words in quotation marks are taken from what I recall of his term paper. When he used similar expressions in class he was quietly jeered by Lopakhin and others.)

It is quite likely that he fears money. He would accept it, I think, if it were given him, and perhaps insist on signing a note; but with his looks and attitude, as he grows older, there is little chance of that. (He *was* helped financially by a girl for a while.) As for his taking the steps needed to acquire money, there is no chance at all. He therefore deprives himself of the surest discipline his society offers, the discipline of money, of doing what is required to get it and increase it. In a new sense he is a man without a country, a man who goes against his culture because he believes his culture goes against him. His energy was long ago introverted from reality to fantasy, and he seems to lack the enormous skill and will—always required of anyone who would succeed in an art—that might give his dream world a value for those who have stayed more prosaically among hori-

zontal realities. For him the marketplace is a profanation of all
that he holds dear. He gives little or no thought to those who
carry on the everyday chores that make his own marginal existence possible, except to admire them undiscriminatingly when
they are "workers" and dislike them undiscriminatingly when
they are "bosses." If he ever "makes a splash," and presumably
he wants to in spite of his scorn for it, it will be among readers
whose defeat comes close to his own.

In his occasional classroom brushes with Lopakhin he
screamed like a madman, while Lopakhin restrained himself
good-humoredly to the soberest common sense. Lopakhin felt
superior to him sartorially, economically and philosophically.
He was confident that he could make his place in the world,
and everything he did would have weight. His taste was also
better. He liked the ever-solid Beethoven, Trofimov the capricious Stravinsky or the ridiculous Varèse. His preference for
Shakespeare was also more intelligent than the other's for Joyce.
Everyday he gave meaning to his existence by his own efforts.
Society provided a firm clear discipline; it would reward him if
he made money according to the rules, and punish him if he
did not.

Trofimov seemed to be dominated by some obscure
religious scruples which he understood none too well. He allowed
them, however, to prevent him from looking after his own legitimate interests. He seemed to *want* to be a scapegoat, to load himself with the worst failures of the community and then to beg
for violent expulsion from it as an unsavory reminder of its own
crimes of omission. His discipline, such as it was, seemed to come
from a highly idiosyncratic imitation of Christ, with a bit of
Prince Myshkin as well. He used the word "sacred" so often that
I recommended some books on religious history to him, and then
he used it even more. He talked as if all action were profane, and
only inaction sacred. When I suggested, as if speaking of someone else, that such thinking could be a rationalization of an incapacity for action, he assured me I was wrong. The word "sacred" appeared to give him a feeling of superiority to Lopakhin
and others like him. He had held onto the essential thing; they
had been "desacralized" (a word he got from an author I told

him to read), robbed of their innate dignity by their worldliness.
(I will give less personal interpretations of "desacralize" later. It
means getting rid of an unconscious awe of the sacred.)

Trofimov arranged, in short, to set almost every social
force working against him. He was aware that the marketplace
had traditionally, in classical times and long after, given health
to literature, by pitting the truth-seeker consciously against his
group and obliging him to sharpen his skills in a dialogue with
those who were less sensitive and more authoritative. He referred
nostalgically to similar conditions that had brought out the
talent of Flaubert, despite his "ivory tower" disdain for "the
mob," and that had even helped Joyce, during his years of obscurity, to develop more "cunning" in his "exile" from Dublin.
But dialogue remained impossible for *him*. His enemies did not
test him, or make him bring forth his best; they made him
sputter with rage and refuse to say anything at all that they
could understand. Communication he rejected as beneath his
dignity. His talents, therefore, were permitted by an indifferent
society—or nonsociety—to lose their edge in pointless debates
with abstract chimeras and in powerful emotions that meant
little or nothing to anyone else. Since he lacked well-defined opposition, and spoke only to his own kind, his talents shriveled
in their hiding place.

He wanted to take his time, he wanted it desperately,
but every day he was told by me, as well as by others, to "get a
move on." The art, science and philosophy that he so passionately
admired had been the work of men who had not been high-
pressured into premature fruition. His own three B's, Blake,
Bohr and Bergson, had had "all the time in the world," he said
with frank envy; but now, in the most feverish of periods, when
individual talent needed more carefree years than ever to produce
something really new and worthwhile, he was told to make good
and soon. Thus he was put in the position of seeming anti-
historical, to those who want new voices to come in loud, strong
and early, when actually he maintained a better connection with
the best of the past, however inarticulately or impotently, than
those who yielded—like Lopakhin and many others—to the worst
of the present.

About a year ago I learned, through another former

student, that Trofimov tried to kill himself by jumping under a subway train. The motorman was able to stop the train in time, and Trofimov was picked off the tracks, weeping, and taken to a psychiatric ward where he had been before. After a few months he got better when another patient tried to attack him with a knife. He resisted, fought for his life, and soon behaved normally enough to be discharged. That is almost the last I heard of him, but I think of him often. His wet handshake stays in my own hand.

Not many students suffer so obviously from his literal agoraphobia, but a great many more share his difficulties than are willing to admit them. Many students feel that if they only had a little more time they would be able to hold their own in the marketplace and on their own terms. Sometimes they marry industrious wives who are willing to forego children—if their husband is an artist, they already have one—and toil in offices or schools, so that the talents of their men may have a chance to ripen properly in the sun of leisure. The formal education of such men cannot be of much help to them. It has not yet found a language to describe their situation to them. So complex a language would require a synthesis of the most useful passages in sociology, psychology, history, philosophy and literature, not to mention extraordinary imagination in the teacher. The students would also have to learn to think rigorously and express themselves exactly. The education they now get seems to be taking them in the opposite direction. A recent article by a well-known teacher in a newspaper's Sunday magazine, along with many similar documents, makes that clear.

> The most fundamental and pervasive "stress" to which [the students] referred over and over in their discussions they called "alienation"—though they never succeeded in saying precisely what they meant by it. Indeed, the discussions at the conference were annoyingly clumsy, intellectually; the students seemed to feel no responsibility for precision or style. Their manner, in fact, deprecated such qualities as indications that the speaker must be inauthentic and insincere or too detached from his experience. Many of the students seemed also to value their own ignorance and imprecision as proof that they were "democratic." . . .
>
> The students were probably justified in calling one of their

major sources of stress "alienation." By and large, we adults had
great difficulty in understanding that what made their experience in
college stressful was that they felt it to be meaningless and isolated.
This kind of statement conveyed nothing to most of the adult par-
ticipants; we wanted to hear something quite different. Partly, this
was because we suspected that a lot of the youngsters were only
pretending to be alienated because it was fashionable. . . . But a
more important reason . . . was that as adults we had largely lost
the capacity to understand anyone who was trying to speak of his
total state of being. . . .

The students, as they finally became convinced that we really
did want to understand them, began to realize that they were wasting a real opportunity through posing and the linguistic and philosophical ineptitude that a decade of pretentious but bad education
had left them with. They became ashamed of their own inauthen-
ticity.

The moment of truth came . . . when the Swarthmore dele-
gate was attempting a critical summary of the proceedings. Each
time he became blocked by his own inarticulate emotion, the audience applauded him warmly and indulgently—until he finally lost
his temper. "I don't know why it is," he almost snarled. "Whenever
anybody here becomes especially incoherent, the conference seems
to like it better. The hell with it!"

New favorites among authors have lately been introducing powerful negatives into the once overbright lexicon of
youth. Students have also been seeing a bit more of the world's
darkness without going outside their university walls. Even when
they cannot put into words what they see, they have been
piercing their teachers with a cold eye that Mad, CBS and Newsweek have sharpened. They have noticed that scholarly "discipline" often means buck-passing of a kind that would make a
postal clerk ashamed. They have seen professional insights as
rigidly departmentalized as if they were canned goods in a super-
market. They have seen personal validity and the actual problems of living men put last in discussions of value. They have
seen the style of every period of the past, including the recent
past, employed to defeat the stylization of the present, since it
would require a far harder confrontation of the very problems,
peculiar to our own time, that earlier stylists did not have to
face. They have seen administrators playing a war game, not

with missiles and helicopters, but with buildings, grants and tenure. They have seen degrees, won by avoidance of life, used to bar newcomers who have learned from it. They have seen professors take royalties on their assistants' inventions, grow rich on government money for future warheads and be spared the indignity of having to teach.

In spite of all they now see, however, a great many students still feel unprepared. Is it because their mothers wanted them to inherit a world as pretty as that in the women's magazines? Did their fathers give them no firm example of male clarity? Was it churches that trimmed on every important issue, and looked for popular social causes to cover up their intellectual and moral failure? Schools that promised an "ever normal cookie jar"? Peer groups that wanted them to be as thick-skinned as Indians? A time that despised wisdom? Or their own taste for coasting?

Sooner or later every student makes his own decision about how he is going to meet "the ubiquity of techniquity," as Trofimov called it in his term paper. The decision will depend upon the depth of his consciousness, and how much energy he can put at its disposal. If he is as simple as Lopakhin, he has no problem; he will go, with a minimum of inhibitions, after money. If he has any of Trofimov's painful complications, he cannot slide out of a distressing dilemma unless he joins "the happy victims."

If he looks closely at the happy victims, he will find that they laugh at their critics because they believe they have exchanged a merely symbolic place in society for a real one. They pity anyone who is not getting in on the excitement and benefits now offered to intellectuals who are willing to enter a crowded scene of action. If their field is economics, they can help justify the men whose tax-exempt oil money has made the last five buildings on the campus possible. They can also help their government in its peace offensive against the Viet Cong with their thoughts on the future development of Southeast Asia. To remain aloof from the great events of the day, they believe, is more often than not a kind of quietistic impotence. Intellectuals can now play an active part in shaping events, and they will get the very experience they need most when they do. If they are historians, they will see firsthand history being made. The happy victims do not feel at all like victims; they feel they have just begun to live. Their books can wait until they are ready to go back to writing them. If their books turn out to be not so good, *tant pis!* They have fallen in love with action.

Action gives intellectuals a sense of liberation and vitality. It means they can move freely and boldly among critical Aztechs, who will now applaud them. At an artists' party, I have often noticed, the loudest gaiety comes from dealers and museum curators who were once painters. The real painters are quiet, usually already burdened with tomorrow's canvas. They cannot be as carefree as those who live *off* art, not *by* it. A public-relations man, having quietly bullied artists into giving him pictures with the tacit promise of publicity—he writes articles for magazines read by collectors—is delighted to promote a university symposium on just those painters whom he has gently blackmailed; it will send up their prices and increase his own stature as a tastemaker. A painter who specializes in "optical art" is not displeased when one of his pictorial effects is used by a dress manufacturer, or when it appears on the body of a model in a fashion magazine at the same time that his latest emulsion on masonite is appearing on the walls of a museum. He knows this blessed synchronicity is not an accident. Presses, looms and walls require months of preparation. He hopes he will be rewarded as tangibly as the model, the magazine, the manufacturer, the museum curator. Even when his hopes are disappointed, as they usually are (he has not yet learned that making a thing is worse reimbursed than selling it), he appreciates the general attention that has momentarily given him a sense of belonging to a world that has order and meaning or at least a place for him.

If the student's heart sinks at such intricate corruption, he had better transfer quickly to an agricultural college or a divinity school—or marry an heiress and live as a permanent tourist on some virgin isle. Unless he can arrange to stay outside it (and neither agriculture nor religion nor inheritance will spare him very long) he is certain to encounter just such maneuvers, or a lot worse, especially in those places where there is officially a wholehearted absorption in beauty and truth.

The professor, the PR man, the op artist are quite willing to cash in their mastery of symbols for real usefulness and real money. Nearly all other professional men agree with them. How else can they keep alive? One's special talents must be bought, or else one "starves." We are back at the "Madisonian" catch in the new technical order, its need to rely, whenever the stakes get high enough, on the misuse of symbols. Words now play a larger part in the creation of wealth than sweat. Words can always be abused in subtle ways that will not be noticed by anyone except a few out-of-date semantic moralists.

People soon become expert in detecting this misuse in others, but seldom in themselves. Students are quick to jump on any fallacy, especially in political statements, but rarely apply exacting standards of logic to their own papers. Specialists put the guilt of well-known evils on other specialists. Journalists blame politicians for mistakes that are in full view. No one goes back to old newspaper files to check on the journalists' many mistakes. Psychiatrists blame parents; parents blame psychiatrists. Whites blame Negroes; Negroes blame whites. Every minority overdraws its balance of public sympathy, until public patience is exhausted, and a new wave of intolerance begins. Some experts in public opinion develop uncanny antennae, as sensitive as a cat's whiskers, and promptly misapply their skills, to wheedle more money from more fools. These evasions of responsibility become inevitable, as soon as morality becomes social, not personal. The market adds its ulterior accent to almost every word we utter. There was never a better time to recall Spinoza's "What Peter says about Paul tells me more about Peter than it does about Paul," nor a harder time to bear it in mind. Everyone's thoughts, emotions, senses and oldest credulities are being played on by experts, to make him believe what is not true. Most people now *enjoy* being deceived; it is the new *volupté*. And when everyone does it, it seems right.

Long before he graduates, the student must face his dilemma: does he wish to gain power through the misuse of symbols? Usually his consent is taken for granted, and the question actually runs: *how much* power and prestige can he, with his particular talents, hope to gain through the misuse of symbols? The most frequent misuse of them is verbal. It may also be visual or auditory or something else, but ordinarily it is verbal.

Words are perverted to get something one wants. The few laws that govern communication are observed (by the intelligent), but after that the chief restraint on deliberate catachresis is verisimilitude—the effect desired and how it can best be obtained. In some markets the soft-sell works better than the hard-sell. Once again the market determines both ethics and style.

This is so much the case, in all walks of life, that a well-educated person reads his morning paper with a simultaneous mental translation of what it seems to be saying into what it is really saying. This member of the Executive Department denounces that pay boost as inflationary now because if he had said so a week earlier, when his words might have had an effect, he might have lost some of the support of labor. This Senator supports that humanitarian cause with special warmth because some member of his staff has reported that polls indicate that he is generally considered a cold fish and had better counteract the impression. This actor is marrying that actress because they are both homosexual and their agents have been after them. This broker is getting that publicity because it will please the influential minority to which he belongs. And so on. The deception of the public by the powerful has existed throughout history, but never before have so many brains been devoted to it, never before have the results been so carefully calculated, never before has it so quickly permeated an entire society, from top to bottom. Someday a new Gresham will establish in a scientific law the greater capacity of untrue words, over true, to remain in circulation.

The professor, the PR man, the op artist did not look too closely at the real use being made of their symbolic contributions. They were merely pleased by the money and the attention they received. They do not enjoy reminders that the sale of one's wits, though now essential to survival, is a hazard to one's moral health. The sale can be completed honestly or otherwise. One does not have to remain aloof from action; one merely has to know what one is doing; and this kind of self-knowledge is required of the man of thought more strictly than of the man of action. That ethical distinctions between the two go back to earliest times was established some time ago by Paul Radin and other anthropologists.

Penniless Puerto Ricans are reminded each day by the New York police with nightsticks and revolvers that honesty is the best policy, while other men who live below them on Park Avenue, south of 96th Street, with attorneys close at hand, commit other acts that are as unethical and antisocial as any committed in East Harlem. The other acts involve the use of words, words that are waiting, in the eyes of the man of action, for him to use them in any way that he legally can. His action now is chiefly verbal, and he is constitutionally free of the "sacred" inhibitions that prevent more thoughtful or more traditional men from misusing words—until a new society, unobserved by a theoretical French sociologist who has not had a chance to see how it actually operates, convinces the man of thought that, if he wants to get ahead, he will have to act as the man of action does. Then he too uses words for their social effect, rather than for their personal truth, which becomes for him an "old-fashioned" criterion. The pressures on him are such that he wants some of the "good things of life" that "seeing things in a larger frame of reference" can "throw his way." So wealth grows, at the expense of words. And instinct, always conservative, fears catastrophe.

The man of thought can do much to help the public's peace of mind. The public wants his superior mythmaking talents to assure it that, in spite of its ignorance and indifference, it is going forward. It wants the myth of its own progress materially *and* spiritually. Those who can provide this myth (clergymen who talk like insurance salesmen, newspaper editors who "soothe as they inform," scientists who promise a golden future) are suitably rewarded. An abuse of words is required, sometimes in ways that make the Nazis seem like bungling amateurs. This is hardly noticed, because so many statesmen, physicians, bankers, economists, deans, teachers, psychiatrists, painters, composers, architects and writers compete with one another for the privilege of telling the public exactly what it wants to hear. The substance of their myth is this: the world is slipping back, but you, reader, are still going ahead.

The demand for it never dies. It is the latest variation on the Calvinist theme of the elect—without hellfire. (We don't need hellfire when we have the Reds.)

A rich public must be kidded; it cannot be bullied. The source of its power has changed. Power still requires soldiers and factory hands in the background; but persuasion is now more directly important to it than military conquest or manufacture. Once peaceful stability is established, power is won by penetrating the minds of the many persons who can be induced to buy goods or support political programs. New rhetorical skills are therefore in demand. Large numbers of people must be sold ideas, symbols that promise realities.

The symbols *must* be misused if they are to achieve their purpose. Truth is too ambiguous to be of help to men of state and men of affairs. If the public received only truth, the new relativistic truth that confuses even the learned, there would be general inaction and apathy. "The wheels of industry would grind to a halt." Truth must be reshaped crudely by those who do not know how to remain long in power (Mussolini, Hitler and *all* unadaptable persons) and supplely by those who know how to endure. The emphasis of democratic survival is always on *adjustment*—of men to reality through words. The medieval mind of Dante denounced it as "trimming," the sin of those "who were not rebellious, nor were faithful to God; but were for themselves." A great deal of modern maladjustment originates in anachronistic repugnance to trimming. (A desire to be forthright had much to do with Trofimov's anomie.) But success awaits those who can do it with skill.

Symbols must therefore be taken from those who created them, bemused poets and pure scientists, and put to work, adulterated into usefulness. The tenuous creations of the Toltechs must be rendered serviceable by hardheaded Aztechs with their feet on the ground and a stronger will to rule. Revolutionary ideas must be converted into workable formulas.

It is important that the student view this situation, from which no one can hope to escape, as clearheadedly as possible. He is bound to have strong emotions about it, one way or another (that is why its very existence is so rarely acknowledged), but he *can* learn to "give the devil his due," see the other side intelligently, and become aware of his natural prejudices when they rise to cloud his judgment with delusions of righteousness.

A few people, unlike the professor, the PR man, the op artist, *cannot* misuse words. Even if they are not as unfortunate as Trofimov, they soon become *un*happy warriors in a fight that goes endlessly against them. After a while they may also develop considerable self-pity, paranoia and undisguised willingness to join the happy victims, if only the chance is still given them. But here let us confine ourselves for the moment to the rare few who remain faithful, and without too many regrets, even perhaps with enjoyment, to the strict qualitative standards of their unpopular tribe. There are such people. They recognize that they possess little power, and are not likely to get more. The only appreciation they can hope for will come from their own kind. They seek no more money than is needed for continuance. They cultivate their vulnerability to experience, as essential to their insights. They do not shake it off. They refuse to feed the public's appetite for the comforting myth of its own spiritual progress. (The public is now so big and so "fragmented" than any part of it can handsomely reward a flattering mythologist.) Thus the faithful few get much bitter experience to swallow. And much insight as a compensation.

Any student will observe the difference between the genuine Toltech and the other kind; the latter is more prosperous and also more highly esteemed. This is so marked a difference that intelligent students soon wonder apprehensively, as Trofimov certainly did, how long a genuine Toltech can hold out in a situation that is bound in time to demand Socratic clarity and courage, and perhaps also a considerable portion of Socratic geniality and wit.

Many Toltechs fail to "come off" because they are unable to meet the much more complex demands that are made of them than of Aztechs. History is full of Toltech heroes who met the most exacting spiritual tests in times of greater social clarity and therefore of greater opportunities for singleminded devotion to tasks. Also, Toltech heroes (such as Socrates, Jesus, Buddha, Lao-tse) have been presented tendentiously by expert mythmakers who wanted to create marvels. Compare Plato's Socrates, who is a saint, and Xenophon's, who is a boaster. The former makes better reading; the latter is probably nearer the truth. The wily Toltech student will therefore modestly "time"

his effort to match the great standards of the past, and not demand too much of himself until he is ready for it. He will also
take real models, not mythical ones.

Since the justice and subtlety of the Toltech's mind
require that he recognize the superior organizing skills of his
oppressors, even while they do their best to make his own continuance unlikely, most students recoil from his example. He
threatens to load their own future with preposterous self-sacri-
fice. Their hearts belong to their culture heroes, their skins to
the happy victims. So they drift into the easy solutions of affluence, while they *believe* they still believe in austerity. Since they
lack a guide to the new moral dilemmas of the technological
society, since they must make key decisions before they really
know what they are doing, since they do face many new problems with remarkable energy and courage, they can hardly be
blamed for their mistakes. Sooner or later, though, the moment
arrives when they must pass from a defensible use of symbols
to an indefensible one if they wish to get ahead, be promoted,
buy a house in the country, take a trip abroad, send a child to
a good school. This is the moment when their moral dilemma
becomes an old one, not a new one, and when, usually, their
respect for strict qualitative standards declines.

Ortega y Gasset attributed the decline in prestige of
quality to "the most important fact of our time . . . the ac-
cession of the masses to complete social power. . . . The principles on which the civilized world . . . is based, simply do not
exist for the average man of today. He has no interest in basic
cultural values, no solidarity with them, is not prepared to place
himself at their service. . . . Civilization becomes more complex
in proportion as it advances. The problems which it sets before
us today are of the most intricate. The number of people whose
minds are equal to these problems becomes increasingly smaller."

In short, the authority of the Toltechs has declined
with their numbers. New problems, together with still newer
ones Ortega could not have foreseen, have obliged the few remaining Toltechs to speak a language that grows less intelligible, while the power of the masses grows both greater and more
suasive. (Actually, not the masses but their manipulators gain

the power.) Weary of all but the prestige of their ancient role, more Toltechs desert every day to join the smiling victims of technolatry—while demanding, and getting more often than scrupulous rivals, the honors traditionally accorded the arts and sciences. The slang word "slick" is used to describe their behavior, as admired in glossy magazines called "the slicks." Character weakens before new temptations, and minds abandon difficult tasks while pretending to have performed them.

Historically, some students will know, Ortega's insight owes much to Kierkegaard. Long before anyone else, in the middle of the nineteenth century, the lonely Danish philosopher concluded, on far less evidence than we have today, that society must drift toward mass values and the decline of the individual. In recent years his ideas have become so familiar, though more by hearsay than by actual reading, that Aztechs and Toltech deserters, especially the latter, call them clichés, with a contempt that is meant to dull their cutting edge. People, he said, would grow fearful of solitude, would huddle together like new savages in ever larger groups. And each group would seek to establish its prejudice as the sole criterion of truth.

This meant that sooner or later words would have to be misused to maintain mass supremacy or, more exactly, the supremacy of men who know how to appeal to the mass minds. The Toltech deserter, however, does not want to hear any words that might trouble him in the small hours of the morning, certainly not the same words that are already troubling him in the small hours of the morning. He does not want to find himself calling himself a phony. He is "definitely bored" with references to a "mind-body split" that, some psychiatrists say, entered history as a conquering force in the seventeenth century, after the philosophical labors of Francis Bacon, René Descartes and others had cleared the way for men to take not only a more scientific but a more exploitative attitude toward nature. Men learned, for instance, what coal meant, chemically and geologically, and then they learned how to strip hills and ruin farmlands faster. Similar science created the Dust Bowl. Soon they applied their improved methods of exploitation to men—first to their bodies, later to their minds. Child labor was followed by child

corruption via electronic circuitry. Technically the advanced
countries are in the phase where mind-exploitation pays better
than any other kind.

The new exploitative attitude was a longer step toward
"desacralization," or ridding themselves of the early belief that
everything real was sacred, than men had ever taken before. It
coincided with "the Protestant ethic," or a theologically justified equation of money with goodness, that at about the same
time, the time of a rising bourgeoisie, preached ever greater efficiency as against the easygoing folkways of the past, body-saving
work habits, established seasonal rhythms. The time of the time-
clock was at hand. The mind-body split, meant, in brief, that
clever men had found great power and good consciences at the
same time, but at the expense, not noticed extensively until our
own stock-taking time, of physical, psychological and moral
health. It was an expense that wealth was able to conceal for
centuries, and still manages to, in the more grossly self-deceived.

However prodigious their "reading gaps," well-informed
students are aware of all this. Rarely does their study include
all the disciplines that are collected here in a synthesis, however,
and they cannot really understand the synthesis until they have
gone "out into the world" and *felt* the mind-body split at work
in themselves and in their antagonists. Their intuitions are
already prepared, I have noticed, to perceive it in the alertly
empty face of a Du Pont executive on the cover of *Time* or in
the abuse of Greek mythology in a Western. For some time their
better books have been telling them that the same skills that
made our technical advances possible are not always a source
of happiness or the best guide for everyone. The favorite poets
and novelists of the student often hate technology—Yeats and
Lawrence, for example—with an eloquence that begins to awaken
him from a long dream. Other artists continue the note of reveille.

He looks for someone who will tell him what to believe
and what to do, at the same time that he begins to realize that
an old chain of instruction is broken; he is going to have to find
his own faith and his own action himself. He also notices that
traps have been set for him by others who can make a very good
thing out of his continued ignorance. Education is not the simple
straightforward blessing he was led to expect. Not at all.

He admires, but he also perceives the grim irony in the heroic effort of Negroes to be admitted to universities in the Deep South where, to gain social and economic advancement, they will get a poor introduction to learning. Their persistence might be better rewarded in the North, or still better in France, but not because France is not racist. (The Algerian war and such writings as James Baldwin's *Equal in Paris* exploded that complacency.) However, a less technicized France still offers the student of any color an intellectual and emotional discipline that he will respect if he really seeks an education. The United States offers the student total immersion in a revolution that few members of the faculty understand. He is rarely educated; he is more often processed. Even so he might get a better preparation for present realities than more traditional training offers, in France or elsewhere, if he were made aware of the hazards that lie ahead.

He is not. Efficiency prefers him, black or white, as he is: uninformed but hopeful. His dumb animal faith or glandular confidence, freshened daily with slogans, is essential to progress. We would all "grind to a halt" if it weren't for that. Usually it is left intact.

Man has been called the "symbol-making animal." Many thinkers believe that in his ability to use symbols, especially words, lies his chief distinction. Through them he has created the civilization that ordinarily prevents him from behaving like a beast. When he misuses them, when efficiency obliges him to misuse them, he is sure in time to lose the civilization that it took him so long to create.

Einstein said that if there is an atomic war, the next war will be "fought with bows and arrows." If this catastrophe occurs it will be brought about by misused words, or more exactly by destructive emotions that have been whipped up by misused words. Some men will know just enough about verbal symbols, which are required for the detonation of bombs, to misuse them.

The bomb is something we can easily blame on someone else. Responsibility for it escapes in a mushroom cloud of social morality. Responsibility for the right use of words, however, we can each demand of ourselves *in principle*. Actually we almost never demand it. If we did, the technological society (which is *not* an immoral conspiracy but simply the most effective way of getting things done these days) would punish us as memorably as the first time we put a childish hand on a hot stove. Sound technique requires a sound misuse of symbols.

Traditional ethics have been turned upside down. Any conventional moralist who dwells on them has failed to examine his own behavior, and is all too well acquainted with the public's demand for the myth of its own continuing progress.

The student, who is usually much more concerned with ethics than he dares to let anyone else observe, is confused by the situation that improved efficiency has created for him. Animal spirits bid him plunge in and conquer it; animal caution bids him withdraw. Historically he has arrived on the scene in a time of prosperous skepticism, when there are more opportunities than ever, and more misgivings. One of his responses, as expressed to me in the classroom, is a doubt that things can go on much longer as they are. (The Trofimovs speaking, not the Lopakhins.)

Perhaps the millennium will not last a full thousand years. It may eat up the previous civilization, on which it feeds at present like a shark, long before that. Beneath its rich sleekness there is intense self-hatred and a strong inclination to suicide: anything rather than the one adjustment that has been neglected, adjustment to the truth about oneself and one's real place in the world.

It is not an easy world for the student to study, and he has barely begun to look at it.

THE OVERSTUFFED VOID

4

Now and then Lopakhin complained about the inter-disciplinary method. "It goes around in circles," he said. He was right; it does, and it must. It must drag in astronomy, medicine, literature, painting, psychology and anything else it needs, if it is to do its job. It must try to be as fluid, as passionate, as entertaining as a good novel. It is therefore better when it is embodied in one mind than when collected in a group of experts. It must unseal compartments, soften rigidity, bring back personality. Knowledge it habitually subordinates to the student's natural rhythms of understanding; he is not learning the multiplication table. With Freud it realizes that science is a form of mythology, and with Rank that truth is insupportable unless one is sustained philosophically by a substratum of myth. (Lopakhin threw up his heavy-fingered hands when I mentioned ideas like that. They would have threatened his whole cosmos if he had tried to understand them. But he took notes on them, and correctly answered questions about them at examination time.)

Trofimov liked a circular method of instruction. "It's like the way my cat does things," he said. "It makes me feel at home. I don't need dex. I can stay with it all the time. And when I feel like taking a nap I can take a nap. Say, that's Zen!" But of course Trofimov was a total failure, most likely did not wash often enough, and the class, except for one girl (an actress who thought he might write a play some day), regarded him with suspicion. He had, however, understood what was said better than anyone else.

Each of them agreed with about half of my lecture called "The Overstuffed Void," which led me to believe that it must have rolled right down the middle between them. It started out with the effect of technology on education and ended up with the chief controversies that every student must face today. It is essential to the story I am telling here. It does "go around in circles," but I hope some readers will not mind. Engineers like to lay out roads in straight lines; I like to curve with the countryside.

Today, in most civilized countries, when a person has a cold and wishes to cure it, he is told on the bottle of his medicine what it contains. When he is hungry and opens a can, he can read what is in it. But when he goes to college and takes a course he is rarely informed what purposive ideas it seeks to implant in him. When he reads a newspaper or a magazine he is never told what strategies lie behind its articles. Medically and nutritionally a few concessions are made to him; intellectually none. And concealéd intellectual maneuvers may prove to be still more important to him than the medicines he takes or the food he eats.

Aside from the fact that chemical analysis is both simpler and further advanced than idea analysis, this means that he lives in a time when some kinds of vigilance are preferred to others. Occasionally it may mean an open-minded hospitality to ideas. More often it means that his intellectual docility is advantageous to those who would persuade him to take one course of action or another. It means he will be encouraged in his docility, frequently by men who express the highest respect for, and give the largest sums of money to, education.

The deception of students, even when it leads the docile into disguised tyranny, is not a plotted assault on their liberty. Socialist thinking will have to reconsider its denunciations of capitalist plots, denunciations which originate in primitive religiosity. It will also have to try to understand the human cost of improved technology if it is to regain its relevance and its true usefulness to the working class. Students are deceived by able but limited men, in positions of great responsibility, who believe they are acting for the best. They are simply not aware, and they will be greatly surprised when they read, that great technical power, which has brought so many obvious advantages —better sanitation, better roads, better housing, more schools, more travel, more leisure, more apparent hope—also promotes falsehood in education. If they were as devoted to logic as their efficiency suggests, they would soon see how and why they have reversed their position toward education, which they believe, waving their canceled checks and their honorary doctorates, they still want to be a genuine search for truth. The obvious fact is that a genuine search for truth is not good for efficiency. It might lead to self-knowledge, and self-knowledge is the last thing a reliable cog in a smooth-running machine can stand. Historically it has always led to indifference to promotion, profits and things and to the contemplation of naked meaning. Naked meaning does not put automobiles on the road. Or get good jobs for students.

Massive self-deception, as near unanimous as possible, is essential to advanced technology, which must regard an ever-increasing number of questions as foes of efficiency. Most departments of philosophy restrict themselves prudently to "linguistic analysis"; most psychology departments to unintrusive gadgets; most sociologists to the most timid of "value-judgments"; not much promotion otherwise. Since steadily advancing technology is essential to power, it follows that a state must suppress education (genuine education which might abet the individual's fullest development) when its economy is poor, as in the Soviet Union, and can only tolerate it, when its economy is rich, as in the United States, so long as it does not impede production or enthusiasm for production. It thus becomes evident, to those unwilling to make the new sacrifice of mind that any state will demand (as rigorously as any church ever did, and less openly) that genuine education must begin with clear recognition of all intellectual strategies which seek to escape attention.

Education begins today with ideological awareness. It can go beyond ideology, and should; but that must be its starting point, even for those who dislike its rigidity. Humane, many-sided minds are under the withering attack of dogmatic, one-sided minds. The alert student will therefore seek an introduction to the principal ideologies of our time, as they seek to influence him in his principal decisions. He will want to understand such important ideologies as Christianity, Marxism, Freudianism, Existentialism and many others which are not so well known. He will want to know whether—and if not, why not?—any of them has been able to cope with a new cultural phenomenon which presents unforeseen and in many ways unprecedented problems to our best thinkers.

Briefly, this new cultural phenomenon is an extraordinary side effect of advanced technology which no one could have anticipated. Technology improves itself (and it must continually improve itself, to keep its competitive fitness) by sternly functional insistence on scientific abstraction. Vivid particulars, which might appeal to the emotions, must be sacrificed daily to dull working principles which satisfy the practical intelligence. Enjoyment, intuition and speculation must yield to technique. As a result, the mind of the technician is systematically drained of folklore, superstition and in time the habit of reflection. This gets rid of much dead wood and also much live timber. It creates a void. The void must be filled, and the untraditional substitutes that rush into it become the chief sources not only of contemporary journalism but also of contemporary literature. We live in the time of the overstuffed void. Our heads are drained of principles that no longer work, and then refilled with cigarette ads, popular astrology, advice to the lovelorn, miracle drugs in brushless lather, cheesecake thighs, beer ballads, diplomas for those who never got through high school and improvised theolgies.

Foremost among the improvisations is "the new supernatural," which has already been introduced as an important theological invention of the myth-starved victims of industrial progress. It is a term that requires another brief glance at prehistory.

In the beginning was the beast. Diggers unearth a time when men respected animals more than themselves. Their gods were animals, which they considered more powerful and more beautiful than their own new and inadequate kind. As their skills increased, they domesticated beasts that formerly had impressed them, and their animal-headed deities gave way slowly to other deities that looked like human beings. They became civilized.

Now, after a period of civilization that once seemed long and durable, but turns out to be a brief candle that frightens us with its fragility, our respect appears to be passing, in significant quantities and in a significant pattern, to another power that again seems stronger and more beautiful than ourselves. It is not an animal; it is not a heaven-sent savior; it is not our own minds; it *is* a product of our minds. Our awe has shifted from our own fleshly, untrustworthy kind to the feelingless creations of our hands. We have found a new idol to worship in our own handiwork, or more exactly in the godlike powers we have conferred upon it.

Our technology, which started out as no more than a way to improve our material condition, has taken over the emotions that were formerly commanded by miracles. Mechanization has not remained mechanical, a sensible means of controlling nature. It has attracted feelings and ideas of unpredictable potency, and reached out for control of its creator, man himself, in his immaterial as well as his material life. The complexity of his mind has not been appreciated. Rational intents have produced irrational results. Technolatry has become subtler and more widespread than anyone, with his eyes still on its benefits and not yet on its disadvantages, cares to recognize.

Technolatry operates by deception. If industry were content to produce nothing more than a higher standard of living, it would have nothing to conceal. But along with that higher standard of living go many other things: profit-seeking, prestige-seeking, efforts to transcend routine, efforts to defeat classification, efforts to indulge in private fantasy, new habits of efficiency, new dislike of inefficiency, new contempt for nature, new belief in one's power to outwit nature, scorn of natural laws of compensation, hopes that life has become essentially easier, substitution of comfort for meaning, loss of fellow-feeling, loss of identity, loss of a personal sense of reality, loss of reason. In man's quest of happiness, the evidence suggests that far more often than not he has been "depersonalized," a term frequently used to describe his new condition. Serious contemporary literature deals with this theme more than any other. The term "alienation" has gained enormous currency among its victims and its doctors, so much that it has long been denounced as a cliché by those who would like to believe that thus they can cause it to cease to be.

We need not conclude that all our technical improvements are wrong, and have led only to disaster. We shall continue to drive automobiles, not mules. We shall rejoice in the fastest possible trips by plane. But while we eat up the miles we may conclude that the effect of our improvements upon us deserves closer examination, and of a kind that it has not received.

Lopakhin sighed in a way that asked me when I was going to come to the point. My "circular" presentation did *not* please him.

The new supernatural might be nothing but the latest twist in our venerable capacity for illusion, and not worth more than brief satirical mention, if it had not already by-produced effective means for its own perpetuation, means that may be undefeatable. Its ingenious manner of rewarding the worst in human nature, and covering it with prestige, seems more likely than any political or economic system to dominate the next thousand years. This group-creation to make the line of least resistance pay, to turn apathy into a civic virtue (while quietly flattering the arrogance that lurks behind it) outdoes Machiavelli. What does technology seek? It seeks a foolproof device that everyone can operate and will mortgage the next few years for. Americans fear that Russian methods of education will prevent exposure of communist errors. Russians fear American affluence will prevent exposure of capitalist errors. Both of these great powers remain indifferent, except for an unheeded minority within them, to a more central error they jealously share, the belief that man can win great technical victories over nature without great peril to his own nature. Though only our unheeded minorities speak openly of it, the majority is also worried. It is one of the most frequent causes of concern in every social class, even those adverse to complaint. A most definite promise has not been kept, except for heathens who have not yet had a taste of industrial blessings. The newest omnipotent father, wrapped in the white smock of science, has let us down. Our professional hysterics (our writers) scream at him with rage. Our professional stoics (our businessmen) say he is still a good provider. In private, however, they are not so sure.

Whether we bow to the new religion or jeer at it, we soon discover how omnipresent it has become, how imperceptibly it has entered all our minds, when we examine a few common controversies that rage in magazines from *Partisan Review* to *Reader's Digest* and in colleges from Harvard to West Kentucky Wesleyan. One familiar controversy can be stated rather simply. There are optimists who believe that although our "Faustian pact" with technology has had some disastrous but laughable side effects, such as a decline in craftsmanship, we have not really jeopardized our rapport with nature or ourselves. The same "Promethean courage" that led to technical advances will also lead in time to common-sense solutions of many of the new problems they have engendered. Professors of the new chair called "American civilization" often hold out this hope to donors and public. There are also pessimists, especially in the more advanced clergy, who believe that our situation has gotten out of hand, that men through their control of nature have become self-inflated to the point of self-destruction, and nothing can prevent a worldwide catastrophe that may depopulate the earth. In many cases the optimists and the pessimists merely proclaim the source of their income: whether they get if from hopeful payroll-meeters or fearful *rentiers*. Temperament plays a role in their attitude, but so does the market for their particular talents.

Optimists also say that although democracy suffers from a fear of freedom similar to that which led to totalitarianism, all people everywhere who have had a taste of political freedom will never permit dictatorship to reappear among them; and those without a libertarian tradition will soon demand it. Lawyers with trust funds to look after like that one. Pessimists say that men's aggressiveness and preference for ignorance are such that they cannot hope to rule themselves well, and democracy as we know it is sure to go, most likely to the accompaniment of nuclear detonations. Psychoanalysts like that one.

In domestic problems the optimists believe that although many homes and children have been injured by new forces of dehumanization, men and women are going to find better ways of living together as material conditions improve and they are educated to a more scientific understanding of themselves. Home life is already better for the masses than it was in the past, and children will be better trained than ever as we learn more about their minds. Trustees of progressive schools like that one. The pessimists believe that sexual relations have been brutalized to an astonishing degree by the new knowledge. We have found no way to channel humanely the new libido released by laborsaving devices and increased urbanization; children are badly trained, home life is a mess, psychiatry a failure, women worse off than ever. Southern novelists like that one.

Of science optimists say that rational study and control of nature are proceeding as well as could be expected by any reasonable person, aware of the slowness of history and humanity. Pessimists say that science is now so highly specialized, and so subject to bureaucratic and military pressure, that it injures the scientist as a person in a manner that more than offsets his services to the community. Many Californians incline toward the former; a few New Yorkers toward the latter.

Of art the optimists believe that, although the new scholarship has dropped a heavy avalanche of knowledge through the artist's studio skylight, and new merchandising methods, along with the cynicism they generate, have further complicated his task, he will yet be able to triumph over his new cultural impediments and find a new lyricism. Pessimists say that mass art gets more and more brainless, and elite art refines itself beyond natural frequencies of understanding. This debate is between Tenth Street and Morningside Heights.

Of religion, the optimists say that there are many needed services that it alone can perform, while the pessimists say that it merely encourages ignorance and immaturity. This is between the village pastor and the *Village Voice*.

Out of these debates emerges a prime fact: *not* to believe in the new supernatural is almost always to disqualify oneself for effective participation in contemporary life. Our Aztechs, charged with practical responsibilities, had to find a sustaining faith. Our Toltechs had to be pulled down from their old authority, they were living in the past. They opposed the mechanistic mind. Affluence has already created a new mechanical morality which has displaced all earlier ethical standards, religious or secular, in our centers of power. It rewards its adherents, and only tolerates its opponents so long as they cooperate. Children give it their spontaneous veneration. ("What will become of them?" we all ask, and dare not stay for an answer.) Its initiation rites are far more binding than those of Judaism, Christianity or any exotic faith that seeks to replace them. In all probability there will not, in the foreseeable future. be any effective opposition. One finds a barely adequate metaphor when one says the millennium is here. It really is—for the Aztech. For the Toltech, however, it is a time of bitter defeat which can mean either surrender or lonely defiance.

Each time I mentioned the optimists' position Lopakhin made it clear to everyone, merely by the way he twisted his vibrant body, that of course they were right. Each time I mentioned the pessimists' position Trofimov made it equally clear, merely by his sorrowful silence, that he agreed with them. I was therefore curious to hear what they would say when the lecture was over and questions in order.

"You make it all sound so hopeless," said Trofimov. Later, in his exam answers, he discussed hopelessness with an eloquence that suggested it was his constant companion.

"You go around in circles," said Lopakhin. But he wrote the most in his notebook when I presented the arguments of the pessimists who made him squirm.

AZTEC INTO AZTECH

5

In a ten-cent store I see a cheap bib for babies. On its terrycloth is printed, in dyes sure to run after one thrust into a washing machine, "His Majesty." The thought occurs, "Every baby, however poor his family, is now born a five-star general, subject to constant demotion." The pride of the destitute, the upward glances of the lower depths. the competition in baby-spoiling, provide a far more lucrative market for the mercantile imagination than all the luxuries of the rich. The time will surely come when the purchases of outcast Negroes and Puerto Ricans, no less than their inexpensive labor, will sustain the economy. Perhaps they already do. The humanitarianism which seeks a decent standard of economic and political life for under-privileged mass purchasers is finally pragmatic. (And the word "pragmatic" meant "businesslike" in ancient times, and in Samuel Johnson's Dictionary, long before Peirce and James raised it to philosophical status.)

If any student is justified in feeling himself the victim of a businesslike tyranny, because his self-fulfillment is so often at the mercy of whatever is good for General Motors, he must nevertheless recognize that there is no deliberate despotism such as was practised by the ancient Medes or the ancient Aztecs. "The tyranny of public opinion" (Stendhal's description of America) avoids the guilt of obvious persecution. Whenever a tactless official makes a statement such as "What is good for General Motors is good for the country," he is immediately set straight by public-relations men, who dislike the bluntness of his phrasing and ignore the truth of his statement, which recognizes the fact that the American economy requires the constant sale of automobiles. "Technique's proper motion," says Jacques Ellul with Calvinist finality, "tends irresistibly toward completeness . . . There is no place for an individual today unless he is a technician . . . No technique is possible when men are free."

Once again he means that we are up against something impersonal and autonomous. If we find ourselves in a situation where we have lost our freedom of action and must submit to powerful enemies (the student has not yet encountered this: he still has a lieutenant's gold bar on his shoulder; but his father, long since reduced to the ranks, understands), it will not help us to respond with witty rage, or curse the education that failed to prepare us for our plight. Nor will old-fashioned categories of good and evil do more than blow off useful steam. Biblical references are still less pertinent than condemnation of teachers. The familiar religious and humanitarian explosions—"godless . . . materialistic . . . exploitative"—merely miss the point in a smokescreen of self-righteousness. Our technology is not a foreign plot against us; it is part of our own pursuit of happiness. Our situation is too protean, too closely related to the nature of things to be handled with mere moralizing. It demands our closest attention and our greatest respect. Once again it is clarified by historical perspective.

The student will find in pre-Columbian Mexico a remarkable analogy to his own dilemma. If he reads about the one-sided struggle for power which existed in that openly tragic land, before the arrival of Hernán Cortés and his *conquistadores* put all the natives under a Spanish dominion only relatively less brutal than that of the Aztecs, the student will find his own emotions are identified with the subtle and cultivated Toltecs who provided so many misunderstood ideas, and so many living sacrifices, to the bloodthirsty Aztecs. (Other students, more power-minded and more numerous, will sympathize privately with the Aztecs, though never, of course, in public.)

For any student, the best account of what happened philosophically in Mexico, before Cortés conquered it with amazing speed, has been given by an archaeologist, Laurette Séjourné. Mme. Séjourné bases her interpretations upon her own excavations at Teotihuacan. She has the intelligence to treat the dead as if they were fully as complex and interesting as ourselves. Her ingenious portrait of ancient Mexico suggests a parallel with our own day.

Why did Cortés conquer a rich and powerful land so fast and with so few men? Many theories have been advanced. Mme. Séjourné says it was because he had an "undoubted talent for intrigue and betrayal, which enabled him to orientate himself quickly in the maze of native politics. Soon after his arrival he discovered resentment and rebellion simmering among Moctezuma's subject tribes, and at once formed the military alliances which made his dazzling victories possible. An indomitable will, not shrinking from assassination or wholesale slaughter, accomplished the rest."

Also, the simmering rebellion against Aztec rulers had been aided by a revival of the old Toltec philosophy of Quetzalcoatl, or the plumed serpent, which contained refinements of thought—"among the highest manifestations of the human spirit"—that the parvenu Aztecs disconcertingly repeated, to the confusion of later historians also confronted with their cruel executions, but obviously did not relate to their behavior. When they conquered the civilized Toltecs they took over their religious and scientific ideas, to fill a primitive void and to further their own military and commercial enterprise. When Moctezuma feared that his kingdom was about to be destroyed, and that he was responsible, he punished himself with a twenty-four-day fast, but went on killing as usual.

> On the calends of the first month . . . they killed many children, . . . removing their hearts in honor of the gods of water. . . .
> On the first day of the third month they held a feast to the god named Tlaloc. . . . At this feast they killed many children in the hills. . . .
> On the first day of the fourth month they held a feast in honor of the corn god . . . and killed many children.
> . . . they killed at the feast a chosen youth who had no blemish on his body. . . .
> . . . in honor of this goddess they killed a woman decked with the ornaments they painted on the goddess herself. . . .

And, says the old Spanish chronicler, "the parents of

the victims submitted to these practices, shedding many tears and with great sorrow in their hearts." Mme. Séjourné adds: "According to Aztec religion, . . . man has no other aim but to feed the sun with his own blood, without which the sun will die of exhaustion. This tragic dilemma obliges him to choose between indulging in massacre or bringing about the end of the world . . . we are dealing here with a totalitarian state of which the philosophy included an utter contempt for the individual."

Yet some statements of the Aztec philosophy astonished the conquering Spaniards, as well as later scholars, with a gentle wisdom. This long-observed anomaly was caused, Mme. Séjourné says, by the now archaeologically demonstrable fact that the Aztecs had taken over the intellectual discoveries of the Toltecs without understanding what they meant, and without connecting them self-critically with their own customs. "Naturally, once they became undisputed masters, the Aztecs established themselves as official heirs to the old civilization. There is no doubt that the power which they received from this spiritual heritage helped them, as much as the bow and arrow, to gain temporal power, a thing which they longed to do. The rapid assimilation, by men who yesterday had been primitive, of a thought, a science and a highly elaborate medium of expression, once again shows the extraordinary strength of will of the short-lived Aztec society."

I am impressed with Mme. Séjourné's insight, which will add something permanent to our understanding of Mexico, I fell confident, even if it should be challenged on minor details by experts. I am still more impressed by the relevance of the Aztec-Toltec drama to our own day.

In our own day, as sudden inheritors of the practical benefits of a long, slow advancement in science and technology, we have produced a new ruling class, here called Aztech, which has achieved unprecedented control over nature through the application of scientific methods it did not create. Like the old Aztecs, the new Aztechs merely took over ideas and skills which had been patiently produced over the centuries by a more peaceful tribe of men. Like the old Toltecs, the new Toltechs must submit to the authority of a more primitive kind of man. For the Aztech it was something like standing at a slot machine which had not paid off for a long time and then suddenly presented him with the accrued investments and unrewarded labor of other men.

The new ruler, the man who now thinks chiefly in power possibilities, having discovered cynically how power is achieved, has been split psychologically and rendered profoundly immoral by his unearned authority. He is fragmented into a mere manipulator and forced to yield his original longing for a good life. He gives no more proof than Moctezuma of the gift for leadership that is now demanded of him under conditions that he cannot possibly understand. His self-division and inadequacy are grotesque in his forms as Texas or Arab oil millionaires, and sinster when he appears as a general or a president determined to use nuclear weapons, which Toltech scientists have given him, if any enemy should question his nation's sovereignty.

But the Toltech is also split by his new relationship to power, whether as a scientist who helps to create it or as an artist who yearns for a gentler day when the handicraft of the forge produced only objects for poetic contemplation, as in the days of the Brooklyn Bridge or the Eiffel Tower. Whether he likes it or not, the Toltech must live in a time when *everyone,* including the most austere and the most unworldly, possesses more power—and feels more powerless.

To judge by the literature, art, scholarship and philosophy that the Toltech currently produces, he has not met the new demands upon him much better than the Aztech. He has made a few halfhearted moves toward an Aztech-Toltech dialogue, but he has failed in the very first step, which would call for a better understanding of the new power and the kind of man who controls it. On the contrary, though willing to accept its advantages, he is content to denounce the Aztech for his mistakes and to overlook his own. (When he finds the world "real doomy," he puts the blame on "the disease called politics.") Indeed, since the audience for the books he likes to write consists chiefly of neurotically exclusivist members of his own hardpressed, highbrow tribe, he would be punished for so much as suggesting the common humanity of the less intellectual foe. ("Business is no good," he says; "power is the enemy of life.") Even though their dispute would remain unchanged in essential hostility, the establishment of a mutually appreciative dialogue between Aztechs and Toltechs might at least help a few of them to recognize that no man is complete in himself and every man can learn more from his natural enemies than from the lulling prejudice of his own kind. Education begins with an understanding of one's limitations. Then one's innate narcissism can be put to work. The world's tragedy continues, but one's own can bear fruit.

Before I go further, I wish to clarify my own position by recounting a conversation I had with the Armenian-American painter, Arshile Gorki, probably in 1939, a few years before suicide ended his brilliant career. He said he wanted to return to the Soviet Union, which ruled his birthplace, because no one paid any attention to his pictures in New York. The Soviet Union had shown hostility to his kind of art; and the recent Moscow Trials had led to the execution of many Russians suspected of unorthodox opinions. I said that if he went there he might be killed. He cried beautifully, "I'd rather be killed than ignored!" I replied prosaically, "I'd rather be ignored than killed." This suggests, correctly, that I have no wish for a violent Toltec end.

On the contrary, I believe that the best hope a Toltech can hope for, in a time congenitally hostile to him, is to be ignored, to be permitted to do his quiet task as quietly as possible. "Cherish your obscurity," Rilke counseled the artificer of our day. It was practical advice, even though a certain amount of publicity may have become essential to the artificer's continuance.

Usually, however, publicity or the substitution of it for an austere pursuit of mastery is the artificer's undoing. The need to see one's name in print, or to hear it on the air; the belief that one will somehow be vindicated if one receives enough dubious homage; the tactical assent to expediency that turns into sickening surrender: this familiar defeat has marked the conversion of more than one Toltech to Aztech salesmanship. The appetite for being puffed, on which the newsdealer counts so confidently, has worked its way into the Toltech's Deadly Sins. We all know, and are quick to point out in others, the ludicrous harm it can do. This smells far worse in Toltech lilies, which were meant to be merely beautiful, without too much attention, than in Aztech weeds. Presidents and party-girl

panders should get the headlines, not biologists and abstrac-
tionists.

The Aztech-Toltech dialogue, if it comes off, will call
not only for tolerance but imagination. Both disputants must
expand or expire. In the event that it takes place at all, it will
be the central social dialogue of our time and one that a *norte-
americano* is especially well placed to observe. The power is
greater in the United States, and so is the power-split.

A celebrated, intramural dispute of Toltechs was opened
by C. P. Snow's *The Two Cultures and the Scientific Revolution*
and violently closed by F. R. Leavis's *Two Cultures?* When we
reach the dilemma of the Toltech in modern England (Salvation
by Teamwork) it will be reopened, together with Aldous Huxley's
comment on it in *Literature and Science,* which received less
attention in the press because his superior insights could not be
turned into headlines. The Snow-Leavis controversy in no way
resembled an Aztech-Toltech dialogue. It had the bitter intellectual limitations that editors prefer to display, since anti-intellectual readers enjoy them. For that matter, there was no appreciation of the Aztech position in Huxley, who had already made
it clear in several other books that he considered any concern
with technical power a form of idolatry.

> Technological idolatry is the religion whose doctrines are
> promulgated, explicitly or by implication, in the advertisement pages
> of our newspapers and magazines—the source, we may add paren-
> thetically, from which millions of people derive their working phi-
> losophy of life. . . . So wholehearted is the modern faith in tech-
> nological idols that (despite all the lessons of mechanized warfare)
> it is impossible to discover in the popular thinking of our time any
> trace of the ancient and profoundly realistic doctrine of *hubris* and
> inevitable *nemesis.* There is a very general belief that, where gadgets
> are concerned, we can get something for nothing—can enjoy all the
> advantages of an elaborate, top-heavy and constantly advancing
> technology without having to pay for them by any compensating
> disadvantages.

Many Toltechs applauded this statement when it appeared in 1945. After a long period of painful *guerre et entre-
guerre,* it was pleasant to turn to the delightful mystics whom

Huxley anthologized in his *Perennial Philosophy,* and away from the dreary and dishonest technolaters whom he correctly attacked for the disasters their self-deceit had brought to all of us. However, when he praised the mystics "not only as the ultimate source of our knowledge of the soul and its capacities and defects, but as the salt which preserves human societies from decay," he did it with a gnostic's exclusiveness, an intellectual's dislike of activities, a *yin* mistrust of *yang,* a Toltech's resentment of Aztechs. Although he agreed with his beloved William Law that "Love is infallible; it has no errors, for all errors are the want of love," he showed no love for warrior-administrators who, though guilty of all his charges, still had the merit of organizing the actual world which had made his birth, education and books possible. (As among others his obstetrician, teachers and publishers knew.) Pacifist and technophobe, he fell into the typical Toltech error of refusing to believe that the world is as cruel and ugly for everyone as in its endless power struggle it is. In Aztech eyes he was immature. Revolutionaries, anarchists, beatniks and many other strange bedfellows have fallen far more crudely into the same error, which may originate in the frailer man of thought's many brutal defeats, in childhood, at the hands of future men of action, and his profound resentment of them. There may also be faint race memories of outrages perpetrated on remote shaman forebears, of Aztec knives in Toltec breasts. It is not pleasant to belong to a physically weak and intellectually superior minority. It is not pleasant to suffer injustice, especially when it comes from brothers, shaped on the whole like oneself, whose deepest convictions are entirely different from one's own.

It is more agreeable to find a specialist's half-acre in the now conveniently subdivided wilderness of learning, and to laugh at the underbrained ruffians who once terrorized one's childhood and later, when one was mastering the language of intellect, could not understand a word one said. Now one can safely ignore them. They still run the world, but they cannot touch a hair of one's head. One is snug in one's sanctuary.

Today an intellectual need not feel that he was born to set anything right. He can shed the tragic dimension of absurd predecessors and put on the retainer smile of an attorney.

A short time ago, more often than not, he was ready to

throw in his fortunes with the working class. Now he sees that the revolution was not social but technical, not ideology but ergs (and not ergs but dollars and cents) and there are many ways for him to enjoy the privileges of the bourgeoisie while still seeming, at least to himself, to denounce it. Intellectuals are now allowed to think and usually to say anything they please, so long as they pay their bills on time. Party cards have been replaced by credit cards. Discipline is now provided by a key. If the man of thought possesses the right key—to the house by Mies, the car by Bentley, the vault in Zurich—no one who is up-to-date will care what he thinks.

The kind of Toltech who can make the transition to the key-owning class—the writer who works for Luce, the composer who works for United Artists, the biochemist who works for Pfizer—is heartily despised by members of his tribe who remain hemmed in by sacred inhibitions. In recent years he has been replaced by the absolutely uncompromising avant-gardiste who insults the country club set whenever he can, in the manner of Picasso, and gets still better keys as his reward. The newcomer is nonetheless despised by the die-hard, purist introverts, who say that his advertising methods are merely more adroit. Intransigence, or what passes for it, can also be a formula, and now almost always is. The new avant-garde apes the gestures of the old one, not its innocence, freshness or strength.

The Toltech power game rarely makes page one. That restricted area is reserved for men of genuine might, who really play rough. Readers always prefer athletes to artists. But *homo ludens*, Man the Player, has turned away even from the sports-field, now that the battlefield has become so much more exciting. Football has passed baseball, it is more injurious, but football is tame next to missiles. "Five hundred Viet Cong were *destroyed* yesterday"—that kind of story makes irresistible copy, and it was filed from a small country, inhabited by very small men.

When Lopakhin heard this lecture he ignored its closing references to war (he never mentioned the draft, unless someone else brought it up), and commented only on an earlier reference to power. He said: "I think it's possible to get all the money and power you want, and still have a good life. In fact, I *know* it is!"

Health (Participation)

6

When the discussion moved toward war Trofimov waved his hand nervously in front of his face, as if trying to banish a bad dream. For him a battlefield seemed to be a literary maneuver, invented to speed up the action, which could have nothing to do with reality. He mentioned once that if the idea occurred to him that great accumulations of power might lead to international conflict, he did breathing exercises that he had learned from a book on yoga. Otherwise he had a migraine headache.

Great accumulations of power had no such effect on Lopakhin. They exhilarated him. "They'll back down," he said of the enemy in Viet Nam. Conflict had a similar effect. He was never more tactful or more precise in his desires than when he asked my advice about getting a student loan; whom to see about it, and above all how to establish his need for it. "They may think, just because I wear Hart Schaffner and Marx clothes, that I don't need it." He must have been persuasive, or worn his shabbiest suit, because he got the money at a low interest rate and, as I heard later, invested it in the Stock Market with extraordinary skill. In time he ran it up, by his own admission, to at least fifty thousand dollars.

He was confident that power did not necessarily have to lead to war. "In the right hands," he insisted, "it can be creative." He was also confident of his own ability to make good use of any power that came his way. "I could hold down any job," he once said, "any."

At first I thought he was a simple braggart, which was a mistake. It took me some time to realize that his attitude

71

expressed a norm. Every word he spoke was delivered with the assurance of one who was in harmony with the deepest beliefs of his society. He knew he could count on general approval. When he expressed confidence in himself he was merely expressing his health, his willingness to take his chances in a tricky game. Thereafter I studied him with some care, and listened attentively to every word he said. He was introducing me to a mental world which I, pro-Toltech by nature, would do well to try to understand. I was already getting an opportunity to participate in the very dialogue for which I had asked.

Here I will put down some passages from lectures of mine, as well as I remember them, and then follow them with Lopakhin's comments. I can now see that I did not come off well in the debate.

In commenting on D. H. Lawrence's famous remark in a letter to E. M. Forster, "Business is no good," I observed that many artists felt that business was a waste of time, and most businessmen, if not all, were bores. The commerce of the world was conducted, Lawrence had felt, by men who had never experienced the joy of living, or if they had, had not had the courage to be true to their experience, and they had compensated for their cowardice by trying to take a profit on every encounter with honest and healthy men.

Lopakhin reminded me of an earlier lecture in which I had said that Lawrence had died young of tuberculosis, and had never even admitted that he had that disease. "Some health!" said Lopakhin with a snort that also implied: "Some courage!"

On another occasion, perhaps to cheer Trofimov, perhaps merely to express a conviction of my own, I said, primitive initiation rites exist also in the civilized world—in confirmations, bar mitzvahs, hazing, etc.—but they did not succeed in preparing our young as effectively as the savages had done for theirs, because our world was so much more complex, and our young needed more time to get ready for it.

"If you're strong, you're strong," said Lopakhin. "If you're weak, you're weak. That's the way it is." At that moment I understood him better than before. He had already, before being old enough to vote, reconciled himself to the pain of life, and was not asking sympathy or help from anyone. He had little use for those who did. Artists and intellectuals were *per se* inferior. Or, as he put it more than once, "They can dish it out, but they can't take it!"

On still another occasion I said that the man of thought rarely gets the better of the man of action, except by flight into the subdivided wilderness of "unintelligible" art or learning. And even there, after neatly ridding himself of the tragic dimension, he is haunted by the terror that grass and jungle will take over in time, now that the old brown-eyed Mediterranean humanities have been undermined by pale-eyed, time-study men. Culture seems to have removed itself so far from ordinary life that a general desire for oblivion rather than thought may be moving our society toward total destruction. Deprived of Vertical guidance, the Horizontals may anonymously frankenstein themselves, while prehistoric silence, as Octavio Paz has predicted, descends upon victorious vegetation.

This gloomy speculation brought forth from Lopakhin a repetition of a radio speech by his favorite author, a scientist who believed the world was at last entering its golden age. "It's a frightful error," he quoted, "to assume that the common man reads only comics or is thinking only of the horsepower in his car. Actually, the man in the street is now discovering literature and art. More people buy books and go to museums than ever before. The music on the air is first class. Science is studied by seven-year-olds, and intelligently studied too. In fifty years this new burst of intellectual curiosity will dominate the entire world. We shall have a Renaissance that will put the Italian one to shame."

So ran our many debates. In one of them I said: "You may think you can retire to the country and live simply, but you can't. One way or another, the cost of living will be forced up, and you will have to find new ways of meeting your expenses. You cannot find freedom the way you want to. You may wish to take a walk in Los Angeles, and refuse every offer of a lift (the French ambassador did), but after a few minutes the police will get suspicious and you will get arrested. That is what happened to him. You may think a good washing machine will solve your laundry problems, with occasional repairs, but in time you will find that no more parts are being made for that model, and if you wish to continue a new habit, which is easier on the hands than the old one, you have to buy another machine. You may think your children can get along better with old schoolbooks, because they were written by Coleridge, Milton and Sterne, not by Slater, Burglon and North, but if you try to make the experiment you will estrange your child from his playmates and jeopardize his ability to make a living when he grows up. Your good taste would be the worst thing that ever happened to him. Also, you may think you can live in another Walden, but if you tried, it would be the most expensive mistake you ever made. It would cost you the love of your family, the respect of your friends—and a large weekly bill from the mental institution where you would soon find yourself. Thoreau is, of course, a great American hero, but he hacked out a tidy path to the madhouse."

Lopakhin's heavy shoulders said: "Nuts!" He did not use that word.

"Abundance," I said. "is revolutionizing even the most established ways of doing things. For some time now the contemplative orders of the Catholic Church have been emptying monasteries to send monks and nuns out into a world of Coke bottles, gas pumps and teenage pessaries. A married priesthood is under discussion. Celibacy seems to have impressed peasants more than it does psychoanalyzed ex-urbanites. The yogis of India no longer go into the forest that lay so conveniently to hand in the good old British days. They write books in English. Zen means less to Japan that is dazzled by technology than it does to a few Americans who have become disillusioned with it."

"So what?" said Lopakhin, in somewhat more tactful language.

It was, however, after I read a passage to the class from a book I was writing, this book, that I got my sharpest challenge from him. The passage went as follows:

A great source of confusion to students is that in the good old days you could tell the Aztechs from the Toltechs without a scorecard, and today it is not always so easy. When the Secretary of the Treasury, Salmon P. Chase, refused to hire Walt Whitman because his poetry was immoral, but kept the letter of recommendation from Emerson that Whitman brought him, for its autograph, you knew at once that Whitman was a good guy, a Toltech, and Chase a banker-prig, the worst kind of Aztech. And when the Secretary of the Interior James Harlan fired Whitman after peeping into his desk at a copy of *Leaves of Grass,* you knew that Harlan was still worse, a snoop. But now of course, even if high officials felt the same way about the creative efforts of a lowly clerk, they would be advised by their public-relations experts to try to tie him up with Moscow or Havana in all the papers before making a move against him. Poetry has become so harmless that it cannot be attacked. It would be like hitting a man who was down—before a camera. If anything is sacred still, it is an art that no one any longer reads. (The student may be quick enough to understand this, but it still disturbs and confuses him. His tolerance of cynicism is not yet as great as he would like it to be.)

If the student has been reading the papers, he can guess that no responsible American statesman of the present day would act with open vindictiveness toward any member of any minority that might strike back. And poets, though on the whole a hang-dog lot and not as alertly mobilized for retaliation as less oppressed, more militant minorities, do have their champions among the word-dazzled wives of board chairmen and other atavistic misfits who do not realize that words are meant to be used for a purpose, to lower sales resistance or vote resistance, and not to provide an as-if experience which no laboratory will verify. (Some poets have caught on, and turned their harmlessness, by adroit appeals to the maternal instinct, into fairly cozy forms of secession; and no one can honestly reproach them, except for the harm thus done to their verse. We want our artists to suffer for us.) Almost everyone who rises high in Washington knows that poetry is read only by other poets or by students whose hormones have not yet been healthily harnessed to the production curve. Whatever tribal, anti-poetic passions the well-trained Aztech may still feel, he is shrewd enough to refrain from actions that might, in his prudent phrase, boomerang.

Unlike the leaders of the Soviet Union, he does not live in a culture that is still close to ancient oral bardcraft. Because the printing press has not had long to work on the Russian

masses, the Soviet, to protect the ideology of its political revolution, had to suppress its poets for fear they might injure its plans
for its peasants. Eloquent symbols still meant so much to Russians that Stalin sacrificed Mayakovsky to Dnieperstroy. (Leaders
of the new Arab lands, where the spoken word also possesses
magic, now face the same problem: djinns or dams?) But the
American politico lives in a land where whatever remained of an
ancient oral bardic tradition among the aborigines, when the
whites landed, was soon extirpated by highly literate divines
who went ashore with books in their hands and genocide pre-
pense. (Connoisseur descendants of the divines are highly critical
of Spanish priests who burnt Toltec libraries in Mexico; but the
Spaniards let the natives live with a tolerance that did not occur
to Puritan bibliophiles.)

Walt Whitman sought to revive the ancient druidic
word-magic of his Anglo-Saxon forebears with books that he
printed himself. His naïveté delighted upper class English
readers, despite his attacks on their older land. They wanted to
arrest utilitarian corruption of their language, and his "barbaric
yawp" could therefore be fitted in, without too much of a squeeze,
with the medievalism of the Rossettis and William Morris. Hard-
hit Toltechs everywhere are always quick to recognize an ally
in any costume.

It has become customary in literary criticism, ever
since D. H. Lawrence threw out a suggestive remark, to divide
American authors into redskins and palefaces. Whitman is generally chosen as most representative of our more savagely extra-
verted writers, while Henry James stands for the civilized introverts. "The creative mind in America is fragmented," says Philip
Rahv, "between intellectual and roughneck, patrician and
plebeian, highbrow and lowbrow." Stung by the challenge, more
than one novelist and poet has tried to heal the breach with his
own books.

When this division is seen in the context of the Aztech-
Toltech drama and the technicization of man that gave rise to
it, it becomes clear that the problem was definitively resolved
some time ago, without appropriate notice to literature. We
now know which path the Toltech must follow. The separation of
human beings into intellectuals and roughnecks, patricians and

plebeians, highbrows and lowbrows will continue, with the latter in each case always heavily outvoting and outbuying the former; but the effect of technicization upon human beings is of such a kind that only the former, the intellectuals, the patricians, the highbrows—and only a fraction of their fraction—will be able to understand it. Neither the anti-literature simplifications of the redskins (once symbolized by Ernest Hemingway and now by C. P. Snow) nor the pro-literature complexities of the palefaces (once symbolized by T. S. Eliot and now by F. R. Leavis) have suggested any capacity to understand the new sociological, psychological, philosophic, historical and *literary* problems that technicization has raised. This is because technicization coincided with, and would have been impossible without, desacralization, which went deeper and farther than the secularization that is sometimes confused with it.

The nature of desacralization is such that no more than a very few palefaces (having, among other qualifications, a naturally close affinity with the redskins, the roughnecks, the plebeians, the lowbrows) will know how it came about and what might in time (centuries) be done to oppose it with a force as persuasive as its own. Desacralization has gained steadily in momentum since it got its intellectual accreditation in the seventeenth century, and has encountered little resistance (less than anywhere else) in the United States, where the abstractness of puritan thought, the temperateness of the climate, the low development of the aborigines (no Toltecs), the richness of natural resources, the need for mechanical improvement, the chance for rapid advancement and many other often debated elements soon produced a new national character that even in de Tocqueville's day was noted for its restless practicality and its distrust of sacred traditions.

If our writers had not been told by science, or what passed for it, to overlook religious factors, even scientifically, they would have understood long ago that they were actually in the midst of a revolution that was infinitely further-reaching than the Russian, sure to affect them closely in every aspect of their personal lives, also sure to alter their literary strategies. They would have reexamined their uncritical Marxism, which they had usually embraced out of laziness—to give them a quick,

unearned faith, to resolve their doubts with fanaticism, to turn
envy into a virtue or to let religion in by the back door—and
realized that a quieter, less exotic but more important seizure
of power was going on all around them. The Aztechs, whom they
then contemptuously called Babbitts, had recovered from the
1929 panic, which was supposed to have been their end, and
were taking over again. This time they used methods borrowed,
without excessive signs of gratitude, from a Toltech economist
named John Maynard Keynes. During the 1930's shrewd laws
were passed to save American capitalism with socialist devices
(minus the fatal adjective, of course) and prepare it for a strong
reemergence after the Second World War. Our writers were once
again faced with the choice of resisting or writing what Aztechs
wanted them to write, in magazines, radio shows, films and books
that were aimed with ever greater skill at emotionally vulnerable segments of "the great audience."

Now they no longer need to resist. Now the Aztechs
have prospered splendidly. These post-war days have slowly
acknowledged their opulent, undemanding revolution as the only
one that seems likely to sweep the world, even in those areas
(like Cuba and China) where poor defiant proletarians still hold
out against a confident, gift-bearing bourgeoisie. Now, no American writer need face a cruel dilemma. Let him merely persist
long enough in his "sullen art," and a place will be made for
him. Shrewd businessmen, secretly worried, have found a place
for his naïve avant-garde faith. If his talent is popular, it can
address itself lucratively to numb status-seekers who can always
be prodded by a full-page ad into buying the newest story about
Lincoln's mother's sad-eyed dog. If the writer's talent is unpopular, there is sure to be an artist-in-residence bunk with a
mere fifteen-hour weekly lecture-load for him at West Kentucky
Wesleyan, while in his off-moments he describes with some ele-
gance how he was led astray in an organloft by a prominent
citizen of Joplin, Missouri.

Some Aztech is always ready to befriend any Toltech,
now, the queerer the better. His culture-hungry money tribe has
made the discovery that six percent is better than removing an
enemy's heart and suffering a bad conscience. (The new Aztechs
are much more humane than the old Aztecs.) If you take a

public-be-damned attitude you not only ask for trouble, you convict yourself of the worst folly—not knowing the rules of the game. A Cabinet member, who fired a poet today, would make his President wonder why he had ever been appointed in the first place. The Chase Manhattan Bank would not approve of Salmon P. Chase. Literature has become a national Hyde Park, where the most subversive views are heard with complete indifference, because they have nothing to do with gross national product. In fact such views are printed regularly in fashion magazines to help sell the *haute couture,* which seems to need them.

There is none of the cultural clarity that still prevailed at the time of the Civil War. If the student is inclined to be antisocial, he may bitterly enjoy the multiple ironies of the situation, which permit him to retire all the sooner into whatever "cool" detachment he can find. If he is at all square (and he is always much squarer than he lets on), he tells himself that these facts, which have foreborn from harsher truths that every adult would recognize, cannot really be facts. He secretly wishes some genuine Toltech, better informed than his teachers, would come along and tell him what to believe and what to do.

Were such a Toltech to appear providentially, what would he say? Before we can even guess at his reply, it will be necessary to look at the historical circumstances which led to his tribe's reduction from a real office of leadership, so real that it invited sanctimonious reprisal, to a titular eminence that is expected to cajole him into silence and decorum. Is it astonishing that his writing often retreats into a private language, almost as secret as that of the mathematicians? To regain his rightful leadership he must not only assimilate many important insights of many experts, he must take them with him into the great loneliness (if he can find it) and bring back an intelligible picture of the world as it is likely to be (during a period he cannot be expected to enjoy) for the less heroic Toltechs and the more receptive Aztechs, who desire his guidance more than their present posts of unchallenged command allow them to admit.

When President Kennedy invited a poet to his inauguration, it was a token admission of this desire, politically less important than routine invitations to prayer-stretching clerics, but still a portent of a need for Toltech guidance that is sure to increase with time, and indeed has already been recognized in less thoroughly Aztech cultures. During the interregnum of their titular eminence and their real unimportance, the few genuine Toltechs will naturally be restricted to an incomprehensible private language. Authenticity must take priority in their slow preparation for a social function that indeed may not be theirs again for another thousand years. (How strangely Hitler's prediction of a "new millennium" is being fulfilled! Not a master race but a master-method is conquering the world.) Toltechs are potentially the most valuable human beings we have, the nearest to a qualitative norm, the best balance of the masculine and feminine minds, the best intermediaries between society and solitude, the only reliable check on Aztech *hubris;* but a very popular hurricane, unless they timidly take shelter with the happy victims, is determined to blow them down.

After class Lopakhin said he wanted to ask me a question, but there were other students with other questions, and he waited until they were gone and then suggested that we have a cup of coffee together. I had intended to hurry on somewhere else. My wife and some friends were expecting me in a restaurant; but something in his manner made me decide to go along with him for a few minutes. He seemed to have an important announcement to make. By this time I was observing him closely. Almost a year had passed since I first saw him.

His dark gray suit had been cut by a good tailor; he was no longer wearing ready-mades. His fingernails had been polished by a manicurist. A dark front tooth had been replaced by a light one. His high-collared shirt and wine-colored tie looked as if they had come from Paris. It was not until later that I heard of his success on the Stock Market, but I was already being shown some outward evidence of it. In retrospect I now realize that his voice grew more musical about that time, and he began to choose his words with greater conservatism. He would no longer have implied "So what?" to me. On the contrary, he handled me with consummate tact.

He began by praising my ability to use words. I have forgotten exactly what he said, but the idea was that I had a skill and I was not using it well. I got the impression that he referred specifically to the lecture I had just given. Why sit like Canute and command the tide to roll back? The tide was sure to wash over me unless I tried to understand its movements. Now I was going against it. But if I were to devote my skill to something really worthwhile, he had a friend who was the director of a complex of computers in a place near New York, and he knew they were looking for someone with just my kind of talent. It was all said with such finesse that I could not possibly take offense, but he meant that in such a job I would be doing something useful, while now I was wasting my time. The pay would be much better than any university could afford to pay. (He knew faculty wage scales better than I.)

He was young enough to be my son, and he was trying to be nice to me. (His face, by the way, was more mature than mine had been at that age.) "Throw away all your crazy ideas about the Aztechs and the Toltechs," he was saying to me in effect. "They'll never get you anywhere. The only people who will like them are the ne'er-do-wells. Get wise to yourself. Come on over to the sunny side of the street. I'm doing all right as it is but when I get out of law school—and maybe when I do, the draft will be over—I'll be able to throw a lot of things your way. You're my favorite teacher. It isn't what we learn in college that counts, mostly that's a lot of nonsense, it's the people we meet. I like you, and I want to look after you. I'll always be sentimental about my favorite teacher. I don't always agree with you, but you make me see new viewpoints. You don't know your way around, and I do." Of course none of that was put into words, but that was what he conveyed with great exactitude.

I said I would be glad to meet his friend who ran the computers.

Lopakhin looked pleased, and insisted on paying for our coffee. Formerly I had always paid the check for all students who had anything to eat or drink with me. We said goodbye.

On the way to the other restaurant I realized once again what a *solid* young man he was. He was already facing the big world that most students feared and not only facing it, but moving around with great clarity in the very midst of it. He was playing the most complex game that the ingenuity of man had

been able to devise, and playing it with the coolness of a master.
My Toltech prejudice against his type amounted to nothing more
than a rationalization of my own inability to act with his decisive-
ness. I would do well to listen to my own lectures, and learn
from my own student, who might have been my own child. He
had just given me a lesson. If there had been a debate between
us, I had come off second best.

SICKNESS (WITHDRAWAL)

7

Soon afterward I made the mistake of mentioning my new interest in Lopakhin to Trofimov. In a misguided attempt to rouse the "permanent student" to action, or at least to a greater awareness of his inaction, I said to him during a private conference in my office (when he asked me to recommend a psychiatrist) that Lopakhin seemed to be the new norm.

"How can you say that!" Trofimov looked as if his last remaining friend had betrayed him. "You wrote something entirely different!" He cited a passage in a book of mine, where I had written that psychology had received a "much-needed norm" from "the Remnant," those who represent man not in his averageness but in his highest capabilities. They are "necessarily few" and they "retain a sure sense of 'the best that is in them.' " They have inevitably a hard time.

"Since you admire him so much, let me tell you something about Mr. ——. (He gave the real name of Lopakhin.) He needed some typing done. He gave it to Nellie Rankin. You know, she always sits in the front row. He was going to pay her thirty-five cents a page; the commercial rate is sixty. But when he got around to paying her it came out to twenty cents a page, and he forgot to sign the check, and so she had to stall her landlady for a whole week. That's Mr. —— for you!"

"Are you sure? He's looking prosperous."

"He's rich! But he didn't want to pay Nellie. So he's your norm now!"

"Only in the usual sense of adjustment, not the Remnant sense."

"Hmmm."

I returned the discussion to Trofimov's search for a psychiatrist. He had received some "help" in free clinics, but had found no one sufficiently "imaginative" to suit him. I said I would try to get some names from a professional friend. I steered the conversation away from any mention of money, which I had noticed before had a particularly distressing effect on Trofimov. His mother had inherited some real estate, and it had been sold for much less than it would now have been worth. The proceeds were long since gone, partly in payment of his educational expenses. If he had had a small but steady income, he seemed to feel, he might have had the time to bring his gifts to maturity without strain. As it was, he felt under a strain whenever he came upon any reminder that others could make money more easily than he could.

"He actually feels guilty," I thought while we chatted, "because he's not both rich and already famous as a writer! This is not the usual case of a rebel without a cause or an uncommitted, passive drifter. He has the cause of a real talent, and he's committed to it, but he can't do much with it because he can't get outside it. He can't see himself as an object, he identifies with his own emotions. He gets all worked up over the injustice to Nellie Rankin, instead of first examining his emotions and questioning them. It's his own relationship to money he should be thinking about, not Lopakhin's or Nellie's. He's caught in the amateur's vicious circle: emotion for its own sake, not cool study of the self that produces the emotion. There are so many others like him with real talents that never get untracked, while the clever fakes run rings around them. How can the talent of America be helped to express itself? What can I do? Well, the first step would be to make something of my own talents, such as they are." And my thoughts ended on a familiar note of self-admonition.

My next lecture, as I look back on it now, must have been in part an attempt to rouse Trofimov to a greater awareness of himself. It mainly dealt with literature. Most of it was meant, of course, for the whole class, but a few words seem to me now, when I try to recall them, as having been especially

addressed to him. Among other things, the lecture included
the following:

Some men of thought, after discovering that thought
impedes their progress toward better pay and the right dinner
parties, dim the beam of their intellect—usually without strain.
They do not have to read Griboyedov's play to appreciate *The
Misfortune of Being Clever.* Uneaten birthday cake, unopened
party favors, sincere peacemaking overtures rejected with scorn
—these heartbreaking come-uppances have convinced them that
wit wins more enemies than friends. So they learn to hold their
tongue. They rebuild careers with ripened flattery. By the time
prudence has won them tenure and the chairmanship of the
English Department, or a desk in the State Department, or a
secure job on a national magazine (if there can long be such a
thing when electronic entertainment daily replaces the pain of
reading), they may seethe with unexpressed emotions, suffer the
mutiny of pancreas and liver, delight their analyst with really
new twists to the old plot, get drunk every night on Third
Avenue, holler down rainbarrels on weekends in East Hampton;
but their ideas, long atrophied from lack of chance-taking improvisation, will not bring any postprandial misgivings to their
dean, their Secretary or their publisher.
     The talent that is death to hide is lodged in them use-
less, except for the poems, plays, novels and above all critiques
they continue to pour out in Caslon or Bodoni, along with photographs that preferably make their wan, conformist features look
as savage as those of Queequeg. They pour for a small circle
of fellow-secessionists whose every back tingles from nape to
bottom with friendly scratching. They seek to convince the
world and themselves that literature can flourish (painting and
music too, if they bring in any readers) in uncontaminated
purity, far from rockets, rivets, computers, tax laws and all the
other licensed enemies that daily drive the common reader, if he
still exists, into listless apathy. The desire for fulfillment in
enduring form obliges these overliterary authors, whose plight
invites derision in newsmagazines but actually is no more ridiculous than that of anyone else who is born athwart his time or

his place, to ignore a general apathy that alert psychiatrists have already been describing as the most prevalent pathology of their patients. It is this apathy that empties bookstores as soon as a newspaper strike ends the full-page advertisements, in double great primer type, that are ordinarily required to prod readers into glancing at the first and last paragraphs of the latest account of Lincoln's mother's greathearted dog.

The new seceding Axels say: "Live? Our relatives will do that for us." They no longer can find the servants on whom the original Axel, as conceived by Villiers de L'Isle-Adam, relied to spare him the details of existence. With the total recall of plainclothesmen, our less popular authors put down every syllable uttered by innocent kinsmen who did not know they were speaking the new four-letter prose. If it can still be said that we possess a folk, in the sense of those who spontaneously produce folklore, it would seem to consist of semi-illiterates, from Georgia to the Bronx, born in humiliating proximity to note-taking symbol-pushers with phonographic ears. Our folk is the kin of our writers. By and by its natural poetry will be reprocessed by newsprint and kinescope into the puffy, white harmlessness that most consumers prefer; but as recorded on the fleshly tapes of word-loving blood-relations, it still retains some of its unbleached graininess.

At times the novels of our vanguard are better, word for word, than some of the hallowed masterpieces of the nineteenth century. Usually, however, they fail to convince anyone, except perhaps a few Sarah Lawrence wives, that it is not a waste of time to read them. Serious fiction sells worse every year, publishers report, even those who prefer to print it.

This is not because, as Ortega y Gasset says, there is a shortage of good subjects. It is because there is a shortage of good readers. An understanding of narrative symbols requires a high degree of personal culture, a leisurely freedom of mind, a playful seriousness that prosperity, in defiance of Engels' Law (quantity passes into quality), has obviously failed to deliver. On the contrary, prosperity and a growing conviction among economists that soon there will be no poverty anywhere have had the effect of turning readers toward how-to-do-it directions and other useful handbooks that might add to their prestige.

Nouveaux-riches behave like *nouveaux-riches*. Symbols, the stock in trade of literature, are either suspect among those who fear leaving arithmetic too far behind or overvalued by those who fear leaving literature too far behind. Usually the only symbols worth studying are those that help salesmen to sell or rulers to rule. In a few cases, however, they may lead to a better job in the English Department. Almost never are they enjoyed for their own sake.

As for retrieving them from nature, from that "forest of symbols" that Baudelaire calls nature, this becomes more difficult each year, even for the truly talented writer. Literary communication requires shared experience. When nearly evey member of his potential audience resists experience, and above all the distinctive experience of his time, the writer can at best hope to share his experience and his symbolic discoveries with a few of his own kind. And sometimes he does not want to speak to so narrow a group, but to others different from himself, to all whom imagination can unite. But if he does not consciously limit himself to a very narrow audience and acquire a technique for speaking to them and only to them, he usually ends nowhere, and speaks only to himself.

It is a hard time to be a writer. He must acquire the fullest possible experience through the thinnest possible skin, and then serve it up to readers who are determined to let *no* experience into deliberately toughened hides. Literature may someday become important again, but only when our thinskins can become strong again (and not corrupt) through daily exposure to the marketplace.

Trofimov's response was almost a scream. "But if one sees literature as a thing in itself," he protested, "something that does not have to justify itself to squares and fatheads who don't understand it, I mean, why judge it by the standards of those who never did dig it and never will? A writer can't have anything to do with those people. He'd go crazy if he did!"

His attitude, though no different from that of many writers of present and past, made me realize how different he was from the Russian student, the original Trofimov, in the play by Chekhov. On stage, in the last act, when Lopakhin offered

Trofimov some money, he refused it with supreme assurance that he could get along without it, and nothing in the future presented a serious problem. He was not filled with despair but with hope.

On stage Lopakhin said: "Look, I've just made forty thousand rubles. You're broke, flat broke. Let me lend you some money. Don't be so high and mighty. I'm a peasant—there's no nonsense about me!" He took out his wallet.

On stage Trofimov replied: "Your father was a peasant, and my father was a chemist, which means nothing. I won't take your money! If you offered me two hundred thousand, I wouldn't take it. Listen, everything that you like—that's just what *I* don't want. I can get along perfectly well. People are going ahead; toward truth and happiness, toward a paradise on earth, and I'm going with them."

Lopakhin sniffed: "Do you think you'll get there?"

And Trofimov replied on stage with supreme confidence and no fear of being laughed at: "I'll get there. And if I don't, I'll help others to get there."

Never did my own student show anything like the prerevolutionary exuberance of his Russian predecessor. As I think of the American student's fear of the future, I also recall his response to another lecture, which went something like this:

An expert in constitutional psychology (William Sheldon), after studying many thousands of typical responses to the factual and the symbolic, has reached the conclusion that the vast majority of men and women have heavy-gutted bodies and slow minds that are sure, for very old evolutionary reasons, to mistrust any but practical symbols. The nineteenth century, progressive belief that all men would evolve toward the urban intellectuality that progressives admired in themselves, and general prosperity would in time produce general culture, is now being tested by the predominant psychophysical structure of man, which seems to have been shaped by a will to survive in brute aggressiveness, not to progress toward enlightenment. Progressives have overlooked biology.

It is a phase of the Aztech-Toltech drama that the student cannot overlook, if he wishes to see it as it is rather than with a wishful astigmatism. Politically it means there can be little progress toward humanitarian goals, unless these are enhanced with appeals to intelligent self-interest. (Desegregation of Southern schools is currently baited with the promise of more Southern factories, once Negroes are given a fair chance to work in them; and this appears to be the most effective argument, surest in the long run to overcome ignorant poor white hostility.) Culturally it means the end of the hope that the man in the street will one day throw away his tabloid for *Women in Love*. There is more chance of political progress than of cultural progress, because the former depends on group reasonableness, which *can* be achieved, while the latter depends on the private needs of a few mavericks.

The very phrase "cultural progress" has been challenged by many cultural critics, as a misuse of analogy, ever since Hazlitt wrote "Why the Arts are Not Progressive" in 1814. "What is mechanical, reducible to rule, or capable of demonstration, is progressive, and admits of gradual improvement: what is not mechanical or definite, but depends on genius, taste, and feeling, very soon becomes stationary, or retrograde, and loses more than it gains by transfusion." To a Toltech his reasoning is self-evident. To an Aztech it is depressing and reactionary, because it argues against the dearest hope of the new ruling class that their manifest talents for external organization can now be applied to matters of taste and feeling. If taste can be created by merchandising "tastemakers," to improve the look of chairs, walls and dresses, why cannot the sensibility that lies behind taste be created early in students, *en masse,* so that in time everyone will appreciate the best in the arts, and if he has talent, be able to create more of it in a super-Amityville?

This is one of the most seductive appeals to the happy victims; it promises not only prosperity but peace and productivity. Also a possible invitation to the White House. What mother's heart can stand up against it? What teacher? What publisher? "Peace, it's wonderful!" As soon as the war was won, the conquerors wanted to behave like saints. And, their press agents artfully suggest, who can hold it against them? What is more to the point, who can hold out against them?

Unfriendly Toltechs are thus forced into an unattractive

corner; they have to look like dogs in the manger. They are holding on to a treasure they do not want to share. Actually, of course, they would like nothing better than to share it. Artists want everyone to have their art. But they know that art is a matter of experience, and experience cannot be taught. Facts, methods and ideologies can be taught, but not experience.

Trofimov raised his hand. To my surprise he was not agitated. "You're saying that experience is unteachable," he remarked quietly, "and I agree. Why should a writer have to teach anybody anything? All he has to do is to put down what *he* has experienced, and let others get it or not, as they please." A disturbing idea then seemed to occur to him; his voice lost its calm. "But don't people *fear* experience? And isn't that what depresses us more than anything else? People don't listen to a word you say. I think that's the most depressing thought in the whole world." He shuddered. Nellie Rankin turned around in her seat in the front row, to look at him, with a concerned expression on her face.

I said as soothingly as possible that the tragedy of time-lag was one that every original artist had to suffer. After all, how could he expect others to understand him right off, if what he said was really new? Stendhal had had to wait until long after his death to find his audience.

"It's horrible, horrible," he murmured, and shuddered once again. "The most depressing thought in the whole world."

"No, it's not a thought, it's a fact, and a fact that is probably truer today than it was in Stendhal's day. Why expect to be understood? Isn't it enough to be able to write what you please without police interference?"

Nellie Rankin shot me a look that meant I was being a cruel monster. But Trofimov was no longer listening. An impenetrable sorrow seemed to have kidnapped his mind and spirited it from the room. I went on:

Writers traditionally have prided themselves on being more open to experience than their parents, their teachers, their neighbors. Writers "travel light," carry a minimum of baggage and prejudice, see things as they are, report them without fear and with style. They do not want to blind themselves with property or degrees or marriage or party alignments. Or so at least the story once ran. Now an entirely different story is more often apt to be true. Writers gain a special stance that is essential to their trade by their party alignment, their marital status (or lack of it), their specialized studies or their desire for property. They regard the universally shared experience of man as a myth in which they can no longer believe, and serve more often as attorneys for their clients or their own prejudices than as spokesmen for man. No one wishes to hear any more about man, except as that overvast subject affects him himself personally. The very possibility of impersonal insight is under suspicion. And even in universities it does not pay.

Yet every day we produce young writers who want to serve as spokesmen for man. They have had some experiences, and they want to communicate them in the name of everyman. They believe they can leap straight into universals from their particulars. And their education, insofar as it is traditional, and uncorrected by modern technically inspired doubt, leads them to believe that they can.

They get caught inevitably in what a psychiatrist has called "the double-bind." They have taken two mutually exclusive courses of action, as a result of two wholly unexamined assumptions. They have assumed that what is true for them is true for others, and that others will want to hear about it. They have acted to report their experiences in a manner satisfactory to themselves, and then attempted to sell their report to others. They have presented their case both to those who love truth and to those who hate it. They have assumed that the former outnumber the latter, and then discovered the extent of their error. They have believed that the world will always surrender to goodwill and intelligence. They have believed that ancient hatreds, though long existent in the Old World, cannot survive in the cleaner air of the New. They have, in short, behaved with a naïveté for which everyone will commend them, except their publishers (if they get them) and their own disillusioned selves, years later.

Their errors are of such magnitude that they lead to complete psychic withdrawal from society, and in some cases clinical schizophrenia, unless society steps in and reclaims them from limbo with war duty or the need to make a living. Usually, since their self-discipline was not sufficient to save them, they end by taking on the only discipline that is currently given, the discipline of money, and acquire an attitude toward truth that is closer to that of an attorney than the one which originally created their illusions. Such is the customary record of American literary genius.

Can any American writers still speak for man, instead of for their own prejudices or their clients? It is possible. First they would probably have to be as big fools as those I have just described, and then they would have to persist in their folly until one day they became wise. Wisdom would mean that they became *objects to themselves*. As a psychologist has put it: "The individual enters as such into his own experience only as an object, not as a subject; and he can enter as an object only on the basis of social relations and interactions . . . only by taking the attitudes of others towards himself is he able to become an object to himself."

What does this mean? It means not withdrawal from a dirty world but total immersion in it. As another psychologist puts it: "The individual dies for the birth of the universal. . . . Let us recall that the 'nature of things' is for us the best, the most affectionate, the most humiliating of masters; it surrounds us with its vigilant assistance. The only task incumbent upon us is to understand reality and let ourselves be transformed by it."

It is not easy to find joy in humiliating reality. It is easier to become a purist or a psychopath, a don or a MacDougal Street demonist. It is disgusting to see oneself as an object, shaped like everyone else by history and society. It is worse to have to trace every depression to a personal comedown. It is hardest of all to stay vulnerable to experience, especially when one has learned how to shut it out forever. What writer wants to open his mind to facts, above all the shapeless facts of the scientist and the dirty facts of the businessman? It is much better to put one's curse on them, "business and science—no good!"

Someday, of course, our crybabies will be stoics. Who can expect less in the land of the free? The tender of mind (and feet) will become tough. Thin-skinned writers will be as indifferent to pain as the hardy shamans who centuries ago started them on their path of purely spiritual conquest. But it is hard to imagine it now.

After class Lopakhin said, "You're right, facts are what count. You can only feed facts into a computer."

I disagreed. "No, you feed into a computer the facts that you see. There may be other facts that you don't see. If you programmed them, the computer would come up with a different answer." I looked to see what had become of Trofimov. How had he taken my lecture?

Lopakhin laughed. "I know what's a fact and what isn't a fact. When are you going to come and see my friend who runs the computers?"

While we were making an appointment I saw Trofimov leaving the room in what seemed like a very gloomy state. Speaking cheerfully and holding onto his arm was Nellie Rankin.

THE RAINCOAT MIND

8

Since Lopakhin was so sure that he knew all he had to know about facts, I addressed some of the next lecture to him. It went roughly like this:

Every student here knows that the empirical method of science obliged overdeductive philosophy long ago to take a more respectful attitude toward fact. Whitehead's description seems to me best: "The sixteenth century of our era saw the disruption of Western Christianity and the rise of modern science. It was an age of ferment. Nothing was settled, though much was opened—new worlds and new ideas. In science, Copernicus and Vesalius may be chosen as representative figures; they typify the new cosmology and the scientific emphasis on direct observation. . . . Galileo keeps harping on how things happen, whereas his adversaries had a complete theory as to why things happen. . . . Galileo insists upon 'irreducible and stubborn facts.'" Whitehead takes the last phrase from William James, who wrote his novelist brother Henry about his own *Principles of Psychology*: "I have to forge every sentence in the teeth of irreducible and stubborn facts."

Every student here knows that the most brilliant logic can go all wrong if it does not humbly check its conclusions with observable fact. What few students know is that this famous scientific victory is constantly being flawed, even now, by disguised abstractions which have not been corrected by concrete facts. All thought, including scientific thought, tends to become too conceptual and too confident. Or as Whitehead puts it: "You cannot think without abstractions; accordingly, it is of the utmost importance to be vigilant in critically revising your *modes* of abstraction. It is here that philosophy finds its niche as essential to the healthy progress of society. It is the critic of abstractions. A civilization which cannot burst through its abstractions is doomed to sterility after a very limited period of progress."

Now what I am saying today is this: you and I, because we are Americans, have to be especially vigilant about our facts. We are much more hemmed in by disguised abstractions than we realize, *because* we live in a country that is quite sure it lives by facts and facts alone.

The United States believes it is the most fact-minded nation in the world. Whether we look at the orderly procession of automobiles from our assembly lines, or at the steadily safer performance of our planes in the air, or at the ever more delicate adjustment of earning, saving, spending, taxation in our economy, or at our greater awareness of remaining difficulties in housing, agriculture, transportation, water, air pollution, medicine, racial prejudice, poverty, we believe that we have made greater progress than any other nation, and we owe it all to our greater respect for facts. We may have slipped up here or there, but on the whole we have done well; and we intend to do better, because as our education improves, so will our respect for facts. We are not handicapped by either tradition or ideology; we can see things as they are, and be guided by them. That is why we are healthy. That is why we are going forward.

It is a pleasant self-portrait to carry about in a well-stuffed wallet. Is it true? In some respects, yes. In other respects, not at all. It all depends on who you are and how you look at it.

If you are a student, you cannot seriously believe that you are being offered in college a fair chance to acquaint yourself with "the best that is known and said in the world." If you desire to be able to understand books, in Arnold's sense, if that is a fact about you—and occasionally it is—you have already had the wit to discover that your desire is better hidden from your college and pursued in private. For your college is a fact too, or rather a composite of many facts, just as you are. Preeminent among its determining data is the much more persuasive desire of those who make its existence possible that there be no undue emphasis on the personal side of education. Individual curiosity or development does not interest them. Education is regarded by them as a social instrument, and only by keeping it such can they truly believe it to be moral or "constructive."

If you are a student who seems headstrongly headed for that unfortunate group whom I discussed in my last lecture— the writers and by extension the other artists—you are still better acquainted with the ability of educational leaders to overlook the fact of your existence, or when it must be acknowledged, to concede it with a sigh which means that you have presumptuously assumed an evaluative role that had been better left to a consensus of sounder opinion. (Unless, of course, your unpopular craft makes you rich, in which case you are at once assumed to have good judgment.)

If however you are plainly destined for a career in industry or the professions or the academy, no concern will be felt for you. It is already known by your educators that you have taken on a discipline that will assure your reliability for life. You belong to an expanding economy that operates as rewardingly and as painlessly as possible; and if you have only a minimum of common sense you will get your proper share of its benefits in due time. You will also learn what are facts and what are not facts.

Respect for fact has been reduced to respect for one kind of fact, that which helps economic increase or, in the day's jargon, "grow power." Other facts, the facts of personality, of truth, of culture, of art, go disregarded, unless they also contribute to turnover. Fact has been identified with the emotions of an apprehensive ruling tribe. The tribe has been called to the satisfactions and responsibilities of world leadership. It may stay aloft on its high wire of domination, or it may fall. If it falls, an important reason will be that it could not burst through its unexamined abstractions, especially the one that yielded all powers of evaluation to its most predatory members.

Some concern has already been expressed by those leaders who have retained some openness to Toltech insights. Even the most enlightened politician, however, must restrict himself to a discussion of political, economic or military facts; he cannot afford a leisurely, relaxed look at all the facts. The more commonplace Big Board pragmatists, so different from the Edwardian gentlemen who gave them their ostensible philosophy, prefer to shut their minds to all original insight. Although it was the insights of gifted Toltechs that helped win their last war for them with new weapons and save the ensuing peace for them with new economic theories, the leaders of America still prefer evaluations that will not require them to realize that the future may be still more complex than the past and call for even more painful thought. They will not encourage a succession of thinkers, except with an occasional check to Alma Mater. They are quite confident that they can get along with old ideas. New things they need, but new ideas inevitably come into conflict with old desires and old alignments. So they live from dividend day to dividend day. The need for a new Keynes, who will have to understand more than economics, goes unrecognized.

And they are quite sure they know a fact when they see it. They have been taught their lesson by the newspapermen, whom they prefer to "book authors."

If a news story begins:

Wichita, Kan. (AP) Thirty-nine employees of the Lookyurbest Casket Co. staged a lie-down yesterday in the company's products as part of a demand for higher wages, shorter hours and more cheerful piped-in music.

only hard facts are presented. If however the story begins:

Wichita, Kan. (AP) While President Lyndon B. Johnson was confronted with a new crisis in Southeast Asia, 39 workers in an important local industry voted to slow down national production.

then it is slanted with "editorial comment." Everybody knows that. It is the first lesson of the cub reporter, and there's no need to go beyond it.

What is a young Toltech, bursting with new facts that may seem like ideas, but only because they require a new way of looking at the obvious, to do when he meets up with mental opposition like this?

There is only one answer. In the face of cocksure

opposition, he must learn the language of his opponents and slowly oblige them to acknowledge *his* facts in *their* terms. He must make them realize that they will perish if they do not respect his superior powers of evaluation, that is, his superior powers of observation. It is a great deal to ask of himself and of them. Usually he expects catastrophe first.

At present, majority rule decides what is a fact and what is not. Truth is outvoted. Our society is silently far more ideological, more dogmatic than it seems to be. Our "pragmatism" has long since hardened into a new orthodoxy. But we do not punish heretics with violence; we merely look the other way. It is the most effective device yet found for avoiding challenge and for ruling without opposition.

What can the Toltech do to make his facts seem at least as real as those of his enemy?

Trofimov raised his hand. To my delight his voice was not shrill, his manner not nervous. Nellie Rankin now sat next to him, and seemed to have a calming influence on him. "Is that question rhetorical or real? If it's real, I think I know the answer."

"Yes?"

"He must go on as if his enemies did not exist. He is being ignored—very well, let him ignore right back!"

I said nothing.

Trofimov looked a shade less confident than before. "Don't you agree with me?" he asked.

"No," I said, "I don't, and I'll tell you why." I resumed my lecture.

The Toltech has a real gift for evaluation, but he rarely uses it well. Instead of using it to understand his enemies and quietly take their moral leadership away from them, instead of giving them their due before he denounces them, he withdraws further into private language and tribal values. He jeers, he shrugs, he walks away. Inevitably, though he starts with broader sympathies and ten times as much imagination, he ends up as narrowly partisan as men who were not born with his intellectual endowments.

In his scientific form the Toltech does not suffer so transparently from a sense of futility, or from wounded pride, as artists do. For a long time now our scientists have been made to feel at home. If we are to understand what a terrifying sense of homelessness can do to men, we must look at our artists.

As soon as they become aware of their difference from other men, they also become aware of their difficulty in communicating it. Their difference originates in their trust of their own experience, and of their ability to communicate it in a style that will be new, durable and moving. They want to share their experience with others. Meanwhile they have discovered that they live in the midst of other men who are resolutely determined, as if their life or their livelihood depended on it, *not* to share anyone else's experience; men who have become strong according to their power to shut out *their own* experience. Artists discover that they live in a city that builds new houses every day, many of them, but houses without windows.

Artists also discover that they are injured by their formal education, which must by law be intellectual and must avoid any mention of their prior need for an emotional and sensual education. They are further injured because their training overlooks the demands of their vocation, at the same time that it pays fulsome tribute to civilization's urgent requirement of the arts. They have been looked through; their essence has been denied; a good challenge to the tough-minded, who move toward journalism, and a bad challenge to the tender-minded, who move toward overrefinement. If they happen to be thick-skinned or to have one-track minds (and such people are increasingly attracted to the arts, as the avant-garde surrenders to mass-mindedness, the only sure source of revenue and publicity) they can pretend to have survived the most adverse of circumstances, which helped them. If they are thin-skinned, they have to look to others with exactly the same delicacy of epidermis to appreciate them. In either case they do not learn much at college except, as one writer says, that "most artists practically have to commit frontal lobotomy after a college education in order to produce anything of value in the arts."

The good artist, aware of all this and a lot more that would be damaged by precise formulation, knows that he is on his own. He has been led close to an education, as close as he wants to get; the rest he must do for himself. He has stumbled into the warlike initiation rites of an enemy tribe (most effective as an impromptu preparation for the new Keynesian trials) and he is a man of peace who needs a different and slower apprenticeship. The first great question in his mind, as usual, is his own relationship to history. What of the past must he accept? What must he reject? How can culture help him? How can it cripple him? What should he do to bring about the best possible expression of his as yet undiscovered self?

The next great question in his mind is his relationship to his contemporaries. How can they be induced to share his experience?

It is here that he encounters, or rather becomes aware of, their principal defense against him. They have made themselves impermeable to his kind of experience; they have developed what I have already called the raincoat mind. It is an ancient device, as old as egocentricity, but it has been brought up to date and camouflaged with an apparent interest in the arts, all of them, the more the better. It is a spontaneous form of inattention that enables its slow-witted possessor, proud of his slowness, to tune out instantly whatever he dislikes. And he dislikes, above all, anything that might disqualify him for effective competition. At the same time he likes to pass, as soon as he can afford it, as an enlightened patron of the arts. If a cover story is written about him, it reads better when it says he devours seven new books a week or has acquired a collection of pictures that have steadily risen in price.

Trofimov's hand went up again. "How can you communicate with such people? How can you say that we should not ignore them, when they shut us out so completely?" His voice had regained its confidence, and Nellie Rankin looked on with approval.

Usually his questions interested me, but this one seemed unintelligent. "I thought I'd made that clear. If you can be content with the tiny little room they have left you, go ahead and ignore ninety-nine percent of mankind. But if you want to be one of 'the unacknowledged legislators of the world,' you will learn how to make people listen to you."

Trofimov stood his ground. "Oh that one! All right, take *him*." And he instantly quoted two lines from Shelley:

> Music, when soft voices die,
> Vibrates in the memory.

"Whose memory? Ours! Not theirs. They didn't even hear him when he said it!"

The class, wishing it knew what our discussion was about, and where the poetry came from, stirred restlessly, as if once more annoyed with a familiar nuisance. I shrugged my shoulders, as if to say, "Have it your own way," to him, and went on with my lecture:

All minds have self-protective devices, and must have, to keep their balance. We cannot take in everything. There has to be an organizing selector, which regulates our receptivity. And it must begin by being as unconscious and as automatic as heart and liver. Later the mind may open slowly, to be educated according to the art of the teacher and the capacity of the student. In most cases, capacity remains greater than intake. Thought creates anxiety. Back-cracking manual labor or routine intellectual tasks are preferred by nearly everyone.

Even artists prefer to avoid the anxiety of trying to understand those who do not, or cannot or will not understand them.

The pain of thought will be accepted by some if the reward is attractive (a bank account, for example) or if the threat of punishment (loss of a sweetheart to a rival) is unattractive. Some of us *will* think when we have to think, but only so long as it is necessary. A few may learn to enjoy thought for its own sake, but only because some unnatural ambition or some natural defect, such as a walleye, or some social defect, such as birth into the family of the town washerwoman, has compelled them to take up a task that is repugnant to sound minds in sound bodies. So runs the popular theory of thought, true on the whole, as far as it goes. (This theory also says that artists and scientists only become such because they lack the robustness of body or mind to get the power and the girl they really want.)

If this popular theory were adequate, the United States would have nothing to fear from the fact that its steadily advancing technology requires an ever thicker layer of raincoat mind. Other nations have also found ways of making their minds impermeable, but their turn can wait. First we must consider the land which I know best, my own, of which it has been said by a visiting novelist that it should change its national bird from the eagle to the ostrich. Americans could go on shutting out every fact that conflicts with their image of themselves as enlightened and benevolent. They could technicize their minds without penalty, narrow them down to making things and selling things, getting along with one another, eliminating social injustice where it still exists, creating new opportunities for all, offering the people in the rest of the world whatever they need, if only they, especially the dark little men in faraway places, will behave themselves. The American way of life would work, and for people as well as for statistics, and for their souls as well as their bodies.

The raincoat mind, after all, is needed to keep a big, new technological society going. From the standpoint of statecraft, its desiccating effect on individuals is unimportant next to its ability to make them move with the astonishing vigor that people can show when the prospect of gain is put under their noses. In American politics, the raincoat mind is never mentioned, of course, but it occupies a place similar to that of the docility of the Russian masses, also unmentioned in the Soviet Union. To be strong, the USA and the USSR need respectively an energetic bourgeoisie and an obedient proletariat. Both lands simmer with minority protest which need not be taken too seriously. If Russians were to demand more political say-so, and if Americans were to demand fuller lives, the two greatest powers in the world would soon become less formidable. Each needs its kind of robot, which nature seems to produce in oversupply.

The Soviet Union has an official ideology, that of Marxism. The United States has no official ideology. Its position has been stated by a historian who has worked for its government:

"Ideology is a drug; no matter how often it is exposed to experience, the craving for it persists. . . . Surely the basic conflict of our times, the civil war of our day, is precisely the conflict between those who would reduce the world to one and those who see the world as many . . . a choice, in short, between dogmatism and pragmatism, between the theological society and the experimental society, between ideology and democracy."

So patriotic a restatement of the virtues of pluralistic pragmatism, coming from a well-known liberal (Arthur Schlesinger, Jr.), will appeal especially to Aztechs, who prefer dated ideas which have demonstrated their harmlessness. It cannot appeal to Toltechs, who want ideas to deal, however disturbingly, and whatever the effect on the applecart, with the realities of the present. Here, they know, the routine metamorphosis of a good idea into a bad one has been speeded by what currently passes for the national interest. They are sharp enough to know that pragmatism has long since hardened into what it originally opposed, an ideology, or worse, a cryptoideology that hides its true face. A dogmatic tone soon attaches itself to pragmatic decisions, once they have met with mass approval (achieved by the cerebral laundromats of the press) in elections that so rarely present any issues with clarity that most foreigners laugh at our "two-party system." A still more dogmatic tone is found in our economic life, where "the tyranny of public opinion" (Stendhal's phrase, once again, which de Tocqueville elaborated with amazing prescience) is so strict, under the watchful eye of public relations experts, that any individual subversion is punished with something better than the firing squad, the inability to make a living. And this "tyranny" can feel no qualms of conscience because it is acting for the best. It does not punish opponents with systematic ruthlessness, that crass holdover from Ivan the Terrible, but with a simple incomprehension which achieves the same disciplinary effect without overt, guilt-forming unkindness.

This incomprehension, of course, means a raincoat mind which can believe itself totally innocent even while it tolerates only those who speak its circumspect language and denies all others their essence.

Hardened pragmatism has not yet had to be as bloody

as totalitarianism, which appeared in lands that lacked a tradition of popular participation in government (Italy, Russia, Germany, China). But hardened pragmatism is spending its inherited capital of democratic assent and goodwill with a speed that the raincoat mind, by its very nature, cannot perceive. There are many new critics in Latin America, Africa and Asia, not to mention more familiar ones in Europe, who say that hardened, uncritical pragmatism has lately shown a tendency to become almost as bloody as its opponents, wherever its neo-imperial will (another of those unfortunate metamorphoses, this time from anti-colonial republic to world-dominating empire) meets with resistance. Whatever the truth of this very complex matter, one thing is certain: the raincoat mind will never understand it.

What does that mean, in plain English? It means that our leaders will never understand it. The men and women who have risen to positions of authority in our land will not be able to understand the dangers that now encircle them. They continue to put their faith in present extensions of other men's insight, not the real facts of our time. In Whitehead's language, we are not aware of the abstractions, the presuppositions which condition our perception of reality. We have not encouraged an honest, fearless philosophy. We may therefore fulfill the prediction that Whitehead made: "A civilization which cannot burst through its abstractions is doomed to sterility after a very limited period of progress."

When our artists see their problems in this perspective they may feel somewhat less enthusiasm for private languages, protected specialities, happy victimage and anaesthetized surrender. They may awaken to their own danger and to their own responsibilities to those who now seem to oppress them most. The first task of the artist is to find his true context in history, and then to go on from there. His next task is to make his facts as real as those of the marketplace, so that his experience may be shared with that of the most demanding minds.

The raincoat mind was born of competition. It imitated its enemies. (And now artists imitate theirs.) It got its strength by studying the most negotiable of human traits, those that can be relied on, in a time of emergency, to bring in the surest amount of money. Its practicality produced a nation of world-conquerors who made Cortés seem like an accidental pygmy. Its efficiency enabled its confident engineers to outstrip all rivals.

But now the other side of efficiency begins to show, and not only to those who have always been aware of it because it slighted them. Among students it can only appeal to the most stolid, the least imaginative. Our intelligent minds begin to be aware that the device of collective deafness, however profitable it may be for the time being, is shutting out too much. They fear that pragmatism, or what passes for it, has reversed its original definition; it no longer contends with all the "stubborn and irreducible facts"; it overlooks those it would rather not face; it no longer "works."

When class was over Trofimov did not come to my desk. He slipped out of the room with Nellie Rankin, and it looked to me as if they were holding each other by the hand.

Lopakhin came to my desk, wearing a new sharkskin suit, beautifully tailored, as I later heard from him, by an English firm which semiannually sent its representative to the Biltmore Hotel. "I liked what you said about efficiency," he said. "Efficiency is for the klucks. The really smart guys live all by themselves, figuring the angles."

AGAINST THE WEATHER

9

I died at Rodez under electro-shock. I say dead. Legally and medically dead. The coma of electroshock lasts a quarter of an hour. Another half-hour and the patient is breathing. But, one hour after shock I hadn't awakened and had stopped breathing. Surprised by my abnormal rigidity, an attendant went to look for the chief doctor, who after auscultation found in me no sign of life. I have my own memories of my death at that moment.

"I can't do it," I said, and then I ran to the curb and threw up, threw up on humanity, threw up on my junkyard past and present and future.

Life will not be a burden for me at thirty-five because I will be securely anchored in my family. My main emotional ties will center in my wife and family. Remember, I hope for five children. Yes, I can describe my wife. She will be the Grace Kelly, camel's-hair-coat type. Feet on the ground, and not an empty shell or a fake. Although an Ivy League type, she will also be centered in the home, a housewife. Perhaps at forty-five, with the children grown up, she will go in for hospital work and so on. . . . And improving herself culturally and thus bringing a deeper sense of culture into our home will be one of her main interests in fifteen years. . . . I look forward to a constant level of happiness.

In the fifteen years which had elapsed since I began my career I had not only proved incapable of supporting myself but . . .

I had substantially increased my debts. . . . Almost the first words out of my mother's mouth, after we had greeted each other, were: "Can't you write something like *Gone with the Wind* and make a little money?"

One nice thing about it is you don't really have to go out looking for a job—they come around looking for you!

After my leaving Frisco he had gone crazy over Marylou and spent months haunting her apartment at Divisadero, where every night she had a different sailor in and he peeked down through her mail slot and could see her bed.

Let's face it, I'll be on salary, not making capital gains, even at thirty-six. . . . Why struggle on my own, when I can enjoy the big psychological income of being a member of a big outfit?

It is not that our company makes us behave in a certain way. That kind of thing is out of date. Most of our people tend to live and talk alike, and think along the same general lines, for the simple reason that the company treats us so well. Life is good, life is gentle. Barring a deep depression or a war, we need never worry about money again.

I used to be a sensitive kid. Things would hurt my feelings. For awhile I had a real inferiority complex. That was in the fifth or sixth grade.

You don't *know* how long it takes you to pick a hundred pound of cotton. The cotton, is, you know, real light, it's nothing. And you have to pick a HUNDRED pounds before you get three dollars, that's all. And you work in the field all week, and you make about . . . you do good if you make $20 a week, really. And like you work in these white peoples' house. In the house you get $10 a week for doing housework. . . . And I don't really think it's different, that much different, between the North and the South, but only in the South people know where they stand; but here people don't really know where they stand, because here, you know, people here do their dirty work under-cover, and in the South it's in the open.

Suddenly I leapt in my bonds and shouted with all my might. C—— had just sent the first electric charge through my body. A flash of lightning exploded next to my ear and I felt my heart racing. I struggled, screaming, and stiffened myself until the straps cut into my flesh.

They dragged her, holding her by the hands and legs, until her hair tumbled loosely behind, to the bottom of the hollow and threw her down on a snow-covered bench, about twenty-five yards from the barrack. She met the first with a furious kicking of her legs, freed for a moment from his grasp, but soon she was quiet again, choked by the skirt which was thrown over her head.

The death cries of the animals whose jugular veins have been opened are confused with the rumbling of the great drum, the whirring of gears, and the shrilling sound of steam. Death cries and mechanical noises are almost impossible to disentangle. Neither can the eye take in what it sees. On one side of the sticker are the living; on the other, the slaughtered.

The distance between my mother and me had grown. My life was now so hopeless that I wrote a book. All day I scribbled while listening to Beethoven's *Moonlight Sonata* on the phonograph. My mother staggered about, dropping a kettle or a frypan, and finally turned to me, begging, "Please turn that funeral stuff off. I just can't stand it, my son."

They were interrupted when a young Negro pansy was brought in crying and looking very roughed up. One of the cops imitated his swishiness much to the loud delight of his colleagues. The Negro boy had a big lump on his head where he had been smacked with a blackjack by the arresting cop, just for fun.

I made the round just once for kicks. You know how old people lose all shame about eating, and it makes you puke to watch them? Old junkies are the same about junk. They gibber and squeal at the sight of it.

The district officer at Tuhlung ran away and was captured after about two days. His lips were cut off and he was bound and brought naked to Tuhlung. The Chinese were not satisfied with his rate of progress; being a fat man he could not walk very fast and he was poked with bayonets to make him walk faster.

The witness saw him covered with bayonet wounds. The Chinese tied him to a tree and invited Tibetans to go and beat him, accusing him of cruelty. They were told not to beat him to death since he would benefit by this.

Unless for some reason we choose to escape back into your anxious world (where the competition is so hard and pitiless and your ego is constantly under attack), we will each enjoy a comfortable journey to what our house organ calls "green pastures," which is, of course, retirement.

When I read these typical scraps of contemporary reading matter to the class they had a strong effect on Trofimov. He was still showing the effect when he came to my office the next day for a conference.

"I still can't get over those people!" he said. "What they went through!"

"Some of them had an easy time. The man who knew exactly what his wife was going to be like, and the future."

"Such people don't count. Such people don't exist!"

"Oh, they exist, all right."

In his eye was the boldest, most challenging look I had ever seen there. "That man was an Organization Man. Organization Men don't count. They're as unimportant as the people who built the pyramids in Egypt or the cathedrals in France."

"They run the world, don't they? If you vote in an election, don't you have to vote for one of them? If you want to go somewhere, you have to travel with them, don't you? Who keeps you fed and clothed and housed? Who taught you your ABC's?"

"I know, I know, but they're all so dreary."

"You mean they bore you?" I must have been getting ready for my answer. For several months now (he was my student, along with Lopakhin, over a period of almost two years) I had been hoping he might get in the classroom the clarity he sought from a psychiatrist. Needless to say, I was mistaken about that. "They don't bore me, they humiliate me. They make me realize how dependent I am on them."

"I can get along without them," he said.

"Well, I can't. I need them. What's more, I admire them."

"Admire them? Why should anyone admire people who are so bourgeois?"

"You admire Flaubert, don't you?" His great enthusiasm of the moment was *L'Education Sentimentale*.

"Yes."

"Nobody loathed the bourgeoisie more than Flaubert. Yet when he was old and saw two very bourgeois relatives of his he suddenly said: "They are right! *'Ils sont dans le vrai.'* "

"What did he mean by that?"

"I suppose he meant he couldn't go on hating them any more. They were part of him, and he was part of them."

"I wish you wouldn't talk like this. I came here to invite you to have dinner with Nellie and me, and now you talk like this."

"I hope you do invite me. I'd like to come."

I managed to get an invitation from him, for the week following.

When Lopakhin came to my office I mentioned the quotations that I had read in class, in the hope that he would respond as forthrightly as Trofimov. All he said was, "Ugh!" He said it in such a way that I knew he did not like them, but still was not going to commit himself to any utterance that might be held against him.

My next lecture contained some more quotations:

"The escape of many gifted if unstable young individuals into a private utopia or, as another patient put it, a 'majority of one,' might not be necessary were it not for a general development to which they feel unable to submit, i.e. the increasing demand for standardization, uniformity and conformity which characterizes the present stage of our individualistic civilization."

"The new style of Technical Philosophy is remarkable since it expresses something about the philosophy itself. The style tends toward the telegraphic code. One reason for this is that the paper must be capable of being read during office hours, and make no demands upon the weekends."

"It became known that I had had some previous training in psychiatry. Presently I found that if I were to have any time for my own work I had literally to lock my door for a few hours each day. Otherwise, almost every afternoon, young colleagues and sometimes older ones would drift in to talk, not about scientific issues but about their personal problems."

"To play his role as a bureaucrat at all adequately is to pay a heavy social and psychological price. The official has to repress certain prebureaucratic sentiments that may have been instilled in him as a youth."

"Questioning my old acquaintances, I cannot find one over the age of sixty who did not witness the last agony of at least one near relative; I do not think I know of a single person under the age of thirty who has had a similar experience."

"Manipulation and exploitation for the benefit of the operator or of the subject is the chief danger man incurs through the decline of the humanities. The humanities are his defence against emotional bamboozlement and misdirection of the will. The student of science—without the support of that which has been traditionally carried by literature, the arts and philosophy—is unprotected; the main doctrines and positions which kept man humane are insusceptible, at present, to scientific proof."

"I was attacking the dominant delusion of our time, that creativity is the criterion of human worth. But illegitimate creativity, creation without immediacy, is no criterion, for it is no reality. It is an illusion and I believe in the absolute eye before which it cannot stand for a moment."

"I can hardly understand the importance given to the word *research* in connection with modern painting. In my opinion, to search means nothing in painting. To find, is the thing."

"Modern man is progressively losing his understanding of values and his sense of proportions. This failure to understand essential realities is extremely serious. It leads us infallibly to the fundamental laws of human equilibrium. In the domain of music, the consequences of this misunderstanding are these: on one hand there is a tendency to turn the mind away from what I shall call the higher mathematics of music in order to degrade music to servile employment, and to vulgarize it by adapting it to the requirements of an elementary utilitarianism—as we shall soon see on examining Soviet music. On the other hand, since the mind itself is ailing, the music of our time, and particularly the music which calls itself and believes itself *pure*, carries within it the pathologic blemish and spreads the germs of a new original sin."

"The poet finds and makes his mask in disappointment, the hero in defeat. The desire that is satisfied is not a great desire."

"When I hear modern people complain of being lonely, then I know what has happened. They have lost the cosmos.— It is nothing human and personal we are short of. What we lack is cosmic life, the sun in us and the moon in us. We can't get the sun in us by lying naked like pigs on a beach."

"The artist, like the God of creation, remains within or beyond or above his handiwork, invisible, refined out of existence, indifferent, paring his fingernails."

"Abstract art . . . is dominated by desire for perfection and for total liberation in the same spirit that has produced saints, heroes and madmen. Extreme as it is, only a few creators and admirers can sustain it."

"Nothing is so poor and melancholy as an art that is interested in itself and not in its subject."

"Existentialism is the endeavor to understand man by cutting below the cleavage between subject and object which has bedevilled Western thought and science since shortly after the Renaissance."

"Cultivate that which the public reproaches you for— it's you."

"If I am sad, it comes primarily from the permanent sadness that destiny has imprinted forever on my emotions, where the greatest and purest joy can only be superimposed and that at the price of a great effort of attention."

"Vitality depends upon the clue of the Holy Ghost inside a creature . . . When the clue goes, the vitality goes. And the Holy Ghost seeks forever a new incarnation."

When class was over Lopakhin left without coming, as usual, to my desk. The quotations must have bored or antagonized him. They pleased Trofimov, however. "They're beautiful!" he cried. "The first weren't so good, but they got better as they went along. I recognized the one from Yeats, and Joyce of course. And the one from Lawrence—no, two! And Picasso and Stravinsky, but who said that about abstract painting? I liked that!"

And he had many other questions to ask.

10

The students in the class to which Trofimov and Lopakhin belonged were shown not only the negative aspects of the technological society, but some realistic ways of coping with it that had been suggested by responsible thinkers. The course attempted to pull together the thoughts of sociologists, psychologists, historians, philosophers and literary men who had addressed themselves to the very problems with which the students now found themselves, quite unexpectedly for the most part, face to face. The course was "interdisciplinary" in a new sense of that word. Specialists were not brought in bodily from other departments to debate with other specialists; the men who had given the specialists most of their ideas were brought in via their most important books, and the most important passages in those books, as seen from the standpoint of a teacher and students who could make personal use of their ideas. The emphasis fell always on *personal* application of ideas to lives that needed many kinds of clarification.

Such a method implied inevitably a confession on the part of the teacher. At least at first he was saying, "These thinkers have helped me. I think they will also help you." Later, after getting acquainted with many students of different backgrounds, different degrees of talent, different capacities for self-confrontation, he was able to expand his range of citation until it applied to almost any degree of ignorance or aptitude that came along. And it seemed to him that he and his students had been put into a position of privilege, such as he had not enjoyed in his own student days, the position of being able to draw upon a new and generally unrecognized kind of wisdom for their new and generally unrecognized dilemmas. Modernity was being used to combat the confusions that modernity had created.

A book would be required to give an adequate impression of this modern "wisdom of the West." (Perhaps I shall try to write or rather compile it some day.) Here it is only possible to suggest it with a few familiar names. There were social insights from Marx, Veblen, Weber, Durkheim, Ellul, McLuhan, Riesman and others; psychological insights from William James, Freud, Adler, Jung, Rank, Benoit, Fromm, Horney, Sullivan, Sheldon, Binswanger and others; historical insights from Ortega y Gasset, Spengler, Toynbee, Giedion, Frazer, Eliade and others; philosophical insights from Kierkegaard, Nietzsche, Heidegger, Sartre, Whitehead, Berdyaev, Unamuno, Dewey, Cassirer, Wittgenstein and others; literary insights from Dostoevsky, Kafka, Pasternak, Baudelaire, Rilke, Joyce, Eliot, Valéry, Camus, Péguy, Yeats, Beckett, Lawrence and others. The selection was not as encyclopedic as it now may seem, not when it was applied to everyday problems of students which were everyday being overlooked in more formal approaches to knowledge. Unlike any of his ancestors, the typical student in my class had been exposed to questions and answers for which there was no test but personal experience; *all* the old answers were under attack. To understand the rush of daily experience (largely unconscious) he needed all the clarity he could get, and from as many clear heads as he could find. The clear heads, of course, disagreed with one another, but out of their disputes he might dig his own truth.

The teacher's task was to collect many insights from a large *dramatis personae* and connect them up, put them into the context of everyday life as it seemed to be lived by himself and his students. It was a task that called for an ability to *pull things together,* an ability that he tried to acquire.

He soon discovered that almost no students, certainly not Trofimov and Lopakhin, were able to integrate all the insights put before them. Truth, manysided modern truth, was too much for them. They could not accept more than some congenial portion of it, and of that only a little at a time. Nevertheless, since "time bombs" might go off in their minds years later, it was his obligation to put as many useable insights before them

as he could, in the context of the daily existence that he shared
with them. In all likelihood, no doubt, few of the insights would
ever actually be used, because common daily existence punished
sharply those who named it with any accuracy. An encounter
with truth can be an exciting intellectual experience in college;
but to persist in seeking it after graduation, when it must be
lived as well as studied, is to ask for chastisement rather than
reward.

To plant his time bombs, the teacher asked his class
to ask itself certain questions. These were not an exam, but a
mere invitation to personal scrutiny of personal behavior. The
questions included the following:

How typical am I? Do I see myself as an object that
has been plainly shaped by historical and social forces?

Do I wear clothes that suggest I am more of an artist
or intellectual than I really am?

Am I able to manipulate others? Do I manipulate
others? Sexually? Economically?

How well do I formulate my problems? Do I become
angry when I cannot formulate them?

How many opinions about books and works of art have
I formed entirely on my own?

How much am I really interested in the civil rights
movement?

What does the war in Viet Nam mean to me, aside
from what I feel obliged to say about it? How much do I know
about it?

Am I a "new puritan"? Do I want both power and sex,
without overconcern for those who give them to me?

Do I believe that help will come to me from the outside?

What is sacred to me?

On the whole the students seemed to like these questions. Each time I put them, I was asked to repeat them in a

later class, so that some earlier absentees might write them down. They also liked an oral test which required them to be familiar with one of the most famous scenes in history, the decision of Socrates to take the hemlock, as reported by Plato.

Socrates has been condemned to death. He has refused to be tactful to his judges. He has adopted an attitude that outrages the public-relations experts of a cunning, keenly political Athens. Nevertheless there is still hope for him. His death sentence is by no means final. He is now expected to propose a lesser penalty—exile, which as a philosopher he is especially qualified to support. It is fairly certain that his proposal will be accepted. The Athenians do not want to have to kill him.

After a long fortuitous delay of execution that increases a general reluctance to insist on capital punishment, his friend Crito comes to his prison cell to tell him that it will be easy to bribe his jailers. He can escape and live outside Athens, in some other place where he is sure to find friends and to continue his work as "midwife" to other men's thoughts. But again he shows his indifference to death, and asks eloquently if it is ever right to oppose evil by doing evil oneself. He takes the hemlock.

I confess I reached certain rough conclusions about students, according to how they responded to this story. If a student merely praised the nobility of the Socratic language, he was relatively untechnicized in mind, I decided, though probably due for technical enslavement in body. In type he was a dupe, the kind of student whom cleverer men, sometimes without education, would most likely control as soon as he got out of college.

If he said, "Ah, death wish!" or "Maybe he was trying to make some kind of a deal, and it fell through," I concluded the student had the kind of mind that might move on to power. He was already reducing everyone else's experience to his own search for power. Perhaps he was already "doing all right" for himself by cashing in on his status as a student. (Lopakhin immediately suspected Socrates of a deal, a deal that did not work.)

If he said, "At a certain point the only effective philosophy must be an *act* that reveals your indifference to everything but truth," he had an unusual mind, and a less predictable career lay ahead of him. He had understood that Platonism would mean far less without the death of Socrates. The odds are, I decided, that such a student will get a job, most likely on a college faculty, a job that will offer him at first a better chance to act philosophically, a job that later will slowly undermine his capacity for philosophic action. But there is also a chance that he will work out for himself an independent life that no one can foresee. To the concern of his parents and colleagues, and to the economic disappointment of his wife and children, he may follow his own unknown rules, after years spent discovering what they are, and go where they tell him to go. Trofimov fell into this category, at least to a certain degree. He said, "But Socrates had to die! It wouldn't be a story if he hadn't!"

I did not need, however, to look back to antiquity to study the effect of mental technicization on students. I needed only to glance now and then at their daily actions.

Does the student greet his teachers with a condescending smile? He usually does, and it means that he believes that, because things have changed so much lately and youth is in a stronger position than ever, he can intimidate them by his great advantage over them, his later birthday. They have to recognize their limitations and their failures. But he, because everything is different *now*, can ignore him, and suggest confidently that failure will never overtake him.

Does he talk almost exclusively about himself and his plans? He usually does, and it means that his future achievements, being infinite (somewhat like exploration of the planets) naturally take precedence over the measurable and miserable finitudes of his seniors.

Does he derive special satisfaction from his better acquaintance with the new inventions, the new customs, the new language of his day? He usually does, and it means a sexual technolatry that prefers girls when they look as if they had come from machines rather than from wombs (as indeed they do when they appear from the beauty shop) with a new sleek, lean style that they cunningly cultivate, as a way of catching him. They suggest to him that they have miraculously transcended the demanding, sick-half-the-time weightiness of their mothers and will never burden him with the cares of which their fathers daily complain. He is easily manipulated thereafter.

Does he talk of a plane trip as if it represented a triumph of his own over gravity and history? Does he use only the newest slang, and ridicule earlier slang (it dates almost as fast now as cars, and for somewhat similar reasons) in a manner that suggests that time has at last come to a satisfactory halt?

Does all this mean that at heart he is scared to death, beneath a pretension of "playing it cool"? It does. He cannot cope with present or future, and he had already forgotten the past (except when he crams), but he has learned from the success stories of his time that bluff pays off better than confession. No one outside the bedroom or the battlefield can check up on the secret failure that passes so convincingly in print as "grace in action." An advertisement for himself, and he runs a great many, will pull better if it relies on plausible appearance rather than on sad reality.

Long before they go out into "the new marketplace," most students have mentally prepared themselves for it.

Trofimov, however, felt quite unprepared for it. He attributed his apprehensiveness to his own fidelity to "the sacred." Others could cheerfully rush into a situation that was sure to make liars and nonentities of them all; he had been called to a sacred vocation, the purification of the word. Like his hero Stephen Dedalus, he bore a pure chalice through a world of enemies. (He said this more than once.) In time, he believed, he would be justified; he would write a book that would make his friends realize that they had been wrong, and he had been right, all along.

He had believed this before he came into my class, but I had reinforced his convictions when I discussed "desacralization," or removal of the sacred as a category of the mind. All other members of the class, Trofimov concluded, had been desacralized, but he had not. I had been presenting the ideas of a historian of religion, as adding one more useful insight to our understanding of our situation, but Trofimov read into "the sacred" a personal vindication.

"It should be said at once that the *completely* profane world, the wholly desacralized cosmos, is a recent discovery in the history of the human spirit," the historian had written.

Nevertheless, in spite of its recency and its possible incompleteness, "desacralization pervades the entire experience of the nonreligious man of modern societies."

This interpretation is by Mircea Eliade, the Rumanian historian who has been called "the Frazer of our generation," because his erudition in the field of primitive religions possibly surpasses that of the famous author of *The Golden Bough* and because his conclusions are so different. Instead of accepting the Scottish anthropologist's abstract opinion that archaic man's thought was "nothing but a monstrous accumulation of madnesses, cruelties and superstitions now happily abolished by the progress of mankind," as Eliade summarizes Frazer, he concludes, after a detailed examination of the evidence from the past as well as the present, that archaic man continues to influence us more profoundly than we care to believe, and the way back to clarity and health lies in understanding our still remote ties to remote antiquity.

The typically nonreligious man of our time, he says, "regards himself solely as the subject and object of history, and he refuses all appeal to transcendence. In other words, he accepts no model for humanity outside the human condition as it can be seen in the various historical situations. *Man makes himself*, and he only makes himself completely in proportion as he desacralizes himself and his world. The sacred is the prime obstacle to his freedom. He will become himself only when he is completely demysticized. He will not be truly free until he has killed the last god."

This means, when Eliade's idea is integrated with the realities of the unexpected millennium, as I have described it here, that our elimination of the sacred from our way of life, signified by such expressions as "Anything goes!" and "Nothing is sacred!" (popular expressions that became the titles of films), has helped us to be more scientific and to achieve more control of nature. No longer intimidated by tabus or false reverence, we have developed a Faustian fearlessness before the unseen, and been rewarded with better command of the seen. One of the many hitches to our progress, however, is that we were not born yesterday, much as we might like to be, but remain the product of long prehistoric conditioning, and a more complex conditioning than even psychoanalysis revealed. Our external mastery is rarely accompanied by a better understanding of ourselves.

We seethe with dreams and fantasies which do not serve us as they served our physically more helpless ancestors, "because they are not experienced by the *whole man* and therefore do not transform a particular situation into a situation that is paradigmatic." Our torpid, technicized lives cease to be symbolically meaningful, which makes it easier for us to misuse symbols. We serve time, and lose the perspective of timelessness, or regard it as a device of obscurantism. Instead of being enriched culturally by our new wealth (one of our foremost justifications for "hardheadness") our days turn into "one damn thing after another." We pay an exorbitant, perhaps ruinous price for our new group technical skills, and our private acquiescence in the depersonalization they inevitably exact.

Desacralization, then, is a necessary step in the development of human beings, if they are to attain their maximum efficiency. It *must* be followed by personal fragmentation, because only a quite oversimplified specialist can hope to exploit, more skilfully than his competitors, the new abstractive talents that demysticization makes possible. We must compete in waterproofing our minds against unprofitable experience. The halfway specialist, who genuinely enjoys the quasi-religious satisfactions of gardening or hiking or Sunday painting (without turning them into a publicity stunt) is soon eclipsed by the genuine monomaniac who thinks only of his press-created "image" and his bank account.

The new hollow men cannot tolerate a spare ounce of authenticity. The people they dominate, moreover, must be trained daily to take the sound of emptiness for the sound of fullness. Otherwise the managed peepshow cannot go on. People prefer such leadership to having opinions of their own (they want the illusion of having opinions of their own) because opinions of their own can only lead to loneliness and failure. Technology facilitates "escape from freedom." Successful political leadership must therefore be affable but ruthless—on the surface as charming as Kennedy and in performance as ruthless as Stalin. The man who can seem all tenderness and be all toughness (without taking *our* son or *our* money) is the man we want to rule us.

The elimination of the sacred was the first step toward the improvement of manufacture and later, when making became easier than selling, the improvement of new verbal techniques. Desacralization was needed some years ago to turn folksinging hillbillies into efficient attendants of assembly lines who hummed tunes from the Hit Parade while they worked. Now desacralization is needed to turn their descendants into regular consumers of soap, automobiles and revenue-stamp whisky. The assembly lines will go on, even on a ten-hour week; but sales may drop at any moment, and that would mean disaster for everyone except the enemy.

In 1910 it was easy to wipe the Bible out of the hillbillies' minds with Henry Ford's promise of five dollars a day. But the newspapers and magazines that took the place of the only book they knew, though carefully purged of anything that might stimulate thought, have nevertheless set benumbed brains ever so slightly on the move. There is more talk now of Viet Nam than of the county fair. The Cumberland Gap is still a helpless tributary of New York, but every so often a solitary voice suggests that consciousness may someday awaken, even there. If there is ever a recovery of the sacred, it will come from those who have experienced the profane to the limit. They will *know* what is sacred and what is not.

The student, however, must deal with the conditions that exist, and these are a confusing mixture of the pseudosacred and the disguised profane. When he opens his Plato he cannot count on the tacit values that sustained Socrates in his defiance of Athens. The stern qualitative standards of human behavior that were established in classical times after a long, bloody fight, cannot be taken for granted. Such standards can *never* be taken for granted. They have to be reestablished with great effort by each new generation, because the innate aggressiveness (or evil) in man always works against them; but now the appearance of external order as achieved by our new technology has acquired such a high finish that the student likes to think he can take them for granted. And his mother, who wants to believe that peace on earth has come at last (she has a deep psychological effect on him long after he leaves home), confirms him tenderly in his self-deception. She cannot realize that she desires the impossible: the material benefits of desacralization and the reverence for life that only a sense of the sacred can give.

By comparison, Socrates was *spoiled* by his environment. If Athens had not been deeply interested in the questions he raised, if Athens had been able to ignore them with continual front page war crises and back page bull markets, Socrates would never have been offered the hemlock. He would merely have been ignored.

To be ignored is the best a student can ask for today. If he is willing to be poor, he can hide away for a while. It gives him a chance to get his bearings. It gives him more time to ask himself slowly, "What do I really consider sacred?" Upon his reply will depend his life.

So ran some of my commentary on desacralization, as well as I can recall it now. From the perspective of a better understanding of him, I see only too clearly how it reinforced Trofimov in his delusion that he belonged to the privately anointed few who had "recovered the sacred" for an uncomprehending and undeserving world. "It was only because I was so completely pissed off about *everything*," he told me jubilantly when I had dinner with him and Nellie, "that I could find the sacred again—and find it in *everything*."

Lopakhin's response to the discussion of desacralization was different. "Sure, you're right," he told me, "we had to get rid of all the phony religion so that we could get real religion back again. You watch, we're going to destroy communism with God!"

OTHER STUDENTS, OTHER QUESTIONS

11

The class to which Lopakhin and Trofimov belonged had other students, mostly older than they. And when my two "Russians" returned to take a second course with me they sat in a still larger class, once again composed chiefly of adults who had already made their acquaintance with the marketplace that attracted Lopakhin and frightened Trofimov. On the whole, these adults were better prepared, by virtue of personal experience, to understand the frequently conflicting insights that were put before them. They asked better questions. Often I found myself saying, "That's a good question," to play for time while I framed an answer.

A lawyer said: "I get the impression that you are not exactly optimistic about education. Is that correct?"

"That is correct," I said. "Education is our great cure-all, but no one will get a good education today unless he gets it for himself, in spite of his teachers."

"Does that include you?"

"Certainly."

An accountant asked: "What is Engels' Law, and why is it not true?"

"Scholars disagree about the exact meaning of Engels' Law, but it has been accurately defined, I think, as 'the passage of quantity into quality.' In my opinion, it is not too well understood, even by the most erudite scholars, because they fail to examine the psychology of the man who formulated it, Friedrich Engels.

"Friedrich Engels was the partner and 'angel' of Karl

Marx, coauthor of *The Communist Manifesto,* and the victim of a delusion that arose from his limited observation of *bourgeois* progress in the 19th century. Engels' Law has been reversed by the court of modern experience. Quantity, we now know, does not pass into quality. The reverse is more likely to be true. Cities do not inevitably become better when they become larger; they turn into such bad places to live that their inhabitants, as soon as it is possible for them to afford it, push out to the suburbs. People do not inevitably become better when their number increases; on the contrary, they lose touch with their own natural resources, deteriorate conspicuously, and as an astute psychologist says, long for wars that will thin out the mob. The atom bomb was one answer of science to the population explosion.

"Education does not become better when it is conducted on a mass scale. In the lower grades it must be leveled down to the least intelligent, and in the higher grades it moves toward television lectures, computer marking and student riots. Bread does not become better when it is baked in larger factories. On the contrary, the natural vitamins, which were left in for centuries, are now removed to make way for the synthetic vitamins that 'enrich' it. This is done with such efficiency that nutritionists have found an alarming amount of sterility in males who have eaten the puffy white bread of our big cities, a sterility that could only be corrected by change of diet and large doses of synthetic Vitamin E.

"These results of the rule of quantity are so well-known that intelligent people live, when possible, away from the polluted air of the big cities. They try to find rapport with themselves and those nearest them, and to avoid the psychological epidemics of mass-dominated society. When possible they send their children to smaller schools where there is individual instruction. They eat the good, new breads that have been produced as a protest against the bleached stuff that makes people sick— enough good bread to create a new industry.

"Engels was capable of such bad prophecy because he was a romantic ideologue without much power of observation— nothing like the empirical skill that had already made such novelists as Stendhal and Flaubert denounce the very nonsense he helped to spread. A sociologist who does not read novels, or understand them, is a poor guide. The rootless hope that he expressed can only have meaning now for those who are still born close to feudal obscurantism. Those born close to democratic progress, technological progress, have had a chance to test out his hope, and to find that it has been turned into a demagogic lie.

"Engels, like Marx, was the victim of a bourgeois delusion. He had observed that a few members of his own middle class were able to extend the culture of the aristocracy from which they had wrested power in 1789 and after. He therefore jumped to the conclusion that in time the proletariat, after wresting power in turn from the bourgeoisie, would move on, *en masse*, to a life of culture. It was a typical mistake of 'the sociological imagination,' which dearly loves to have ideas that can be turned into weapons. (In this case, as it turned out, the weapons were bayonets in the hands of Russian peasants, who could not rip up the Matisses and icons that had been hidden away in Leningrad, as they would have liked to, but had to be content with ripping up the readers of Chekhov.)

"A few proletarians have heroically moved on to a life of culture, and are already being punished (as well as rewarded) for it. Their personal victories only emphasize the falsity of large, social generalizations like that of Engels, which insinuate that what demands the utmost of the individual can be accomplished easily by large numbers of people who are afraid of thought, afraid of solitude, afraid of looking at themselves. To paraphrase Spinoza, if qualitative success were facilitated by quantitative success, a worldwide revolution would have been accomplished long ago, and our children could coast into culture, without cracking a book. But real education is as difficult as it is rare.

"The irony is that nearly all millionaires, while rejecting the valid side of Marxism, its insistence on the class struggle, for instance, admire this soft, beery, romantic delusion which means that all you have to do is get rich—they have already done that—and the mysteries of the symbolic life, which you have kept out with a heavily raincoated mind, will suddenly be opened up to you. They want to have their power and cheat it too.

"Engels' Law was quietly and sensibly forgotten by the

rulers of the Soviet Union, who had an illiterate peasantry to train and future wars to fight. They established a tough program of utilitarian education which produced factory hands, engineers and soldiers. We do pretty much the same thing, over the protests of our womenfolk, who didn't raise their boys to be soldiers or wear anything but a white collar to work. Now our factories are getting so complicated that the foremen need college degrees, and it looks as if our mothers and our machines are going to be satisfied if only we can get our message through to our enemies in the East.

"Some of our students go in for the humanities, which are needed more and more for the sale of the stuff the machines make. After all, you have to know something about symbols if you are going to misuse them to any effect. Once in a while you might even want to read a book, not more than five pages, the publishers privately predict, but still, it's nice to have it around. It looks good on the wall.

"Soviet education has no time for the humanities, unless they help to produce linguists for the embassies or curators (women) for the museums. There, literature almost occupies the same place that it occupies here in the curriculum of an engineering college. However, every book is read straight through there, and many times, with all its implications sought out hungrily. Every printed word is still taken seriously. In Russia for a long time after 1917, the year of the revolution, printing presses could not print words that had not been in use at that time. Slang and neologism abounded in private talk, but were banned from books. The Soviet government feared new words might confuse the new literates, still moving their lips as they read. Russian peasants had a reverence for the printed word, and this reverence would have been lost if printed words had referred to life as they knew it, in the salty terms that they used every day. Literature had to seem to come from afar. This is hard for us to understand, because printing reached us centuries sooner.

"Our fund raisers would not dream of admitting how tightly utilitarian our education has become. There has to be an illusion of idealism, of a disinterested pursuit of truth. When President Clark Kerr tactlessly reminded the students of the University of California that they were going straight from the 'multiversity' into electronic factories, the Berkeley riots occurred, amid war cries of 'alienation.' It is now fashionable to give more latitude to the humanities, to show that we are not all barbarians. Who knows, they may pay off some day. More important, if the millionaires' dream of quantity becoming quality were disturbed, endowments might drop suddenly, and the jobs of fund raisers too.

"It *has* to seem easy to get an education. It has to seem easy to pour many antagonistic insights from art and science into a single person, who will straightaway assimilate them and not show any of the tensions they set up in him. The myth that education will solve all our problems *must* be preserved."

"Why is that a myth? I believe it."

"You are justified in believing it for yourself. You are not justified in believing in it for your society. You can get an education, and the truth you discover will set you free, as free as you can ever be, if it reaches all of you, and not only your head. But your society can only get an intellectual education, a negotiable education which requires a denial of all other values except its own. Societies are set up to organize the conflicts among warring individuals. Educated people are happier when backward societies adopt more humane laws, but they do not expect even the best society to do more than keep order and be reasonably enlightened. It is a sure sign of self-deception when an individual expects any state to give him a real education. He has a right to expect a socially useful education from society, but a real one which implies a fundamental criticism of both society and self, he can only get for himself, and in the fiercest kind of opposition to and from his society. If he is intelligent he knows this from the start. Technicization has sharply intensified the anti-individualism of society."

A union official asked: "Did I hear you say that the technological society is autonomous? Do you believe that?"

"That's a good question. No one can say for sure, but it certainly seems so. The world appears to be divided into those who can concentrate powerfully on unworthy ends and those who cannot concentrate at all well on worthy ends. It is hard for 'the good guys' to be effective because they cannot concentrate their mental energy to conscious purpose. They lack *will*, or at least they seem to. Why? Because by comparison with their opponents, they get no response from 'the people.' The people are being rewarded by the new prosperity for following the line of least resistance, doing what is expected of them by a society that treats them as objects. They will not listen to anyone who makes moral demands, unaccustomed moral demands of them. Anyone who seeks to prod them into awareness soon finds himself all alone, or practically so, without the social base on which he was trained to count. He therefore cannot concentrate effectively, and seems to lack will, unless he can learn to speak without expecting any response at all.

"This is painful and calls for real strength of character. We all expect a yes to our yes and a no to our no. When we do not get it we usually collapse into a private language or take our revenge by concentrating on the acquisition of money. Only the hardy uncollapsibles who can face a very great loneliness will be tough and tender enough to survive morally on the technological tundra. Perhaps they will make their voices heard some day above the lathes and the cash registers. To do so they will have to become stronger than a system that is all but foolproof and 'autonomous.' "

A copywriter asked: "You talk as if the so-called millennium were really here. That's a figure of speech, of course—or isn't it?"

"For you and me it's a figure of speech. But if you were to see what I saw yesterday from the windows of a Long Island Railroad train, if you saw the excitement of our fellow citizens when they beheld a new shopping center at twilight, all aglow with pink and tangerine lights and apromise with steaks, beer, macaroni, apple pies, bleached oak consoles, easy chairs, bikini dolls, bouncy beds, you would realize that all this is a lot more real than anything the Bible promised. The rule of Christ after a thousand years, that was a figure of speech, but not this.

"Christianity began as a poor man's religion that promised salvation in a world of sorrow and persecution. What we have now, if it can still be called a religion, is a set of facts that intellectual austerity can never really understand. Apple pies and easy chairs are there for the taking, if only we are willing to work hard and limit the scope of our minds. This millennium is so real to the instincts of ninety-nine percent of the population that any stock market or defense department or foreign office, or social scientist or poet, for that matter, who fails to take it into account is not living in the world that exists. You can't understand what is happening to the Americans or the Congolese, the French or the Chinese, the Cubans or the English, the Russians or the Italians, if you don't understand how much they demand this tangible realization of all their more childish dreams. Once those dreams are satisfied, we'll see if they are followed by mature ones. But first the children must have their pie."

Over the years a favorite classroom question has been about "the sacred." What does "the sacred" mean? The answer, with slight variations according to time and place, has been that its definitions differ, and the word has become one more way of determining whether one is inclined to horizontal adjustment to society or to vertical development of self. Most Horizontals will accept Ellul's definition of the sacred as "that which men decide unconsciously to respect." Its emphasis is legal. Most Verticals will desire a more psychological definition which calls the sacred a capacity of the mind that men possess but usually neglect; a capacity that may charge reality with beauty and meaning, and may influence behavior for the good. The last sentence is a paraphrase of Rudolf Otto, and somewhat related to Kierkegaard's description of despair, "the sickness unto death," the unhealthy state in which we all live unless we can heal ourselves with a sense of the sacred or a leap into faith.

There are many other definitions of what is sacred and what is profane. My experience with students led me to believe that it was unwise to attempt to be specific about these words. There were almost as many interpretations as members of the class, and usually the student, as indeed both Trofimov and Lopakhin had shown, adapted them without shame to his own blind spots. For a while I tried to illustrate them with homely incidents taken from my own life, and then I gave it up as a bad job. Although what I had said until then had not been challenged on grounds of clarity, I was soon accused of being anything but lucid. I retreated from the field with more discretion than valor. But with a resolve to return to it later.

"I don't see any difference," said Nellie Rankin with much effort, "between your Aztechs and the tough-minded, or your Toltechs and the tender-minded. Aren't they just extraverts and introverts?"

I replied that there was a significant difference, even though the Aztechs and Toltechs obviously have certain things in common with types invented by William James, Jung, Spitteler, Sheldon and others. The Aztechs and Toltechs were not drawn from philosophical or psychological observation, but from history (or history deduced from archaeology), from a familiar conflict that has existed from earliest times to the present. Aztechs are "primary" (Yeats's word), or quickly adjusted to material wants. Toltechs are "antithetical," or concerned with spiritual wants. The Aztech needs the Toltech's creativity; the Toltech needs the Aztech's materialism; but each tries to minimize the other's contribution.

Culturally we are still somewhat under the influence of the Bible, which spoke of the children of light and the children of this world, and favored the former. The Bible was written by priests with priestly self-interest. Now the prestige of priests has declined. We are almost totally under the influence of the market, which favors the Aztechs. It looks as if this situation will continue for a long time. In fact the Toltechs have lost their power so precipitately and so thoroughly that honorary power is granted them by enlightened Aztechs, somewhat as farmers (the original creators) are granted government subsidies when other occupations, nearer the market, corner too much economic privilege to make agriculture self-sustaining. Maintenance of power demands a steady flow of ideas from scientists, as Promethean (forethoughtful) as possible, since there is sure to be a superfluity of Epimethean (afterthoughtful) managers to adjust their wildest thoughts to the customers or the enemy. Novelists give new phrases to copywriters, composers give new tonalities to soundtracks, painters give new designs to fabrics. By granting these useful Toltechs a small margin of the profit, wily Aztechs prevent them from making a new bid for spiritual power, such as they might make if they had no place in the market at all.

But isn't it wrong, a student suggested with an incoherence that has to be paraphrased, to divide people into types or classes? It's better, isn't it, to see them as just people? There is so much of the Aztech in every Toltech, and vice versa.

There is indeed very much of the Aztech in every Toltech, and very much of the Toltech in every Aztech. Often they fight a fratricidal war within a single bosom. It would be better to be able to treat their many differences in the ceremonial way of cultivated Hindus, who even now wear several different costumes every day, according to whether their functions are to be active or thoughtful—one for early meditation, another for breakfast, another for a ritual bath, another for the office, another for lunch, another for tennis, still another for dinner, and sometimes a change between lovemaking and sleep. Sartorial recognition of man's diversity (and unity) comes harder in the antimetaphysical, that is, the more modern lands. There is not enough time in the West, except among its actors, for so many changes of dress and attitude. Furthermore, the demands of the market require us to slough off any eccentricities that might make us less effective competitors for the new wealth that is being so lavishly thrown up for snatchgrab.

"Almost everything you say," observed a student with a foreign accent, "applies only to the United States. What about the other countries?"

"They are being technicized too, each in a different way. I'll come to them later. We are the pilot plant. You can't understand what is happening to them, unless you understand what has already happened to us."

"You imply," he continued thoughtfully, "that the Toltech, to survive, must face his full complexity. Then you say that it is much more difficult here than anywhere else. Why?"

"First of all, because the United States was created by documents in 1776 and 1789, in the Age of Reason. We lived in tiny settlements near an unexplored wilderness. What little we heard of the inner life we got from clerics who could only give secondhand, conventional reports of it. Our best energy had to be available for public, not private tasks. The atmosphere was overtheological at first, and then, at about the time when Emerson left his pulpit for the lecture platform, overromantic, overliterary.

"We therefore welcomed tougher-minded thinkers when they came along a little later and fought hard to establish the validity of scientific intelligence. Science corrected the mistakes of theology and literature. We liked the scientific emphasis on biological and sociological contexts, its interpretation of human thought as an effort to improve environment. We were changing our environment more radically than any environment had been changed for thousands of years. We liked the scientific picture of man as essentially a maker, a technological animal. A belief in technology is still a supreme article of American faith, but now we are no longer wrestling with a frontier, and we do not always feel optimistic about our new mastery of nature. On the contrary, it alarms us often, and not only because of our new weapons. We have learned that technology is drying us up as human beings.

"In the present century there has been an about-face. Earlier our most active spirits welcomed desacralization, as it came to them from John Dewey and Thomas A. Edison, along with many others, because it freed them from the mortmain of theology and literature. Reduction of the human being to biology, sociology, psychology and technique helped to liberate earlier American Toltechs from old theologians. Now, however, with private worries at last pressing down on him more frighteningly than public ones, the individual has become more critical of the historical forces that helped to shape him. What is the good of his new wealth if it does not permit him to look at his real concerns? He is terribly afraid that his life has no meaning at all, that he has unwittingly done something that now makes him incapable of joy. His reading, when serious, has become more speculative, and his art, when serious, has become more symbolic. Questions keep shaping up in his mind that he never finds time to answer. He is preoccupied with matters that for a long time he put aside. Now they seize hold of him at strange moments, and seem even more important than what he does for a living. He has no traditional European way of dealing with them. His American practicality has stripped him bare at the same time that it has made him rich. He begins to sigh for tradition. He has been given no established way of life that helps him to cope with his problems, he has to do it all himself."

A woman social worker asked: "You don't seem alarmed about automation. Why not? You should see what it is doing to the Negroes in New Jersey."

"You're right. It is already costing unskilled labor a great many jobs and causing a lot of misery. But aside from such cases of hardship, which it is so easy for the prosperous to forget, I believe that in time the practical genius of Americans will find a way to live with automation. It is a big problem, from the standpoint of the underprivileged. For the privileged like yourselves, who can get a higher education, the technicization of your minds is a more serious problem. You all have some of the Toltech in you, you can go bad all the more easily."

"Are Toltechs more liable to go bad than Aztechs?" This was asked with some surprise.

"Definitely. They are more complex. When the going gets rough they have a richer personality to throw overboard. They are nagged by *sacred* obligations. The unimaginative Aztech can keep a sense of duty as a matter of course. The Toltech almost never."

"Why is that?"

"Because he knows how hard the climb out of self-deception is. We're in so deeply now that often we think it's impossible to get out. We'd rather blame everything on the Aztechs."

I worked hard on my answers, and at times I was thanked for them, but they never satisfied me. The reason, I fear, does me little credit. I disliked having to be reasonably well-informed on so many different subjects. I resented having to stretch my mind into so many nooks and crannies of contemporary experience. I feared I was wasting my substance on what might turn out to be mere trivia. I hated the literalness that had been forced on me by my choice of subject. I loathed the many references that I seemed to have to make to money and power and base motivations.

Yet I felt I had to go on. It was dirty work that I had cut out for myself, but it had been forced on me by my time, my place and my way of looking at things. So I went on.

SALVATION BY CHECKBOOK (USA)

12

When an American appears abroad before foreign students, he invites questions about his country, questions that often become aggressive because his country is strong. Might, the might of America, awakens a youthful sense of justified attack, because might, of course, should always be right, and almost never is. Students need an oversupply of paternal scapegoats, unless they are ready to take an undue portion of guilt and responsibility upon themselves. In the querulous atmosphere of great universities, language uniformly becomes fierce in proportion to academic awareness of a ruling monster with no breaking-in at all in the house of intellect. (The monster has no way of harming them.) A visiting American lecturer finds himself identified with slaveholders, witchburners, and germsprayers before he has opened his mouth.

The joke on him becomes still funnier when he is attempting to inform the foreign students that the very same tradewinds that made his country powerful and monstrous are now blowing eastward in *their* direction. Usually they smile at the suggestion. Nothing can "Americanize" them. In the next breath they are boasting of how many kilometers they get on a liter of gasoline, of the excellence of the new superhighway between this ancient place and that, or of how they learned the newest variation of the frug, the latest twist to the twist.

The most rigid opposition to an American lecturer comes from those Europeans who want to continue undisturbed in their belief that all inhabitants of the land between Canada and Mexico must be savages, exploiters of savages or maimed descendants of savages. It is a residual belief, apparently essential to European *amour-propre*, which can be found in the writings of Jean-Paul Sartre, Georges Duhamel, Simone de Beauvoir, the photographs of Henri Cartier-Bresson, and in almost every class-room—at least in the six countries where I spoke. It prides itself on an attitude of "no forgiveness" for the sins of the New World, and represents a considerable toughening of the dignified op-position that was announced by Unamuno and other Spanish intellectuals after their country's defeat by an upstart power in 1898. Above all, it refuses to recognize the possibility that the United States, because its people have been knocked about so unpreparedly by the real wave of the future, may in time produce a hardy few who can at last begin to reverse their country's un-favorable balance of intellectual trade with Europe and to send back a few ideas in exchange for the many they have received. European rigidity will never admit that it has anything to learn.

Fortunately there are some Europeans who are neither rigid nor afraid of former colonials who have demonstrated rather massively their capacity to be materially helpful, artistically surprising and culturally alarming. Some Europeans do want to know more about the United States, if only because it is a fact that has already had a fairly noticeable influence on their own lives. These Europeans are willing to ask questions, and a few of them are reported here, along with the answers that I gave to them.

A German student called my attention to the fact that Max Weber had quoted a passage from an American author as Exhibit A in his description of "the Protestant ethic," in his book of that name. The American author was Ben Franklin, and the passage came from his *Advice to a Young Tradesman* and his *Necessary Hints to Those That Would Be Rich*. The German student wanted to know whether it still reflected the American "spirit of capitalism," or whether new economic con-ditions had changed it. The passage went in part as follows:

> Remember, that time is money. He that can earn ten shillings a day by his labor, and goes abroad, or sits idle, one half of that day, though he spends but sixpence during his diversion or idleness, ought

not to reckon that the only expense; he has really spent, or rather thrown away, five shillings besides.

Remember, that credit is money. If a man lets his money lie in my hands after it is due, he gives me the interest, or so much as I can make of it during that time. This amounts to a considerable sum where a man has good and large credit, and makes good use of it.

Remember, that money is of the prolific, generating nature. Money can beget money, and its offspring can beget more, and so on. Five shillings turned is six, turned against it is seven and three-pence, and so on, till it becomes a hundred pounds. The more there is of it, the more it produces ever turning, so that the profits rise quicker and quicker. He that kills a breeding-sow, destroys all her offspring to the thousandth generation. He that murders a crown, destroys all that it might have produced, even scores of pounds. . . .

The most trifling actions that affect a man's credit are to be regarded. The sound of your hammer at five in the morning, or at eight at night, heard by a creditor, makes him easy six months longer; but if he sees you at a billiard-table, or hears your voice at a tavern, when you might be at work, he sends for his money the next day; demands it, before he can receive it, in a lump.

I told the German student that the passage from Franklin accurately reflected the spirit that had set in motion our prodigious economic growth. Today, in an atmosphere of prosperity, Franklin's style may amuse our more sophisticated bankers, or horrify depositors whose penny-pinching ancestors have permitted them to regard a lifetime of money-getting as undignified; but even now great fortunes are not won or kept by part-time effort. We spend money much more freely than in Franklin's day, but a modest competence can consume all of one's best hours, waking and sleeping. In fact, the ever-wider spread of affluence has meant not forgetfulness of money but the need to pay more attention to it. The independent grocer as well as the chainstore employee, the insurance salesman as well as his customer, the plumber as well as the house-owner all have to develop Franklinian standards of efficiency or run the risk of going under. The same smell of "cash money" that brought the hillbillies out of the hills is now taking the ease out of the easygoing. It also develops precocity of financial interest and virtuoso advertisements. Schoolboys discuss the stock market in the most esoteric jargon of the financial page. Brokers season their market letters with quotations from Proust, in French, and their attempt to treat dollar-chasing as an elegant sport of the *cognoscenti* merely drives home its deadly seriousness as a full-time occupation.

A question from an Italian carried the same line of thought further. "Why are Americans so tense? Why are they so worried about the Communists? They've made all that money, why don't they relax and enjoy it?"

My answer to that was that affluence has not brought the mass relaxation that reformers and revolutionaries once hoped for, so that people might read books, listen to music, look at pictures, study chemistry and be so stimulated by them that they would demand fuller lives of their own. Mass education, instead of awakening mass minds to individual experience, has redoubled mass anxiety, mass escapism, mass apathy. The anxiety has been so acute as to check the genial openness to culture that a super-abundance of wealth and a flexible credit system had been expected to bring. Our good artists are not impressed, as they have said more than once, with the greater sale of good paper-backs, the wider programming of good music or the busier turn-stiles at museums. They fear that culture is being regarded as a status symbol rather than as a cherished personal experience. Their art brings them in return thin conversation and pathetic correspondence. They realize that "art consumers" "mean well," but their best energy seems to be consumed by the strain of keeping abreast of tricky new pecuniary currents. Money gotten with so much strain does not permit relaxation. Communists are therefore regarded overemotionally as dangerous foes by the dollar-chasers, rather than as other human beings with troubles of their own. Anxiety becomes so acute that almost no one can afford to take his eye off the ball.

What is more, the same tricky pecuniary currents surround the artist himself, and everyday it becomes harder for him to take *his* eye off the ball. The "permanent revolution" has arrived, only it is not communistic, as Trotsky hoped, but capitalistic. Its effect upon the American artist is to oblige him to adapt himself ever more rapidly to new things, new words, new salesmanship, at the same time that culture, which he desires more desperately than ever, demands a leisurely evaluation of every act and every word. Each day he is made systematically more schizophrenic, more divided against himself, until his culture-born split reaches a point where it cannot be healed by psychiatry. Correct diagnosis of his mental illness now requires a psychosocial understanding that is all but impossible to find, and correct treatment would require an imaginative and rigorous use of it, if the culture victim were to transform himself into a culture hero.

"Americans work too hard," said another Italian, "Why are they always so busy?"

My reply was that busyness is a way of putting oneself beyond tragedy, the most ingenious opiate that could be found by a people famed for their "Yankee ingenuity." Faced with a complex situation that could only be mastered with an equally complex consciousness, and denied by their very success an adequate technique of consciousness, they have kept their eye on the job at hand. What is more, their "pragmatism" has worked, although there are many indications now that it will not work much longer, because it is too harmful to the minds and bodies of those who use it.

"Would you care to say anything more about that?" the same student asked.

"I'll be glad to. It's the heart of the matter," I said, and gave a detailed reply which can merely be suggested here. My point was that our great technological progress was created not only by the mind-body split that has already been described; it was also the product of what the British physician A. T. W. Simeons calls "cortical conceit," which may be a better way of saying the same thing. Cortical conceit is the belief that man can rule his body with culture-inspired directives that originate in the outer layer of his brain. The newer and more presumptuous cortex refuses to recognize the priority of the much earlier diencephalon, or thalamencephalon, which lies nearer the center of the brain and determines our instantaneous "instinctive" responses. The person who is so estranged from his animal origins that he chronically disregards his "lower" impulses— toward terror and flight, for example—and favors instead the "higher" orders that issue from his culture, will fall such an easy

prey to psychosomatic illnesses that he may in time, Dr. Simeons
says, be ready for race suicide.

This is a danger that would presumably threaten our
more sensitive Toltechs before it attacked our Aztechs; but once
our Toltechs were gone, our Aztechs would soon follow them.
Commercial civilizations disappear fast. Our Toltechs, who might
have become a "saving Remnant" in the manner I have suggested in a previous book, may instead prefer to die out in the
manner that Dr. Simeons suggests Neanderthal man chose when
confronted with the superiority of his Cro-Magnon rival.

Gradually Neanderthal Man lost his will to live a life in
which the odds were hopelessly stacked against him, and in this
state of perpetual frustration he may well have fallen a victim to
some form of psychosomatic disease which hurried him to his doom.
. . . Thus a possible explanation for the sudden disappearance of
Neanderthal Man is that he committed racial suicide out of fear—
fear of the uncanny and seemingly supernatural beings that appeared in his midst. . . .

It seems improbable that the proud and highly civilized
Etruscans succumbed only to the Roman broadswords; that the
great empire of the Incas was physically destroyed by a band of
fanatical hooligans; that the primitive Veddahs of Ceylon, who have
vast jungles in which they can live as they have done since time im-
memorial, are rapidly dying out only on account of pressure from
more highly civilized races. Even the fact that primitive races have
been known to disintegrate when distilled alcohol was brought to
them can be interpreted as a form of self-destruction through an
alcoholic oblivion from despair.

When the horrors of Nazism were at their height and when
at one time it looked as if this insane doctrine might attain universal
conquest, surviving Jews were often heard to say that in a world so
horribly threatened with barbarity they would refrain from having
children.

The latter example suggests the manner in which the
race suicide of the Toltechs, if it were to occur, would take
place. They would yield to a more brutal foe, only temporarily
stopped, in his German form, by World War II. But before
doing so, they would surrender their own best weapons of survival to expedient imitation of their foe. The symbolic mind

would abdicate before the factual mind, because it could not learn how to use facts to reestablish symbols.

"You suggest that D. H. Lawrence had special insight into the problems of Americans. In fact, you almost put him higher than de Tocqueville. Why?" asked a Frenchman.

For answer to that, to the student's surprise, I obtained a copy of Lawrence's book on American literature, and read him a passage:

> Liberty in America has meant so far the breaking away from all dominion. The true liberty will only begin when Americans discover IT, and proceed to fulfill IT. IT being the deepest *whole* self of man, the self in its wholeness, not idealistic halfness.
>
> That's why the Pilgrim Fathers came to America, then: and that's why we come. Driven by IT. We cannot see that invisible winds carry us, as they carry swarms of locusts, that invisible magnetism brings us as it brings the migrating birds to their unforeseen goal. But it is so. We are not the marvelous choosers and deciders we think we are. IT chooses for us, and decides for us. Unless of course we are just escaped slaves, vulgarly cocksure of our ready-made destiny. But if we are living people, in touch with the source, IT drives us and decides us. We are free only so long as we obey. When we run counter, and think we will do as we like, we just flee around like Orestes pursued by the Emenides.
>
> And still, when the great day begins, when Americans have at last discovered America and their own wholeness, still there will be the vast number of escaped slaves to reckon with, those who have no cocksure, ready-made destinies.
>
> Which will win in America, the escaped slaves, or the new whole men?

Lawrence has asked here, and elsewhere in the same book, I said to the French student, a question that is more acutely pertinent to the American Toltech than anything in de Tocqueville, excellent though he still is. Who are the "escaped slaves, vulgarly cocksure of their ready-made destiny"? They are those who find their cocksureness by letting the new technological society ready-make their destinies and answer every question for them. Who are "the new whole men"? They are those who sail against the weather, "driven by IT," and undeterred by the greater prestige, achieved by publicity, of the phony and the halfway. "If there is any more pertinent question for the American today," I told my questioner, "I am unaware of it."

In another book Lawrence has gone further, and further back, I also said, in his questions about the effect of America upon the individual. In a novel about a woman who goes to Mexico, Lawrence writes:

"And sometimes she wondered whether America really was the great death-continent the great *NO!* to the European and Asiatic and even African *YES!* Was it really the great melting pot, where men from the creative continents were smelted back again, not to a new creation, but down into the homogeneity of death? Was it the great continent of the undoing, and all its peoples the agents of the mystic destruction! Plucking, plucking at the created soul in man, til at last it plucked out the living germ, and left him a creature of mechanism and automatic reaction, with only one inspiration, the desire to pluck the quick out of every living spontaneous creature."

The novel is *The Plumed Serpent*. It is not one of his best fictions, but the questions it raises are nonetheless important. He wrote it some forty years ago about Mexico, but obviously he was thinking of the Mexicans' northern neighbors as well. Certainly its huge rhetorical questions, lacking data, can be made to seem irrelevant in the United States of today—to all but a few Toltechs.

Could its use of "death" be extended to those of us who hope to outwit suffering with busyness? Can planned insensitivity be premature *rigor mortis*? Is the raincoat mind a shroud?

If there is any point at all in his questions, the fact remains, they have not been used by any sociologist as a basis for research. Apparently they are not as important as why we no longer enjoy going to parties, or why Vassar girls now prefer babies to careers.

"We take the trouble to learn your language," a Swiss student complained, "but you don't return the compliment. Or very seldom. Why are Americans so bad at languages?"

My answer was not as good as the question. I have often thought about the question. If it were asked me again, I would answer it somewhat as follows.

The habit of winning their wars has made it unnecessary for most Americans to learn languages. Also, they live far away from Europe. But more important, the demands of their new technology, the new state of mind it has induced in them, have drained off the intellectual energy that might have gone into languages. Their cultural libido is low, because the requirements of the new efficiency and the new competitiveness are high. They live in the center of a world revolution that affects the individual more deeply, more exhaustingly, though less violently, than any other revolution (such as the French or the Russian). Other revolutions were soon over; adjustments to them were abrupt and painful but clear. In the Second American Revolution the individual lacks an ideologue to spell it out for him with guillotine or firing squad; he has to decipher its sinister enigmas for himself. The new crucifixion is not over in an afternoon; it takes a lifetime. There is little relaxed leisure in that lifetime for the study of languages, which call for a cultural sympathy and a sense of playacting that the harassed technolater simply cannot summon.

The linguistic failures of Americans, which have caused some concern in the State Department, are another symptom of the cultural aridity that follows an overpragmatic exploitation of the cortex. Most American education is aimed at just that. Under such practical instruction, life is not welcomed gently and amply through the loins and the solar plexus; it is channeled narrowly—"screened"—through the forebrain. The result is profound unsympathy, to put it mildly, for all other ways of life and the words in which they express themselves.

Even our Toltechs are rarely good linguists, because so much of their energy is preempted by the psychological and philosophical questions that the new "pragmatism" prefers to overlook. Their lack of a fluent metaphysics means the lack of a fluent Italian or even a fumbling Vietnamese.

"In your book on the Remnant you used the phrase 'salvation by checkbook,' " said a Welsh student. "What did you mean by that?"

The checkbook is *the* focal point of modern power, I answered. It buys the action and the thoughts of other men. It is impressive. It makes lonely individual effort seem puny and unimportant. It discourages the young from making such efforts.

Every nation, I said, has its own road to salvation, its own hope of extricating itself from a sea of troubles. The French believe in art, the English in teamwork, the Italians in instinct, the Germans in ideology. The early Americans put their faith in a book that was originally written in Hebrew and Greek. Now their successors have thrown it out as ineffective, and found another book which seems to do the same job better.

When I reported some of these questions and answers to my American class, Lopakhin expressed a polite but distinct disappointment. "You should have been firmer," he said. "Those people hate our guts, after all we've done for them. You shouldn't have been so nice. Irony and sarcasm—it just rolls off people's backs."

Trofimov did not comment directly. " 'No man is an island,' " he quoted derisively. "But I am an island. And so is everybody else I know." He reached out and took Nellie Rankin's hand. We were sitting in her tiny apartment. At last the night had arrived when I was to dine with them.

SALVATION BY ART
(FRANCE)

13

Nellie Rankin's apartment was in the lower part of Greenwich Village. I went there on the evening of a holiday. After climbing five flights of stairs in a shabby building that had garbage cans on each broken-tiled landing, and tricycles on two of them, I entered a white-walled room, lit by candles, that might have been the study of a prioress in seventeenth-century Mexico. A splendid hand-hewn table, a polished chest of drawers and four leather-backed chairs, all of dark old wood in Hispano-Moresque style, made such a contrast with the dispirited disrepair of the hallways that I realized I had underestimated my student. My new interest in her increased when I saw many books, mostly in incongruous modern jackets—and some from my own reading list—in an elaborate bookcase with carved panels that suggested the Churriguera front of a Spanish cathedral. Among the books lay the remains of a candy skull from Oaxaca and a sepia photograph of a fatigued Christ, bearing tropical flowers, in a church in Yannuitlan.

The owner of these unusual decorations, whom I had hardly heard speak until then, turned out to have a trained mezzo-soprano voice and exceptionally clear diction. Moreover, she talked a lot. On cryptlike walls hung framed playbills which showed that her voice had been heard at least four times in the last five years in off-Broadway productions of plays about Latin America. Nellie Rankin was a professional actress who seemed about twenty-seven years old, had large dark eyes, a dancer's lithe figure, and a warm smile that looked sad in repose. At home, instead of staring at me in silence, she apologized for the height and filth of the building, gave an impromptu imitation of her landlord, insisted on hanging up my coat and offered me a choice of tequila or Spanish brandy. Later she told me, with imitations of nearly every character involved, that she was half-American and half-Quebec French, and had been born on her father's father's farm in Michigan, but her face and her facility at accents had qualified her for Latin American roles, in the eyes of producers, and since she had made her greatest success on the stage as a Mexican, she had put her modest earnings into Mexican furniture. She was trying, she said, to create an "image" that would help her to get other parts as "a cute Mexican bitch."

Trofimov was already there, lolling on a daybed that was covered with a mussed Navajo blanket. That evening there was none of the terror in him that I had usually sensed in the classroom. On the contrary, he seemed relaxed and cheerful when he got up slowly to greet me. Soon, while Nellie excused herself to cook dinner in a tiny kitchen that was not out of earshot, he was telling us of a meeting he had had that afternoon in a Charles Street bar with a French journalist, a meeting that had meant much to him. I believe Nellie had heard the story before, but she seemed eager to hear it again.

He told it with a natural relish and skill that seemed part of an Irish inheritance and somehow went with a babylike face. (In real life his name was not Trofimov but nearer O'Toole.) The French journalist had looked him up because he had read a short story by him and had liked it. It had been reprinted in the Best Stories of the Year, and it had also been translated into French. That was why the Frenchman had met Trofimov-O'Toole in the bar on Charles Street.

The story, which I also admired when I read it later, had dealt with the theft of a painting by Chardin from the Louvre, and how the thief had escaped his pursuers and carried it under his raincoat to an apartment in St. Cloud by taxi, subway and bus. More interesting than the theft itself were the fresh and original descriptions of the landmarks passed by the thief on his way to the outskirts of the city, and the final revelation that the author had never been in Paris and the crime he described had never taken place.

"How did you do it?" the French journalist asked. "I could have sworn you were French!"

"I should have been," Trofimov-O'Toole told him mournfully.

But the compliments of the Frenchman had cheered him, and he remained in good spirits, even when he mentioned that he felt like "an island,"—throughout the excellent dinner that Nellie Rankin soon served us; a meal that gave us bean soup in the Quebec style, *boeuf a l'ancienne,* a choice between Bordeaux wine and Montreal ale, cheese made by Trappist monks near the St. Lawrence River, and pralines from New Orleans. In that meal at least, as she said, she felt no need to conceal her French half or to try to seem Mexican.

Naturally I thought of her francophilia, and Trofimov-O'Toole's also, when I gave a lecture soon afterwards on France. I wondered whether they would like it. It said so many things that *seemed* anti-French.

Some people will feel I was wrong when I suggested a while back that France must almost inevitably follow, though in her own way, the United States in the direction of the technological society. They eat French bread, they drink French wine, they love French women and they think, "Who would ever give up all this for the privilege of eating foam rubber, drinking California, or penetrating the heroines of Mary McCarthy?"

They say further that the French people possess many safeguards, both earthy and intellectual, that will protect them against Ellulian disaster. Ellul, incidentally, they seem to regard as a sourpuss *emmerdeur,* and a bad writer, unworthy of the best accomplishments of his own country, who passed from the certainties of Marxism to the certainties of neo-Calvinism in a few weeks of uninteresting personal crisis, and now has dreamed up the technological society as the nearest thing to a Calvinist hell with which to frighten fellow-puritans who begin to feel guilty the instant they bite into a buttery *croissant*. At many times in history, these francophiles say, newcomers like the Americans have gained power, newcomers only too willing to forget their original search for reason and dignity and to let themselves be consumed, through some temporary technical advantage, by their own covetousness and triviality.

Who are the Americans, after all? Killers who destroyed the original settlers of their land—wholly unlike the French in Canada, North Africa or Viet Nam. Employers who have been living off the sweat of immigrant labor—Irish, German, Russian, Canadian, Mexican, Italian, Puerto Rican and African—for over a century, and now are trying to prevent their melting pot from boiling over with rage by offering the cheated new arrivals cars, clothes and homes in the country at cheap interest rates (which they never pay off) or a place in the government if they have learned to think "right." Abroad the Americans mask their true intentions, which are to run the world at a tremendous profit, with pseudo-Keynesian pretensions of benevolence. Their hypocrisy, which begins with the claim that they are ruled by a democratic government, has a particularly insidious appeal to youth, as insidious as their rock and roll, because it is sentimental, discourages hardheaded thought, and slyly suggests that waste is better than thrift. Everywhere the younger generation is being encouraged by the American example, to believe that a demanding attitude toward existence, accompanied by a minimum of effort, will be rewarded.

After a while, say the francophiles, the American madness will pass. People have to live with themselves. Truth has a way of making itself known. Work finally means more than unemployment insurance. Bellies will grow rounder, even on foam rubber, meditation will set in, even on fake Chablis, and the penetration of Vassar girls, even when they come equipped with impeccable bodies, will lose its pathological appeal.

It is rather significant that in the movies, where Hollywood once reigned supreme with a starting new popular legendry, there have been no American stars of any real magnitude for a long, long time. Everyone knows by now that perfect features can conceal the mind of a drive-in waitress or a gasoline pumper. Even sex needs mythology to keep it alive, and the American way of life has depersonalized American screen actors to a point where they can only hope to appeal to children between popcorn and uncomfortable fornication. The stories the actors appear in have also been censored to the point of complete insipidity.

America is afraid to look at itself. It has also grown blind to the beauty that exists even among robots. America is a myth that was.

Mass stupidity will not rule the world forever. So runs the reasoning of several intelligent Frenchmen to whom I have spoken. The Americans have come up with many useful innovations; no one has questioned their ingenuity. It was better to make the president of a republic strong. It is better to let citizens build houses at low interest rates, rather than at the 12 percent or 20 percent now charged in France. Some day a crisis will oblige the French to borrow this latter device; they have already borrowed the former. But such practical improvements are of minor importance in the long run, and should be made only when urgently needed. Otherwise they take too much time from the art of living. It is better to leave, though with the usual legal controls, the dreariness of government and money to those who *must* dominate them. In no country can determined power-seekers be kept long from getting what they want. It is better to make sure that enough political freedom and money come your way to let you cultivate your garden. Planting seeds is still more important to the truly intelligent than getting your picture in the paper. Some injustice is bound to be imposed on you. If it is not more than you can stomach, accept it and get on with your work.

This idea, I think, comes from a traditional belief in art. One of its undiscussed implications is that the more injustice you accept, the better your art will be. You will see more deeply than others. You will feel more deeply than others. You will construct more cunningly than others. It is a conservative and perhaps masochistic thought without much contemporary appeal. It helped to create the French works of art that we Americans love, to shape the old stones that take such a hold on our imagination, but as a way of life a mere handful of us can accept it, and then perhaps only intellectually, without referring it closely to our own lives, because we are all, even our most selfless minorities, being offered new powers that we find almost unrefusable, at least for a while.

I am obliged to admit that I, who as a writer stand to lose most by a decline in traditional respect for craftsmanship and culture, doubt the ability of France to save itself by art. I admire the sentiments of certain French thinkers, such as I have tried to convey here, but I cannot overlook the fact that the new powers being offered everyone, and offered with a minimum of moral demands, are so tempting that traditional happiness, as symbolized by the cultivation of a garden, has lost its appeal for nearly everyone, and especially for the younger generation in its more vigorous and finally more hopeful aspects. Healthy young people do not take the world on hearsay; they have to discover it for themselves. Little understanding can be expected from the early prudent. Discipline, if it comes, must come from experience. The healthy part of the younger generation everywhere will soon face the attractions of freedom from loneliness, abundance of goods, greater longevity, sex with impunity, money in the bank and the myth of progress through mass education. Such attractions, in forms both realistic and unrealistic, if they have not already been offered, will soon be offered young people in France and everywhere else. It remains to be seen what they do with them.

France still attracts more affectionate pilgrims than any other modern shrine. Turbojets bring her as much devotion, at least from Toltechs, as Baltimore clippers or half-steam barquentines did in another time. The bull-leaping in Nîmes and the lonely canals in Burgundy are as beautiful as ever. African and Asian students say they learn more in France, which they respect, than in the United States, which they do not. Money has not yet created insuperable barriers to truthfulness. A desire for orgasm blends occasionally into a desire for relatedness. A false note of salesmanship, among intellectuals, brings a salutary sigh of boredom. Ridicule is ever on the alert for the naively self-centered. Mental toughness actually contributes here and there to *joie-de-vivre*. Daily routine is sometimes not rushed through as a chore, but cherished as a sacrament.

On the other hand, Chardin purity can be offset by French Line whoresdream. Boulogne films can be worse than anything done in Hollywood. The protected insularity of French intellectuals reduces their connection with the world as it is every day. Some *École de Paris* painters outdo J. Walter Thompson in advertising technique. French workers are exploited in a

way that American workers would not permit. A Lyons banker's
son must wait until he has passed fifty, before he is made an
official of the bank. French scientists flee France because they
get no help at all from the rich and their government tells them,
"A scientist's best laboratory is his own mind." Dull authors
have every page of tedious manuscript brought back to them
at the end of each week, by copyboys, in printed form, so they
may see how beautiful it looks. Taxes commensurate to Luxem-
bourg are collected from the richest country in Europe. The
dreariest epigrams are uttered as if they came from the mouth
of La Rochefoucauld. Overeating is habitual. Americans are
preferred when they are obvious monsters, reinforcements of
French complacency. Salvation by art does lose ground every
day to salvation by advertising, even in the land of the honest
baker, the worker-priest, the devoted *lycée* instructor.

An overlooked but significant French debate is that
between Sartre and Ellul, who was his friend in the *Résistance.*
Together they dramatize France's role in the technological society. Ellul scorns individual efforts to outwit the withering
effect of technology, for example by art: "these spiritual movements are totally confined within a technical world . . . technique encompasses the totality of present-day society. Man is
caught like a fly in a bottle. His attempts at culture, freedom and
creative effort have become mere entries in technique's filing
cabinet."

Ellul's death-sentence, even if he has overstated it
for effect or, as seems more likely, tried to cover up some hidden
incapacity of his own, suggests that he is talking more from
logical deduction than from personal experience. Nevertheless,
the few personally observed facts he assembles are impressive,
and imply that Sartre, with whose ideas we are better acquainted,
is being irrelevant when he speaks of "the politics of engagement." Ellul is telling his friend that he should cease the
profitable shadowboxing of fake revolutionism and face the real
antagonists of our day. "Leave off your dreary Marxism," Ellul
is saying in effect, "and realize that the real revolution is technological, not political or economic."

By extension, such a critique of Sartre and many others
like him, not only in France but in the United States and else-

where, means that he and they are guilty of what Sartre himself has called *mauvaise foi*, bad faith, or lying to oneself. They are polemicists who enjoy driving home a point to the lazy or the uninformed, without questioning their own relationship to it. They prefer to overlook the familiar psychological fact that one never denounces *any* fault of which one is innocent. (If one were free of it, one would overlook it and denounce something else.) They enjoy guilt-fixing, a favorite sport of the undetected guilty. ("We can never forgive or forget," etc., a standard device of those who have much to hide.) They are especially rough on the bourgeois, because of the unfaced bourgeois within themselves. (What a tale the concealed bank accounts of socialists could tell!) In an age of hasty acquisition the lies of polemicists pass unnoticed, until they are replaced by still bigger ones that are more to the taste of the oncoming generation.

All this has nothing to do with healthier forms of Existentialism, which despise these conceptualist maneuvers, seek to go "to the things themselves," as Husserl put it, and accept a full portion of personal error and anxiety. The Sartrean adaptation of Heidegger is an ingenious new development of the same mind-body split that Heidegger was denouncing. It has been merchandised for a gullible intelligentsia which wants the thrill of "commitment" without the stern self-examination it implies. Sartre's wartime identification with Existentialism was primarily a public relations job, pulled off in a place and in a profession where public relations are not supposed to exist.

But Sartre is still many times more interesting than Ellul, and so far as I know he has never suggested that all contemporary efforts at art are worthless. How could the author of so excellent a book as *Nausea* say anything like that? It was later that he turned from self-examination to the new sanctimony.

The sanctimonious antibourgeois theme ends fraternity in both literature and life. The Toltech seduced by it is denied his true relationship to the Aztech, which is that of a brother, even when his earthier kinsman turns fratricidal. It is the Toltech's task to understand the Aztech and to interpret him to himself: to give him an understanding that he cannot return except by "deductible contributions." His occasional returns are more frequent in the United States than in France. (Sartre's denunciation of rich *salauds* would have been harder to bring off in the land of the Fords and the Rockefellers.) Without the Toltechs' modest, merely symbolic leadership there can be no dialogue between them, and they may both be destroyed by some new Cortés emerging from the sea on a horse.

A division of men into Aztechs and Toltechs is not a play on words, but an attempt to deal accurately and flexibly with complex everyday realities that have existed since the beginning of civilization. Every Toltech is contaminated with Aztech bloodlusts and moneylusts. Every Aztech, no matter how brutally intent on his net return, longs ever so slightly to be released from his more savage preoccupations. Fraternity is a biological fact, whatever the distance in division of labor or hierarchy of values. It can be felt, however, only at rare intervals. It cannot be insisted on, as it was in some churches or on the day the Bastille fell. In this war there is seldom an armistice.

A foremost obstacle to dialogue between the two tribes is their different attitudes toward institutions. Power-oriented Aztechs quickly acquire "correctly adjusted positive feelings" toward social institutions like churches, armies, corporations, schools and governments, which may, and usually do, move craft-oriented Toltechs to strong denunciation. Aztechs *want* to believe in institutions, which guarantee order; Toltechs want to believe in their own sense of right and wrong. Aztechs adjust their feelings to social facts (saying the right thing to their boss— or to his marriageable daughter) with an instant agility that seems to their critics the essence of corruption. Toltechs prefer to remain steadfast to subjective perceptions, and *their* critics call this no better than a childish fear of change.

In France a litmus test is your attitude toward Malraux. If you admire his switch from the Left to De Gaulle, you are Aztech. If you do not, you cling to Toltech individualism. But all such tests and typologies, when used literally, are superficial. If you are capable of more than tribal rigidity (and the complexity of the technological revolution drives all gifted men, especially those with Toltech complications, toward a humane synthesis) you will, I think, accept André Malraux as an exceptionally interesting man who dramatizes in his own person one of the major fluctuations of our day. Tolerance of this kind does not mean siding with him politically or aesthetically, but seeing him as much as possible as he is, freed of your own demands on him, and as rewarding to a contemplative mind as a swan, a smokestack, a germ or a ballerina. There will be nothing superficial in your perceptions if you address yourself to seeing what is inherently sacred in him and in all other men.

Each day the momentum of an "autonomous" technological revolution makes attentiveness to others more difficult to attain. Technology promotes peace with a plenitude of goods, and war with a rigidity of minds. Only those who have nylonized their minds with commercial indifference or *parti pris* fanaticism can do well in the technological society. Those who expose themselves to the chaos of experience, who try to see André Malraux as he is, rather than as he should be (according to one's own desires), comprise a minority quest for self-respect and justice that cannot make itself heard above the din of self-dramatizing fragments. Therefore, as I have already suggested, true education must begin with helping the student to face the chaos of experience and to see through the various ideologies or concepts which seek to oversimplify it for him.

French students—or at least those I have known—will be held back from true education by the dead hand of the past, the weight of tradition, or the "spirit of seriousness," as Sartre deftly calls it, that offers to reward them if they avoid the perils of openness to experience. Americans will be held back by the dead hand of the future, the myth of inevitable progress through mass education. It shuts out manysided reality with equal effectiveness.

French students still have the advantage of the most closely reasoned way of life in the world. They speak a language that disciplines them in the art of thinking as no other language does. They live in a land that overlooks nothing and forces individual responsibility upon them at an early age. They are well-schooled in the various articles of Toltech faith. If survival as a Toltech did not require each one of them to pass through a private revolution as far-reaching as the social one that is already transforming every moment of their lives, we could be surer of the continuance of the best French values. As it is, gifted French students are better protected against new realities than gifted American students, who must contend with them from birth. The danger is that French students will ignore them, and Americans will be snuffed out in perfect silence.

As a nation France cannot put its faith in art (no nation can), but a few Frenchmen—and a few others, wherever they happen to be born—can and do. If anyone is outwitting the technological society, as it is punitively preached by Ellul or as it exists in reality, it is our few genuine artists. Who enjoys life more than they do? Who faces it more as it actually is? Who is more likely to avoid being caught like flies in a bottle? The radiance of their faces would be enough to recommend artists to the perceptive student, if he had never read of their unpredictable ingenuity, their erotic dash, their dogged faith, their lasting prestige. Now that the ability to become rich is supposed to have been added to their accomplishments—at least in the picture magazines—now that they no longer need be unrewarded heroes, even the most Aztech student can admire them.

By comparison, "how beastly the bourgeois is!" Poor Richard's counsels, as reported by Ben Franklin, would get no response at all in the affluent society; they would have to be rewritten by Rich Richard. And Rich Richard would no longer stress industry but "creativeness." Commerce has long since taken over the vocabulary of the arts, as more appealing to women and to youth than its own grim directives. The most mercenary professions now find a way to add the word "creative" to their recruiting approach to the young. Tellers-to-be are told by banks, along with routine explanations of why the daily handling of large sums of money must be rewarded with only small sums of it, how "creative" their work is to be in their cages. It is the most charismatic, as well as the most pragmatic word of our day. And it came of course from the arts—or rather a shrewd exploitation of the arts.

Meanwhile this commercial tribute to the arts has been reciprocated by many artists. The clever adoption by businessmen of an earlier avant-garde credo of continual progress toward "light, more light" has been matched by the attempt of more and more artists to adopt businesslike methods of studying the public. Since the ultimate source of contemporary power is the

mind of the purchasing public—or more exactly, the minds of
the *many* different publics which can be made to yield a profit—
it was inevitable that ambitious artists, once they had passed
beyond the early private obsessions which drove them into the
arts, should copy the cool analysis of the many-faceted mass
mind that has long been practiced by advertising men and investment counselors. These artists seem to have relied more
often on intuition than analysis, but they have been at least
equally expert in their awareness of how the public most congenial to their individual style might be shocked, cajoled or
bullied into buying it.

The recent success of Pop Art was no accident. It represented an astute fusion of vanguard mythology ("Now's your
chance to get in on genius while it's still unappreciated and
cheap.") and a brilliant understanding of one public's preference
for easy-to-take art it could despise. Pop artists knew in advance
how to win space from cynical editors for confused but contemp-
tuous readers. (One prevalent attitude toward the technological
society: "It's all a phony, so I can be phony too.") But Pop
Art's skill in *épater le nouveau bourgeois,* the more *nouveau* the
better, which proved to be one of the more lucrative of unexpected technical innovations, had been prepared by earlier artists
who, even when they remained faithful to their original freshness
of vision (as they ever more rarely did) showed in their later
work an ad-man's understanding of their audience. The giant
Picasso cleared a path for midgets who try to find victims they
can still shock.

The decline of a once-real avant-garde in France—a
decline that was inevitable when it became a big business—led
to the birth of a completely factitious one in America. (Not to
be confused with the work of a few serious, isolated American
artists.) It was Lend-Lease in reverse and an improved form of
simony, much subtler than that practiced by erring churchmen in
the Middle Ages. Works of art, among the few things left that
the most skeptical could still consider sacred, were being mar-
keted, and by the very latest public-kidding tricks required to
clinch the deal.

Men of goodwill, if that term still has any meaning for

intelligently disabused contemporaries, prefer to think of works of art as sacred, and free of all huckstering. Men of goodwill also prefer to think of France as retaining a pretechnological common-sense, often called "Mediterranean," that will defend it against the various manipulations of the various mass minds and lead in time to a reestablishment of reason. Men of goodwill who indulge themselves in such hopefulness must now question their own goodwill. Can goodwill ever be taken for granted, now that a wholly desacralized, anything-goes millennium is here? Are they really well-intentioned or do they hope that "tradition" will do what human beings now have to do, and have always had to do, for themselves? Are they willing to take on the personal responsibilities that a belief in art now demands? Or do they prefer to issue one more dishonest "indictment of society"?

Men of goodwill cannot deserve that title unless they recognize their new relationship to power. The use of symbols is no longer a lonely gesture of innocent communion, as it was for example in Dada days, when artists registered a refined protest against World War I with works of delicate absurdity, and expected none but their own *je-m'en-fichiste* kind to follow what they were saying. Any use of symbols must now be con-sidered a deliberate attempt to move the minds of others in a preconceived direction. Symbols are always, one way or another, related to a quest for power. The mere proximity of docile publics, or overstuffable voids, was enough to alter the artist's relationship to symbols. He can still be so committed to an unpopular message or an unpopular style that he will fail to make an impression on any public of any size. He may also consciously restrict his appeal to a few. If those few are astute enough, they can get considerable attention for him in the press. He may also discipline himself to speak only from his deepest being, which might have a bad effect on his following, but a good one on the quality of his work. He needs money to survive, if only a bit of it, and the way to it is now more often through publicity than a patron. Patrons need reassurance. He must win *some* favorable attention to keep going. He must recognize his dependence on society.

The earlier cult of the avant-garde led him to think of

himself as entirely independent of group values, but the facts
of the new prosperity have destroyed this hallucination. Romantic protest against an earlier industrialism made the illusion
of complete individualism possible. Now it would be merely
stupid.

Still more interesting than the difference between Dada
and Pop, as a revelation of a changed avant-garde, have been
certain literary developments. I have already mentioned Sartre's
cheapening of Heidegger. The difference between Franz Kafka
and Albert Camus shows how a complex vision and style, addressed despairingly in almost perfect solitude to a handful of
kindred spirits, was converted by a more journalistic and more
political talent into the kind of social indictment that would
appeal to a new intelligentsia that wanted concepts to protect
it from the devastations of actual modern experience. Camus
admired Kafka, as his essays about him make clear, but when
he adapted Kafka's lonely description of the world as he found it
to the minds of readers who for the most part had ignored Kafka
or disliked him, Camus ingeniously dropped the complexity of
his model and gave a life-fearing literati one more indictment
of society that was to its taste. He was writing for time-pressed
intellectuals who wanted to read fast, without too much thought,
and above all craved another round, after the bitter disillusionment of the Moscow Trials, of bourgeois-baiting. The difference
between *The Castle* and *The Stranger* was the difference between
true mystery, created by a mind that had exposed itself nakedly,
or as nakedly as possible, to the chaos all around it and a
readable facsimile of mystery, created by a mind that organized
chaos rapidly into a familiar pattern of social injustice and fixed
the guilt on a well-known enemy who would not reply.

Camus was a good writer, admirable in many works,
who is mentioned here as an illustration of how literature, as well
as ideology, can be used to hold overpainful experience at bay.
We have new reading publics which want only as much life
in their books as they are willing to take. So we get authors who
give them just what they want and no more.

The treatment of homosexuality in modern French
literature also indicates a change in the reading public, and a
consequent change in authors. Marcel Proust was born in Vic-

torian times. Since he wished to keep his own homosexuality a secret from his mother, and had been profoundly influenced by her in his approach to the public, he introduced in his long novel, as the sexual companion of his hero Marcel, not a boy named Albert, but an unfeminine girl named Albertine. André Gide, however, who had found in homosexuality a liberation from his ancestral portion of an overstrict, life-hating Protestant ethic, grew bolder than Proust. In *Corydon* he celebrated homosexuality as not only biologically natural, but historically indispensable to the higher forms of civilization. Jean Genet went still further. In *The Thief's Journal* a tube of vaseline that is found jeeringly in his pockets by Spanish police, and denounced by them as proof of his pederasty, is turned by him with great literary skill into a symbol of his own moral superiority to them.

Since homosexuals now constitute a sizeable public of their own, this unjustly ridiculed group of men has been aided by the proliferation of publics to find a way to reply to their persecutors. In performing this service to his own kind, Genet was also aided by the guilt of heterosexuals, and he knew how to make the most of it. Perhaps in time his work and that of his more traditional predecessors will help homosexuals to obtain fairer treatment and better legislation in other lands than France, where the Code Napoleon already protects them against the police.

Other minorities, in whom persecution has developed special skill in the use of symbols, have profited by the breaking up of a once almost monolithic audience into self-sustaining fragments. Technology is supposed to promote a narrow conformity, but it does not always do so. One of its many positive aspects is that, by enabling men to travel more, read more and open their minds to ways of life entirely different from their own, it encourages them to look at other men with less prejudice.

In art, technicization seems to lead to vulgarization, even among highbrows, but in human relations it has already eliminated much prejudice and opened the way to a better understanding among men.

After the lecture, Nellie Rankin, who had at last found her tongue, made her first objection. "I wish you hadn't said that about *The Stranger*. They're making a play of it, and I hear there's a French part in it I could play. I'm so tired of Mexicans!"

Trofimov said sadly, "And I always wanted to go to Paris! I'm not sure I do now."

Salvation by Teamwork
(Britain)

14

In real life Lopakhin's name was no more Russian than Trofimov's. It was as Anglo-Saxon as my own; in fact, more strikingly so, and at first I thought he had not been born into it but had received it as the gift of a court. I was wrong. His name was Anglo-Saxon, and he came from early American stock. His grandfather had lost a fortune in the era of panics, and his father's dime store in Queens represented an unsuccessful effort at a comeback. Lopakhin-Leicester, as I shall now call my student, had been born in poverty and was as determined to rise from it as any resolute immigrant. He had reached back three generations to a factory-owning great-grandfather for the commercial cunning that now was apparent even in the classroom.

If the marks of the millennium were on him, it was because he had not been genteelized in the manner that so often emasculates young Anglo-Saxons in the United States, especially in the rich Northeast (that had so noticeably weakened Trofimov-O'Toole). He was free to pursue his share of the new wealth without inhibition. His mother had been a pretty German girl of peasant stock, without social pretensions. Mentally he was ready for conquest. He was not, thanks to his grandfather, an insider on the way out, but *an outsider on the way in.* That, my study of modern society leads me to believe, is the most enviable of post-millennial situations. Little enthusiasm is felt now anywhere for a lost cause, however admirable, but a clear chance to get ahead—ah, that awakens instantaneous identification in almost every heart.

It was not until halfway through his second year as

161

my student that I ate a full meal with Lopakhin-Leicester. He kept after me to meet his friend the computer boss, and I declined several invitations before at last I accepted one.

My student, wearing a new suit and fashionable brown suede shoes that had also been made for him in London, picked me up in an equally new Jaguar convertible and drove me to an "English chop house" where he said the best dish was roast beef and Yorkshire pudding. When the computer boss arrived he urged us to drink a particularly good Scotch and soda, and during the meal he ordered two bottles, not of red wine, but of "claret" and one of the five most famous brands, as he explained. At the end of the meal he suggested we have a "sweet." He did not use the word "dessert." For a boy who a year earlier had been saying "bird" so that it almost sounded like "boyd," and had been as "non-U" as possible, he had become "U" remarkably fast, and I marveled once again at the quick pick-up, faster than a Jaguar's, of the status-hungry American mind.

A few days later, when I gave a lecture about the effect of the millennium on England, I knew in advance that Lopakhin-Leicester would not like it.

For centuries England was the foremost forerunner among nations. It led the way in such diverse innovations as *habeas corpus,* colonialism, child labor in factories, reform laws, tolerance of foreigners, independence of colonies and football. (Its cult of sport seems to me no less important than the others, though my reasons, as you will soon see, are different from those of the Duke of Wellington, who liked sport because it helped him win the battle of Waterloo.) Its innovations were to some extent thrust upon it when its distinctly practical leaders found themselves, as a result of their own energy and a post-Rennaissance boom, in the midst of new accessions to power for which they had no rules but must handle as best they could. Because they improvised with success, they soon became traditionalists. Phlegm replaced the emotionalism that had caused Hans Holbein to write home to Germany, while he was painting Henry VIII and other unpredictable Tudors: "These English! They're too demonstrative. They're always kissing one another!"

It was an effect of empire that they became reserved.

Empire also made them value teamwork, though this came slowly, over individual expressiveness. Eccentricity was allowed, even encouraged. The more fantastic the better, so long as it recognized the paramount importance of goodwill (and in those days everyone *knew* what that meant) among men, who after all had the good fortune to play on the same winning team. The underlying message of their favorite historians, from Fielding to Dickens to Kipling, was, "Lots of things are wrong, of course, but we're so *lucky* to be English!" Empire led also to clichés that became the stock in trade of satirists, jokes that significantly were first told by the English on themselves: Being a Good Sport; Muddling Through; Taking It Easy; Never Say Legs, Say Limbs; Putting Women on a Pedestal; and Keeping a Stiff Upper Lip. (Foreigners could not laugh at the English then; they hated them as long as they ran the show.)

Now that the empire is gone, and it is rapidly being replaced by a new way of life, suggested here by the word "turnover," what will happen to teamwork, phlegm and English self-confidence? How has professionalism affected the cult of sport? Can Muddling Through stand up against computerized planning? Who can afford to take it easy? Is never-say-legs puritanism making a secret alliance with sexual promiscuity? Are women better off, off the pedestal? What are teachers to say to youngsters who believe that frank tears and griping are *better morally* than Keeping a Stiff Upper Lip? Are the English likely to become less catarrhal, less Haw Haw, more Beatle? Above all, are they likely to become less prejudiced, more tolerant?

As preliminaries to an attempt to answer these questions, here are two comments by well-known Angry Young Men, open opponents of the old imperial way of doing things:

"Lacking a live culture of our own, we are drawing more heavily than ever on that of the United States. This will turn out to be the most burdensome and expensive of the American loans, but we can't expect to put up some kind of tariff barrier when they start sending over their most particular anxieties and neuroses. America is as sexually obsessed as a medieval monastery. The moral failure of Protestant Capitalism has produced the biggest sexual nuthouse since the Middle Ages. And let us remember, sex is everybody's problem. Even Aunt Edna has an itch under the tea tray."

" 'What, finally, is the practical application of all this? Can anything be done to halt, or even to hinder, the process I have described? I say that something can be done by each one of us here tonight. Each of us can resolve to do something every-day to resist the application of manufactured standards, to protest against ugly articles of furniture and tableware, to speak out against sham architecture, to resist the importation into more and more public places of loudspeakers relaying the Light Pro-gramme, to say one word against the Yellow Press, against the best-seller, against the theatre-organ, to say one word for the instinctive culture of the integrated village-type community. In this way we shall be saying a word, however small in its individ-ual effect, for our native tradition, for our common heritage, in short, for what we once had and may, some day, have again— Merrie England.'

"With a long, jabbering belch, Dixon got up from the chair where he'd been writing this and did his ape imitation all round the room. With one arm bent at the elbow so that the fingers reached the armpit, the other crooked in the air so that the inside of the forearm lay across the top of his head, he wove with bent knees and hunched, rocking shoulders across to the bed, upon which he jumped up and down a few times, gibbering to himself."

These are comments by two interpreters of the Angry Young Men:

"A new hero has risen among us. Is he the intellectual tough or the tough intellectual? He is consciously, even consci-entiously, graceless. His face, when not dead pan, is set in a snarl of exasperation. He has one skin too few, but his is not the sensitiveness of the young man in earlier twentieth century fiction: it is the phony to which his nerve-ends are tremblingly exposed, and at the least suspicion of the phony he goes tough. He is at odds with his conventional university education, though he comes generally from a famous university; he has seen through the academic racket as he sees through all the others. A racket is phonyness organized, and in contact with phonyness he turns just as red as litmus paper does in contact with an acid."

"In any society stratified by caste or class . . . the great majority of marriages or socially recognized sexual relationships take place within the caste or class . . . These bright young working-class lads jump three or four social classes (in the English seven-class social hierarchy) in the second decade of their lives. At the end of that period their intellectual interests, their social horizons and almost certainly their accent and vocabulary, the chief stigmata of social class, are much nearer to those of their fellow graduates than to those of their parents or their less bright brothers and sisters. . . . The assured status of the upper middle-class girl is intellectually seen as desirable, indeed as an emotional reward for all the hard work, so that it would not be satisfactory if she abandoned her manners and habits and became a working class wife; but the upper middle classes and the working class have very different models of ideal masculine and feminine, husbandly and wifely behaviour, and each is seen as destructive to integrity and self respect by the member of the other class and sex. The working-class husband expects, and most of the time gets, far more service and subservience from his wife than does a man of the upper-middle class (whose wife would complain that she was being turned into a drudge), an upper-middle class wife gets far more consideration and physical help, where there is no money for servants, from her husband than does a woman of the working class (whose husband would complain he is being unmanned, turned into a sissy). If both are strong characters—and both are likely to be, the man to have fought his way to his present position, the girl to have defied conventions so far—conflict would appear theoretically almost inevitable; and the books and plays tell us what forms these conflicts take."

If any of these statements by or about the Angry Young Men should already seem a little dated to anyone, certainly that could not be said of the following statements, which have just appeared in print as I write this, and address themselves to the future:

"We've had the push-button revolution and the technological takeover. We've been presented with conveyor-belt production, cybernetics, depth psychology, mass communication, instant-packs, supermarkets, glam admanship, man-made fibers, neon, nylon, perspex, plastic, expanding economics and dynamic obsolescence. It's all there, miraculous materials, magical machines, communication techniques and more leisure. And how can the visual artist serve in this social clime? He can avail himself of all these fabulous facilities and use his creative intelligence and imagination to produce inventive and desirable objects, environments and atmospheres. In fact, supply a visual panorama in this new Golden Age in which culture can fulfill its real function and enhance and stimulate the nonfunctional leisure-time of society."

"If this new world does not appeal to you, it is probably because you are too old. But if, as has been said, the clues to tomorrow's culture lie in the cults of today, it will appeal to the next generation, the generation that has been brought up from birth on television and motor scooters, space travel and Cinemascope and big-beat music, for whom silence is leaden and not to move is to be dead."

The latter statement is by an art dealer in Cambridge, the former is quoted by him from four ex-painters who want to create a "kandy-kolored, kustom-built for kumfort" Merrie England out of "miraculous materials" and "magical machines." Both are sales talks and issue from a less interesting level of being than the four passages that precede them.

All the quotations, it must be admitted, have been chosen first for their proven ability to entertain. They are the work of professionals who know how to catch and hold readers. The student in quest of modern history need not, in my opinion, flagellate himself with social science gobbledegook unless it offers the only way to get a job on the faculty and to make an honest woman of the co-ed he encountered by chance in the library stacks, or as seems more often the case, if he believes that a dull style is bound to be more serious than a lively one, since culture, to his still-theologized mind, must be boring. Here, whether the quotation comes from the playwright John Osborne apropos Tennessee Williams, or the novelist Kingsley Amis on the stuffiness that simianizes his Lucky Jim, or the literary critic Walter Allen on the delight of young intellectuals in finding phoniness in others, or the sociologist Geoffrey Gorer on boys who marry above their station and try to burn their wife when they have to wash the dishes, the bright student has bright copy before him, words that got sharpened in stiff competition with other bids for attention in a land where almost everyone writes well.

The level of verbal expression is higher in England than it is in the United States. The letters to editors of comparable publications reveal this every day. It does not mean that Englishmen are more intelligent than Americans. It does mean that they are given a more precise verbal education, a holdover from the days when words for practical as well as religious reasons *had* to mean what they said. They have been required, by the habit of living in the same place for a long time, to express themselves with more traditional grace, if they wish to get a hearing. Americans are now more likely to get a hearing if they are unaware or incapable of the usual ways of winning it. Unimpeded by long-standing tabus, they are more likely to strike at instinctual responses, to "hit the reader where he lives." Their advertising has long been recognized as far more effective than the English kind. Now English copywriters imitate them, and English consumers no longer "drink Bovril and enjoy the winter," but "think young" in the summertime with another beverage. Pastoral pleas against misuse of the unconscious, grim reminders of how the Nazis misused it, go unheeded among youngsters who were born after Hitler died. Meanwhile American music is imitated so often in England that future archaeologists may decide that the Negroes came originally not from Africa but from Liverpool. And American literature at last exercises more influence on English than the other way round.

Americans who seek more difficult and more traditional acclaim—for instance, in poetry—must unite a greater national proximity to primitive emotions with the refinements of an art that has no lasting appeal unless it meets ancient requirements of mastery. This puts them in such a sweat, and is objectively such an unhistorical demand to make on themselves, that they usually abdicate in favor of one form of advertising or another (some very highbrow indeed and often called criticism), or they apply advertising methods to their art. In a few especially astute cases, they restrict their unpopular craft to a snobbish elite which takes in only a small number of many disgusted fugitives from Madison Avenue. They do not live, as the English do, in a land where writing a poem was once a natural consequence of learning a language (as it still is in Latin America) and their heroic struggle to meet old Toltech standards puts them under a rather anachronistic strain.

Surely their task is much harder than that of English businessmen who wish to meet new Aztech standards, as imported from a lost colony (lost by George III, the goat of English history) that now dominates them economically, militarily and psychologically. It is much more likely, as the last two quotations suggest, that English businessmen will pick up the new barker's spiel (American style) of their trade, and get all the lucrative attention that goes with it, than that American poets will reach more than their own secessionist kind. The language the poets write, though the best language of their time, will suffer from minority dryrot unless it manages to establish some definitions in common with those of its fiercest and most indifferent enemies. It will also suffer if it does not prevent its enemies from making off with such key words as "love," "honor" and "faith."

I can hear the businessmen saying with scorn, "Who cares about the *poets*?" I can hear the poets saying with equal scorn, "Who cares about the *businessmen*?" Sooner or later we are all going to have to care, and to get over the habits of mind that make us think and act so emotionally.

The pullulation of publics among the reasonable French is even wilder among the "ruff, raff, roaring" Anglo-Saxons on either side of the Atlantic. It is also more lucrative to fragmentary minds. To succeed, a playwright need reach only 200,000 expense accounters (twenty weeks of full houses, a smash that could be stretched out for months longer); a novelist only 100,000 readers (a temptation to any mail order book club or reprint firm); a literary critic only 50,000 (in a weekly magazine that also discusses Viet Nam and student disorders); a sociologist only 25,000 (enough to get him called "merely popular" by envious colleagues); and ex-"easel weasels" need only 100 customers to make the renunciation of art in favor of "kandy kolors" a good business proposition.

All of these tiny but profitable fractions *have* been won by *opponents* of traditional English teamwork. They have refused to give up their own ego gratifications for the good of a whole in which they no longer believe, and they have been rewarded for it. They have been rewarded for griping and sniping.

It is enough to make the blood of the positive thinkers, the flagwavers, the traditionalists boil into beef tea. While we are about it, what *has* been the response of the many publics to the positive thinkers, the traditionalists who have preached the doctrine of personal renunciation for the greater glory of the Crown?

The positive thinkers have done better, far better, in England and everywhere else. The biological preponderance of tradition-directed types, over all other types, is at least four-to-one, and psychology for ancient evolutionary reasons still continues to follow biology before it considers economics. A mere glance at the best sellers and the long run hits shows that, even in arts where set ways of thinking count least, they still determine the size of an audience. Roast beef, brown October ale, Dickensian humor, Gilbertian wit, Winston Churchill and musical comedy still make absurd the hopes of more cerebral competitors. Almost all of the many publics are composed of traditionalists, ruled automatically by diencephalon, or what is called instinct, and barely aware of the cortical pinwheels touched daily in print, on the boards and on the air. And traditionalists believe in teamwork. It took a long time to develop the high level of social order that prevails in England, an order symbolized by the bobby without a gun, or the credulous customs official, or countless other instances of trusting, interpersonal relations that have been established for a long time in the face of man's natural aggressiveness. Most Englishmen will not yield easily to any innovation. They will prefer leaders who can incorporate necessary social changes into the old way of doing things with a minimum of fuss or strange terminology. They will confidently expect the young, however indignant or big-beat, to yield to them and their ways, sooner than they yield to the young. They will count on the same forces that defeated them to be again victorious over the young.

"Time is on my side," read a sign in the back window of a hearse owned by a frank undertaker in Dover a few years ago. Time is also on the side of anyone else who profits, if only in perverse emotional satisfactions, by what Lawrence Durrell called "the English death" when he fled from it to Greece. Stuffiness takes an awful beating in literature each night, when the moon is supreme; but it comes back in life the next morning, as strong as ever. The exiles may seem to get more attention; the stay-at-homes run the show.

We have therefore to distinguish clearly between the large historical forces that made England strong, as well as antipathetic to a few individuals, and what, if anything, determined, life-loving, possibly moonstruck individuals can hope to do about them. Wherever we live, we are shaped more by large historical forces than we realize, and anything that approaches self-fulfillment is extremely rare and difficult, because it requires continual thought and a heroic capacity for change. In England, because life is relatively cozy, perhaps more so than ever now that the strain of empire is gone and full employment is at hand, individuals seem to have grown less likely to make any effort toward change. The later work of Osborne and Amis would indicate that anger can subside into entertainment when it gets a response from a sympathetic fraction of the audience. Of course, there are others, though necessarily few, who will not settle for that.

First a look at "the large historical forces." England entered the technological society earlier than any other country, profited by it first and wrote the first literature of protest against it. What its Aztechs did, its Toltechs denounced: a healthy dialogue that led to *Songs of Innocence,* the abolition of child labor, safer coalmines, the independence of India, socialized medicine, Keynesian economics, more prosperity for everyone. There were also uglier aspects of the story that need not be told now. The strong animal instincts of natural leaders were harnessed by earnest teachers to a respect for words, and a national belief in teamwork was created that has impressed subsequent foreigner observers, until very recently, as being second nature to almost every Englishman.

The first lesson taught on the playing fields of Eton, so dear to Wellington, was that others belonged on the same team with you, and you all had to play together. Vigorous young savages were whipped into line with the promise of freedom from loneliness, as well as a chance to get ahead. It was an effective initiation rite which helped to make England the foremost technical power in the world until it was challenged by other countries, and most effectively and most painlessly by the United States, where greater natural resources and an uprooted melting pot culture produced even keener technicians. Rootedness of the English kind became a disadvantage when manufacture finally became less important than merchandising. It was harder for people with an established sense of roots to throw away the respect for words that had made their literature preeminent and their style of life notably plainspoken. (No tradition of *politesse*, as in France.) Today England faces the dilemma: follow the anti-truth trend of the new technology or be unable to compete.

The evidence indicates that it will try anti-truth, and indeed is already doing it. Each year the book ads of Bloomsbury get closer to the books ads of the East Fifties, while campaigns for Coventry cars approach those for Detroit cars. Each year England exports more bearded accents to sell more quinine water. Britons never, never will be slaves of Napoleon or Hitler, but they will be slaves of turnover—or go under. Soon they will be guilty of bad form if they try to fix an old Baby Austin with a spanner; they should trade it in. Lipton's has for some time been subtly suggesting, perhaps after motivational research, that a lack of orange pekoe at the right moment may well lead to frigidity and impotence. And Prime Ministerial addresses have never been known for their scientific accuracy.

A relaxed attitude toward truth has demonstrated its ability to make things easier all around. Economically it has already become an indispensable, if unanticipated and unacknowledged, part of the Keynesian program. Soon it will be

serving patriotically to jog the last romantic out of his tran-
quillities and into an American-tempo attempt to crash the new
televised Establishment. It will not be the solid old Establishment that Lord Snow worked his way into, by a hard fight,
positive thinking in a new key and a stalwart repetition of the
traditional virtues. It will be subject to the caprice of publicity,
a "super-styled and slickline bright new world" that comes and
goes according to mood, but is real to a younger generation that
finds itself so bereft of old English folklore that it has to get its
now from Negroes, and is fed up with the pinstripes, bowlers
and umbrellas that once meant leadership and now can so easily
be turned into figures of fun. (As in the first Beatle film.) The
new Establishment, however fictive, is better for turnover than
the old one ever could be. Turnover means more money for
everyone, as well as more fun.

The imagination of the younger generation has been
caught, even more than by the Angries, by James Baldwin's
neighbors, William Burroughs' needle, Jean Genet's vaseline tube,
which can be used mentally to make them feel that they are
really close to life in the raw, among permanent outcasts and
insoluble predicaments. The Angries can get over theirs, as
everyone knows, if only they will buckle down and knuckle down.
But a truly unmasterable problem, provided someone else has
to live with it and it reaches one only through the printed page,
can be used by young readers to help them forget their own
tragedies, which are never so vivid and always hard to face and
put into words. It is easier to believe that a student who has
"every advantage" cannot possibly have any real problems, to
believe that real problems are to be found only among self-
dramatizing spokesmen for hopeless minorities.

Lord Snow's Stiff Upper Lip, the hallmark of all his
writings, is far from vaseline tubes, hypodermics and dark un-
laughter. It echoes Wellington, Playing the Game, Muddling
Through, the White Man's Burden and Teamwork. It is not on
the Toltech side of the old dialogue that led to Britain's great-
ness, though at first it seems to be.

"There have been plenty of days when I spent the
working hours with scientists and then have gone off at night
with some literary colleagues. . . . I felt I was moving among

two groups . . . who had almost ceased to communicate at all, who in intellectual, moral and psychological climate had so little in common that instead of going from Burlington House to South Kensington or Chelsea, one might have crossed an ocean. . . . I believe the intellectual life of western society is being split into two polar groups."

After that Snow showed a strong scientific mistrust of the literary men, especially the more poetic of them, and later a bureaucratic mistrust of scientists who did not make themselves useful to Britain in an international arms race. He was not on the side of either the writers or the scientists as free Toltechs, but wished to conscript them for an Aztech program of national defense. The Stiff Upper Lip was reminding the individualists and the funlovers of *Realpolitik*.

Art for art's sake replied to him through Professor Leavis, but so insultingly—"he is intellectually as undistinguished as it is possible to be . . . as a novelist he doesn't exist; he doesn't begin to exist"—that the secessionist blind spots of literature became even more evident than the activist blind spots of military preparedness. Also, Leavis showed such carefree academic unawareness of his own debts as an intellectual to the men of action who had made his professional existence possible—by, among other things, a program of national defense— that he embarrassed the Toltech cause with a crabbed arrogance it could no longer afford. Snow wrote like an imperialist without an empire; Leavis replied like a bug in a rug. Aldous Huxley, with a better understanding of science and literature than either of them, ticked them off gently in his last book, which was so much more intelligent, that it got none of the headlines they had received. (Neither did the admirable comments of the American critic, Lionel Trilling.)

Newspapermen gave more space, once again, to intellectuals who sounded as if they were making fools of themselves than to those who did not. The anti-intellectualism of the masses and of the editorial staff had to be pleased. Otherwise public and private anxiety might arise. "The tyranny of public opinion," as Stendhal called it in the 1830's, had triumphed again, at least in the press, though it is not likely to win a lasting victory in the minds of those who are slowly learning how to see through popular timidities and to think for themselves, as their best hope of survival in perilous times.

"Snow or Leavis?" Huxley wrote. "The bland scientism of *The Two Cultures* or, violent and ill-mannered, the one-track, moralistic literarism of the Richmond Lecture? If there were no other choice, we should indeed be badly off. But happily there are other roads, there is a more realistic approach to the subject. . . . Thought is crude, matter unimaginably subtle. Words are few and can only be arranged in certain conventionally fixed ways; the counterpoint of unique events in infinitely wide and their succession indefinitely long. That the purified language of science, or even the richer purified language of literature should ever be adequate to the giveness of the world and of our experience is, in the very nature of things, impossible. Cheerfully accepting the fact, let us advance together, men of letters and men of science, further and further into the ever-expanding regions of the unknown."

More imagination, more self-discipline, more openness to experience went into that statement than was shown by either Snow or Leavis or any of their partisan adherents. It comes, however, from a book which, while dealing in a masterly way with the quarrel between literature and science, retreats characteristically from issues of practical responsibility and yields all power to Aztechs without even attempting to create a dialogue with them. It represents the life of an Englishman who passed most of his mature years in the United States, exempted by his literary eminence from most of the trials that beset all Americans, and especially those with talent as writers. Before that, he had been spared the social bad luck that blights the lives and writing of the Angries.

He wrote from a highly privileged position which knew how to maintain its prerogatives, by a judicious change of scene, in a time that threatened them. He exercised his privileges with rare distinction, used words honorably as well as brilliantly (failing as a film-writer, succeeding as an essayist), but cannot be said to have been exposed to the new perils of his craft which came to a head in his lifetime, the apocalyptic epoch when the power that might be gained by systematic misuse of symbols was made obvious to all first by demagogues, later by businessmen. As an exemplar to the young he therefore already belongs to an extinct species which can be admired historically but no longer imitated. It is another reason why his views on a significant issue got so little attention: they had been uttered by one of the last of the English gentlemen. (An ironic end for the *enfant terrible* of his day, the author of *Crome Yellow!*)

Lord Snow writes from a position, however, which lends itself readily to emulation. He is the social type favored by his time: another outsider on his way in. Even though he is an imperialist without an empire, a Kipling without Gunga Din, he does not become ridiculous; he is dynamic, he is always moving ahead. His every action wins the key phrases of ethical assent in an activist era: "You can't blame a guy for trying," and "By God, he's done it again!" Aztech students would do well to study his every action. He deserves the most sedulous apery.

Professor Leavis deserves emulation by all who would teach letters. Since the new exploitation of language alarms anyone capable of reflecting upon its inevitable consequences, he is put in a privileged position. He is a custodian of the word, which must be kept sacred, or where are we? However crabbed or cranky he may become, he will be forgiven, because someone must guard the Purity of the Language and he is doing it. It does not matter that Purity was stolen some time ago; the barn door must be locked; and there are plenty of jobs for guards.

The significant paths of Huxley, Snow, Leavis and the Angries will interest the young British Toltech, as roads *not* to take, but they will not help him to reestablish a healthy dialogue with his Aztech opposites. He has been brought up realistically, British initiation rites are tougher than the American kind, sometimes even brutal, and he knows that a dialogue between blood enemies does not mean an end of hostilities but merely a chance to make hostilities productive. He is also aware of a historical change. In the sanguinary reign of the first Elizabeth, when action and thought had not yet been ripped quite asunder, the doers were much bloodier and the thinkers lived in constant fear of them; but their tragic feud was carried on in the closest intimacy, and out of it came great deeds and great words. In the benign reign of the second Elizabeth there is little chance that such primal intimacy will ever come again. Hate is more likely, hate and growing unawareness of how the other tribe lives, when restriction to a lucrative minority audience or a minority board of trustees permits young artists and young scientists to see only their own kind. The mention of hate, however, is likely to be public-relationsed away, as an unseemly emotion, and with it will go its old companion, love. (You can now say "legs," but you can't say "hate.") Each man *will* be an island (I picked up that from Trofimov) untroubled by his enemies, but to get clear of the mainland he must pull his oar in the automated ship of state an hour a day. He won't even have to speak to his natural enemies, and the hand of his boss will be unseen. Merrie England *will* come again. The Forest of Arden will glisten with plastic, and one can always blame the Americans.

And I've been telling you to shun the future tense! Forget everything I've just been saying.

It won't be like that at all. No one can say what it will be like. The only thing we can say with certainty about the future is that it is going to be rough on determined Toltechs who refuse to be happy victims.

In England they already live in a technicized society, not yet as much so as the United States, but one that is moving daily in the direction of impermeable minds and misused symbols. Their best teachers cannot help them; they understand the new problems no better than their students do. For the first time in centuries, the gifted and cultured Englishman is going to have to live without much of the traditional help that formerly sustained him, that sustained even so recent a rebel as D. H. Lawrence, the working class master of Huxley.

The young British Toltech already lives in a world that can no longer count on the old teamwork or the old self-confidence. Professionalism encroaches daily on sportsmanship; the shame that outcast races feel makes them run faster and jump harder than privileged fairhairs. The love of play that once made dialogue possible and games fun is one more lost cause. Muddling Through is *not* standing up to computerized planning in foreign markets or bomber runs or cardiology. No one can afford to take it easy if he wants to make even an imaginary Establishment. Never-say-legs puritanism long ago made a secret alliance with sexual promiscuity. The new puritanism exploits employees and sexual partners with equal indifference. Women slowly win better jobs, better pay, and sexually are treated everyday more like boys, catamites. "Mod" clothes become transvestite. The genuine mystery that once put women on a false pedestal, in Victorian days, cannot be perceived by the functional mind, which reduces them quickly to secretions and drives.

Frank tears and gripes have become as phony and as hard to take as the Stiff Upper Lip, while the charm of a progressive kindergarten wears away. The English *are* becoming less catarrhal, less Haw Haw and more Beatle, or seem to, in the public prints. And they do travel more than ever and do get exposed to all sorts of foreign types, but whether this promotes more real tolerance in them is doubtful. Tolerance has become the accepted style of the day, the new formalism; but real understanding among people of different backgrounds, different sexual inclinations, different pigmentations still takes time and above all *self*-understanding. The new speed of urbanized living means less time than ever for giving any real thought to one's neighbor. Persecuted minorities, especially the Toltechs, had better not count on it.

Aside from the nonsense that appears daily in the press about mods who believe they change their luck when they change their clothes, aside from the nonsense that a decade earlier appeared about the Angries—some of which had to be repeated here as an amenity, to give a sense of journalistically recognizable surface—aside from all that, young British talent faces the same problem that confronts young talent everywhere. How to desacralize and then resacralize? How to get rid of false or inhibitory notions of the sacred, usually acquired very young through miseducation, and then to renew one's sense of the sacred, especially the sacred in others? Unless we perceive the sacred in others, unless we daily and consciously recognize others, and those most unlike ourselves, as being equally sacred, there is no health in us, no true productivity, no sense of democratic give and take. We are dehumanized when we desacralize (a necessary step for the intelligent part of "systematic doubt"), but fail to win back our self-respect by a rewon respect for others. Unless others, once viewed properly with suspicion, spontaneously awaken our love, we remain dehumanized. This is the predicament of most artists and intellectuals today, as their books and pictures and music plainly show. It is the key dilemma of young Toltechs in Britain and everywhere else.

The young British Toltech is faced with a "challenge" infinitely more complex than any described by Arnold Toynbee in his formulation of "challenge and response," as the way that hard-pressed talent has managed in the past to survive its worst predicaments. The nature of the young British Toltech's response must be individual, and is therefore unforeseeable.

As I had expected, Lopakhin-Leicester did not like the lecture. Most of what he said I have forgotten, but I remember this: "Why did you have to say all that about Snow? He's dead right, and you know it!"

SALVATION BY IDEOLOGY
(SOVIET UNION)

15

A few months after I dined at Nellie Rankin's apartment I received a telephone call from her. While she spoke, I could see her sad smile, sad but determined. She apologized, in admirably precise diction and with a skill that must have been acquired from many dealings with difficult theatrical agents and producers, for intruding upon my valuable time and for getting my number from a university official on a false pretext, but said most earnestly that she wanted to talk to me. Since she sounded as if she were in distress, I arranged to meet her in my office an hour before my next class, which was not one for which she was enrolled but situated, in fact, in another university. (I taught part-time in two separate institutions.)

While she spoke on the telephone I recalled that for some time I had not seen her sitting next to Trofimov-O'Toole. (What a name to give him!) On the contrary, she had sat by herself and left by herself, except on one occasion when to my surprise I saw her leaving with Lopakhin-Leicester, whom I thought she disliked. Until she called I had forgotten the incident.

She was waiting for me when I arrived, ten minutes late, at my office. How many times she must have waited for producers and directors! Against drably dressed and quiet-spoken secretaries and students she stood out like a professional, almost as if she were already on stage. She impressed me as a naturally shy introvert who had to *learn* how to call attention to herself. The gardenia-like perfume she wore would have reached over any footlights to at least the tenth row. The shyness I had sensed in her from the start had been replaced by a loud, clear voice,

179

an assured semi-English accent and almost enough make-up to
hold its own against spotlights. The blue of heaven adorned her
large brown eyes, which had unusually long lashes, and the
red of war her mouth. A crisp white dress and a white spring
coat set off an olive skin that was almost transparent. Her
dancer's legs looked smaller in exquisite white shoes with high
heels.

In my office she began to repeat her apologies, but I
cut them short, and soon she was telling me "her tale of woe"—
or *playing* it—with what developed into much more frankness
than I had thought her capable of, as well as much more vigor
of language. "Once I get my teeth in a part, I play it hard," she
once said of herself. I had expected to get rid of her in about
fifteen minutes, and to be able to read some messages that had
been handed me by a departmental secretary, and to see two
other students who had more right to be there than she did
because they were taking *that* course; but after half an hour
her tale of woe was still in Act One, and I had to hurry out,
confer briefly in another room with the two students with a
better claim on my attention, and forget about reading my mail.
When the time for my class arrived and the now hypnotic Nellie
Rankin was just getting into Act Two, I invited her to come to
the classroom (where she sat with admirably concealed impa-
tience) and later took her to a cafeteria-bar, where Act Three
was finally performed.

Here I must cut down her drama to a brief synopsis.
She began by telling me that she had "not been seeing" Trofimov-
O'Toole for some time. She spoke of him at first with the greatest
admiration. "He's a fine man," she said of him more than once
with, however, a strong implication of "but ——!" Finally she
corrected herself. "No, he's really a kid, he'll never take any
responsibility," she said, and revealed that she had known him
for some years. Contrary to my impression, they had not met
in my classroom. He had persuaded her to take my course with
him, and she had "signed up" more to try to push him into
taking a degree and getting a job than because she was interested
in my subject or my way of teaching it. (Her original tact
melted fast enough when she got into her performance.)

"He was going to marry me, but he had to get his B.A.

and a job first. Sometimes I thought I'd go out of my mind, with you telling us how easy it is to make money in this so-called millennium, and him unable to make a cent or even take his B.A. Why, even I've got one, and I'm not half as smart as he is. You sound like you know the answers," she said with some exasperation and not much English in her accent. "What's wrong with him?"

"I'm not a psychiatrist. It's not my job to . . . are you trying to get me to talk to him?"

"No, no, it's too late for that," she said quickly. "I've thrown him out. I've slipped him a ten-dollar bill to pay the check for the last time. What a bastard! He even steals tips! No, it's somebody else I want you to talk to," and she spoke the real name of Lopakhin-Leicester.

Here the drama dragged for a while, when she seemed to feel some reluctance about telling me what she wanted me to say to Lopakhin-Leicester and why. She went into an attack on him, and by implication on me, because she *had* met *him* in my classroom. "First he rooks me on that typing job I did for him and I don't want to see any more of *him*. Then Timmy goes (the nickname of Trofimov-O'Toole) and back comes Butch (the nickname of Lopakhin-Leicester). I'm so glamourous, so exciting, such a wonderful actress! He wants to marry me. He takes me out in his Jaguar, he gives me the French wine routine. I drink some French wine, and the next thing you know I'm in trouble. He's so fat, he can hardly do anything at all, but there I am! You understand? I'm pregnant. And just then a lead in a Giraudoux play comes up, and the producer, the director and the guy who did the adaptation, they *all* think I'm just right for it. They want me. They're sending a contract to my agent tomorrow.

"Listen, do you know how serious this is to me? I'm caught, but Butch doesn't want to marry me now. It's the first real chance I've had, but I don't believe in abortions. I was brought up a strict Catholic. What I want you to do is this. Talk to Butch, he thinks the world of you. He's half-Kraut, and you're a *professor*. Tell him he's *got* to marry me. I'm only in my second month now. I could open in that show and drop out later. You got me into all this!"

"I?"

"Yes! You! If it hadn't been for your class, I never would have met Butch. He came sucking up to me right away. Said he saw me in *Juarez,* and I was terrific. Well, I was, but I didn't think it would lead to this."

Her story took, of course, far more time than it takes here. It took hours, and finally it came to nothing. She wanted me to speak to Lopakhin-Leicester, and I refused. When she left the cafeteria-bar, where dozens of students drank beer and ate salami sandwiches, apparently without a care in the world, while a jukebox played on and on, she was on the point of tears. Her theatrical bravado had gone, and along with it her gay, hard way of talking. A mouth that had always seemed sad in repose now became frankly sad. Her crisp white dress, which before had stunned me with its beauty, made me think of the hours of washing and ironing that went into each of her daily professional appearances in public. Her olive skin seemed darker, surcharged with blood and anxiety. If I had been younger, and unmarried, I might have found myself taking on her cares and Lopakhin-Leicester's responsibilities. As it was, common sense warned me not to interfere.

Finally she took a sip of cold tea (it was all she would let me give her) and stood up. "I guess I'm licked," she said. "Goodbye. Thanks for listening." With this phrase from a radio commercial she left.

I did not expect to see her the next day at the class for which she was enrolled, but she came, and so did both of the young men she had discussed so intimately with me. None of them sat next to each other; they were scattered in a fairly large room, amid about seventy other students. No sign of any emotion appeared on their faces. I went about the business of giving a lecture.

It was not until the present century that political ideologues had a chance to test their ideas in action. The First World War led to the Russian Revolution, which gave Lenin and his successors a chance to test the ideas of Marxism. Soon afterwards, Mussolini was given a chance to test the ideas, if they may be called that, of Fascism. And after a while Hitler had a chance to test what he called National Socialism. First Russia, then Italy, then Germany tried to save itself by an ideology. Today, except in technologically undeveloped lands, which need the fervor of ideas to uproot ancient feudalisms, a growing disillusionment with every programmatic solution of political and economic problems has led, in a limited sense, to "the end of ideology." Among the industrialized nations there is not much belief any more in salvation by ideas. In the Soviet Union, for instance, it looks as if political commissars will be on the defensive from now on against technicians; they have already been turned into reactionaries.

Meanwhile, however, the spirit of ideology, the belief in programmatic solutions has transferred itself, in the more prosperous lands, from matters of bread and law, which everyone must take seriously, to matters of art and thought, which only a few can take seriously. As usual the millennium has operated with a confusing complexity all its own. It is invariably rough on dogmatic attitudes.

The concept-loving mind, which desires an airtight intellectual defense against the chaos of reality, has failed conspicuously in projects that are open to public scrutiny, such as the defeat of capitalism or the promotion of agriculture by socialist plans. Wherever possible, that is, outside totalitarian states, it has shrewdly transferred its efforts from fields where there may be embarrassing checkups to fields where there cannot be embarrassing checkups. Ex-Fascists have managed to become authorities on poetry, ex-Stalinists on psychology, ex-Trotskyites on painting by channeling an original one-sided excess of zeal into teaching, therapy or tastemaking. Who checks up on professors of literature, psychiatrists or curators of museums?

And in the United States, and sometimes elsewhere, they have virgin minds to work on, minds that are now fumbling their way toward the arts and sciences, minds that prefer unquestioned certitudes and firm guidance. American pragmatism has made its beneficiaries mentally supple in industry, government and elsewhere. But in fields where taste and judgment are required, they are defenseless before singletrack ideas. Protestantism, while rejecting dogma in religion, unconsciously encouraged it in aesthetics and education. Certitude was needed by noninitiates whenever they encountered the unknown, the new, the unexperienced. Certitude was soon provided by unemployed doctrinaires, masters of absolute conviction.

A Texas oilman is not likely to listen to the economic theories of a one-time Stalinist, but his wife, with a huge new house to decorate, is only too glad to be told in tones of perfect assurance why Dubuffet exists and Buffet does not. Or *vice versa*, if it is Buffets that have to be sold. And their daughter wants to be told with the same conviction, in a college with a solid reputation for solid learning, why Freud exists and Jung does not, or the other way round if she goes to a different institution.

Voids seek to be stuffed, and dogmatic minds are willing to accommodate them. The end of ideology is hardly at hand in the land of the free; it has merely gone underground into harmless matters which involve the mind and the soul. Salvation by ideology is not restricted to the Soviet Union, which needed it to break free from feudal land-monopolies, feudal power-blocs and feudal states of mind. Salvation by ideology also exists among free democrats who are supposed to have been delivered from it by pragmatism long ago. If they didn't have clear, onesided ideas to fall back on, what would they have to say at dinner to the charming stranger who has been put next to them? They might lapse, as their earth-tapping forebears did, into provincial grunts. It is so much better to know clearly why you like Freud and Buffet, or Jung and Dubuffet.

Meanwhile, far from the petty aesthetic and intellectual tyranny now practised in the home of the brave and the rich, there are other countries where ideology may at any moment become a matter of life and death. Russia is one of them. Russian ideologues and Russian technicians are engaged in a primary struggle for power which still favors the former but seems likely in time to be won by the latter. (Efficiency is finally stronger than programs.) Russian ideologues are seeking to deny ever more determined Russian artists their freedom of expression. The land of Dostoevsky is still an openly more dramatic land than the land of Melville, who had to go to sea for adventure. Russia provided Dostoevsky with his chief adventure when it sent him, at its own expense, first before a firing squad and then to prison in Siberia.

Or, as Robert Frost put it, "How are we to write/the Russian novel in America/as long as life goes so unterribly?/ . . . We get what little misery we can/out of not having cause for misery."

It must be apparent by now that I do not agree with him. I think we have sufficient cause for misery and our lives go terribly enough. Only it is misery and terror that are hidden, hard to understand, hard to dramatize. Democracy refuses to accept the guilt of open cruelty; it must always *seem* benevolent. A general catastrophe would be needed to simplify the problems of our literature, to bring our good and our evil out into the open. New abundance now obscures them.

Nevertheless, I must admit, it is a great deal easier to discuss the problems of Russian literature. The case of Boris Pasternak is sufficient to make that clear. Who dramatizes the precariousness of the committed Toltech more painfully or more beautifully? His hero Zhivago was not playing *Hamlet* for laughs. There was no way for him to become a happy victim. Pasternak himself refused to take any path of escape, though many were offered him. When we talk of Boris Pasternak we talk of one of the great modern heroes. All Toltechs can learn from his example.

He gained the authority of suffering in his mature conflict with bloodthirsty conceptualists. He died prematurely, a victim of ideological warfare, when the overpolitical offer of a prize by foreign Aztechs forced him into difficulties with his own kind of Aztech. No other modern shaman has been driven more brutally into the great loneliness. No other Toltech can help but be chastened by his ordeal, which exposed an exquisite sensibility, nourished on the ectasies of Scriabine, to the coarse bodily dangers of a civil war. He began as an overprotected aesthete; he ended a defenseless citizen. By comparison, the suffering of American Toltechs must seem mental and undramatic, none the less real but harder to write about. Once again the land which had produced *Le Sacre du Printemps,* a land close to primitivism and ideology, produced a story of human sacrifice.

As Russia hurriedly technicizes itself away from artistic power and towards another kind of power that it now desires more, its Toltechs face less physical danger (they can no longer be awakened and carried off in the middle of the night; a new law protects them at least until morning) and more of the subtler hazards that have been described here as inseparable companions of improved technology. When the Soviet Union can give its citizens all the cars they want, with the aid of Fiat and perhaps other foreign manufacturers, its artists' problems should become still less Zhivago-ish. American foreign policy would take a cunning step toward world peace if it *gave* the Russians the total output of Ford, General Motors and Chrysler for a year or two, and then made a similar gift to the Chinese. The foremost enemies of the bourgeoisie would be bourgeoisified at one stroke. Soon Russian artists may not have as much to fear as they still do from the traditional pendulum-swing between anti-intellectual "slavophiles" and pro-intellectual "westernizers" who want a dialogue with the rest of the world, but only when the Soviet Union becomes a consumer economy.

When Russia is really technicized, its artists and scientists will not have to fear ideologues, but their own new bourgeois appetite for the good things available to those who can reach affluent, culture-hungry *muzhiks* from the steppes with plenty of rubles to spend. Peasants will begin to despise artists, instead of regarding them with awe. The new Dr. Zhivagos will want what the members of the American Medical Association want: higher fees and more things to spend them on. Pasternak's ordeal will become a historical curiosity, like Galileo's.

The happy day of the happy victims has not yet arrived. If a touring Russian poet (Yevtushenko) indiscreetly lets his unauthorized autobiography be published by a magazine in Paris, he can still be called home and threatened with—not the firing squad; he no longer has to fear that—but something else. What happened to Yevtushenko? He was denied for a while the right to publish again, but allowed to console himself by buying new sports clothes. Later he was allowed to publish and travel abroad again. His government now has to take foreign opinion into account. A new Mayakovsky might not be driven to suicide; he might be given an honorary place on the cultural presidium, a comfortable *dacha* and an eight-cylinder car. That happy day has not yet arrived, however. Bureaucratic anti-intellectuals still lean as heavily on Marx as their Tsarist predecessors leaned on the New Testament. Others poets have to behave more discreetly than Yevtushenko, who is thought, by the American visitor Peter Viereck, to desire psychopathically his own destruction. But the record of the liberalizing and sterilizing effect of technology upon the arts suggests that in the not too distant future Russian poets will have safe jobs and small audiences of well-fed nostalgics, not unlike those who congregate regularly in the Young Men's Hebrew Association and the Guggenheim Museum in New York to hear a treasured minority art. Poetry will have lost its ancient bardic capacity to disturb the public mind. Even peasants will learn, as ours did, that all words must be used technically, to achieve effects of statecraft, and the once-holy words of the poet are no exception to a general rule of desacralization. (Or as Cassirer puts it in his theory of language, words must become "counters" of abstract usefulness, with the metaphorical nap rubbed off them, until they are redeemed for a few by poets.)

There are always people who believe that they, perhaps they alone, are exceptions to this rule. They want the advantages of desacralization—new weapons, new power, new comfort—as well as the illusion that they have retained the *numina* of the poet. Stalin's decrees on art, his presumptuousness in telling Prokofiev to write like Beethoven and Meyerhold to stage like Stanislavski, not to mention his part in the death of Mayakovsky, made it clear that he had this illusion. He was not alone in his self-deception, though he managed to call more attention to it than others can hope for. It is a general hallucination that we all tend to share: we think we can banish the sacred from our minds and still know how to recognize it when it appears. The humility, the daily self-riddance of self, that were formerly required to recognize it, are now no longer needed. This may be the prime modern arrogance. Only those who know how firmly they have desacralized life can hope to resacralize it. And until they make it sacred again, by a conscious understanding of their own hates, they will remain as anti-human as the Inquisitors or the executioners of Auschwitz and Moscow.

Russians were encouraged to cherish this illusion first by their relative newness, in the nineteenth century, on the European scene, and later by the emergence in the twentieth century of the United States as their chief military rival. First they compared themselves favorably to the French, the Italians, the Germans, the English, the Poles—most memorably in the more chauvinist pages of Dostoevsky, who made the specific claim that Russians were superior and alone could redeem the modern world. They overlooked the many ways in which they were clearly inferior to the Europeans (though Turgenev frequently reminded them) and liked to think of themselves as a "Christ-bearing" people, more sacred than others. Then in our own time, they recoiled from the Disneyland vulgarity of American mass culture and overlooked the many ways in which life in the United States was still superior to their own. Once again they were *choosey* in their comparisons. Above all, they refused to notice the obvious fact that the Americans were merely preceding them in the wide application of a jointly admired but treacherous technology.

In all their invidious comparisons they invoked Toltech standards to denounce Aztech evils, at the same time that they were making it all but impossible for their own Toltechs to exist. Hypocrisy so huge is only possible in those who have primitive national delusions about their own religious superiority. In the Russian case these delusions helped the propaganda of a new anti-religious state for a while, until everyone could see that they also helped to conceal the fact that the Russian government was quietly killing, for ideological reasons, still more people than were being killed by the less crafty German government, which had a publicly announced program of hate. The Russians, with a public program of love of mankind and tolerance of minorities, actually caused many more human beings to disappear, as Arthur Koestler has shown, than the Nazis. The primitive cunning which enabled them to invoke gentle Toltech ideals, while pursuing ruthless Aztech objectives, gave them an advantage in the minds of the gullible.

It is difficult for the modern American student, stripped long ago of the barbaric splendor of ancient imagery, and hungrier for it than he knows, to understand the subtle tricks that can be played on his senses and his emotions. With the powerful Byzantine clang of *Boris Godunov* in his ears and the saintly icon of Alyosha Karamazov before his eyes, he finds it hard to realize that magnificent music and literature can help to spread, no less than the Psalms, Revelation or the Koran, delusions of national sanctity. It is especially hard for the myth-starved student who happens to be sensitive to excellence in art, and prefers art that "sends" him or takes him "out of this world," to make critical distinctions between that which moves him and those who use it. He wants to believe in anyone who gives him aesthetic joy. The sensitiveness that he inherited, usually from his mother, is seldom united with a tough masculine capacity to pass from receptivity to action. Maleness was poorly represented in his formative years by his father, who if he was able to make a living in the new society had almost always to subordinate any originality he may have possessed to the leveling demands of capitalist collectivities. The son is therefore "uncommitted," slack, guilty and easily victimized.

Such sons were quickly duped by Soviet propaganda in the 1930's. They were not ready to see that every Toltech creation (in this case the Marxist plan for a perfect state) lends itself to misuse by clever Aztechs who know that the way to control the factual in men's minds is through the symbolic. And today *their* sons are not ready to see that every state—and every church for that matter—must practice this sleight of hand. They do not want to think. They want a chance to feel exalted, no matter what someone else may do with their exaltation.

So it has been difficult for students of Toltech sensibility to get free of Russian influence. More difficult, for instance, than to get free of German influence. Students with an Aztech predisposition will go by preference toward the Germans, because they spontaneously admire Germanic punctuality, care, thoroughness and system. Both kinds of students know, if they have done any reading at all, that most of the contending ideologies of our time owe a primary debt to German thought. Neither Marxism, Freudianism nor Existentialism could have been born without German scholarship (even when they rebelled against it) and all of the sciences and semisciences still lean heavily each day on forgotten German labors. What is more, the original dynamic of the modern world needed Luther's protest of 1521, not to mention Gutenberg's invention, to come into being.

The American student who belongs to the Toltech

minority may know all this, but he usually sends his spontaneous sympathies toward the Russians. He usually dislikes the Germans. He feels that the Russians still, in spite of everything, have *doukh,* or soul, or at least a few traces of it, preserved on LP vinyl, and his own Aztech culture deprives him of it.

More realistic Americans, able to forget wartime hatreds and impressed with the rapid postwar comeback of the West German economy, have made an enthusiastic alliance with West Germany, and both countries have enjoyed more prosperity than either has ever known, in a love-feast of Aztech efficiency. West Germany, in fact, is the foremost test of the dedicated technologist's most important claim that peaceful productivity can demilitarize the most warlike peoples and sublimate their energies into socially useful acts. At present, the evidence bears out the dedicated technologist. While the factories of the Ruhr run twenty-four hours a day, the once-mighty *Wehrmacht* has become such a doubtful quantity that German statesmen beg American soldiers to stay and occupy their soil. A student of mine, from the University of Bonn, told me of seeing something that seemed to him significant of his country's demilitarization: a German sentinel, in a sloppy uniform, who *carried an umbrella* while walking his post in the rain. There have been many such stories, pointing in this direction or the opposite. It is, however, still too early to understand what is really happening.

One conclusion may be safely drawn: good technology likes to forget wartime emotions as soon as possible. They were a means to an end, and should not be allowed to foul up the next transaction. France learned this when, for reasons of moral repugnance, she broke off relations with Franco's Spain and later resumed them when diplomatic technicians convinced the French business community that it was the wiser course. American policy toward Spain has been somewhat similar. The greatest weak spot in American foreign policy is its emotional attitude toward Communist China, an attitude which has promoted war and enabled the rest of the world to laugh profitably at this rare example of Yankee inefficiency. There is evidence, from cultural exchanges of dancers, agronomists and the like, that Americans are already more sympathetic to Russians, who once kept most of their editors in hate copy, and may some day learn to love the Chinese again. The still stronger language of Moscow and Peking may also undergo some moderation. Such is the hope of dedicated technologists, who are all positive thinkers and say that peace on earth and goodwill among men *can* be achieved— within reason.

What chance is there that they are right? How much can we believe that their dream of peace is a realistic one? Are they replacing old discredited ideologies with a new crypto-ideology, less pragmatic than it seems, or have they, as hard-headed men of action, by testing out the schematic ideas of thinkers, actually found a way to make a reasonable Utopia exist? Should we cease lamenting the technological society, and begin to realize that it is here to stay, can be made to work for the common good, and can even be made qualitative in time?

The questions are so central, and awaken so many intense emotions in everyone, that a good answer to them is all but impossible. Besides, the evidence that we have is far from conclusive, as well as confused by many kinds of timelag and many kinds of temperament, conditioning and aptitude.

Nevertheless I am going to give some of my responses to these questions. I shall discuss them as they seem to me to relate to the Soviet Union and Salvation by Ideology. Later on I shall try to relate them to the outstanding problems of economics, politics, family life, sex, philosophy, religion, science and art.

First I must attempt to be fair to Salvation by Ideology. By temperament I am not inclined to like it, and my American conditioning has prejudiced me against it, but I must recognize that historically it is a secular extension of the old ecclesiastical precept, "Outside the church there is no health." The implication of this need not be as cruel or destructive as it has been made to seem. It can be regarded as a practical fatherliness that realizes, after much experience of life, that few unaided individuals can hope to succeed in working out their problems for themselves, and all are better off when held firmly by ritual and dogma to master-ideas.

We need only consider the situation of the gifted American student to realize that he has been trained according to the opposite principle. He has been brought up in romantic individualism. He has been given his head, he has been allowed to think as he likes, because his forefathers rebelled against the dogmatism of the old ecclesiastical precept and the rigidity of its succeeding secular ideologies. And at times, when his name was T. S. Eliot or John Reed, or one of their many imitators, he has rebelled in turn against his forefathers' romanticism, and gone either towards an established church or a dogmatic state.

Pragmatism has now had more time to affect the lives of American students than it had in the decade, between 1910 and 1920, when Eliot and Reed made their anti-romantic decisions and departed, for similar reasons, in opposite directions. Pragmatism and its developments have restored American students to the position of the first thinkers. They have to find themselves and the world all over again. They get almost no traditional help, unless they accept the help of a dogmatic faith. Hence after early animal faith their now chronic sense of alienation. Hence their frantic "quest for identity." The past can only be used, the present also, as hard-won fragments in a collage on their own construction.

As a challenge it is beautiful and murderous. It excites the imagination, and it leads in most cases to a form of race-suicide. In practice it means that the gifted young Toltech, struggling in desparation to piece together a workable collage, is no match for monomaniacal competitors. While he strives to acquire the art of presenting his ideas (and finding what they are), he is inevitably outwitted by those who have only one idea and soon acquire the skill to show it off at its best. He cannot abuse symbols. Usually he ends up a hopeless failure. He may appeal for a while to the kind of woman who prefers helpless men, but as soon as she makes demands on him he cannot help but disappoint her. He is not ready for life in the here and now. He is destined to defeat by less interesting, less sensitive, less imaginative competitors. His alternatives are to make a profession of being defeated (there is still a dwindling audience for the lost cause) or to duck into an organization, usually educational, that will use him according to its impersonal needs. Two centuries ago he would not have expected even a choice of alternatives; he would probably have entered a church.

Pragmatism has meant the defeat of the more complex

Americans and the victory of the cruder ones. Only complexity that can learn from crudity, and then make it ashamed of itself, can hope to survive. This is another reason for Toltechs to stop seceding from the marketplace and denouncing the bourgeois; another reason for Toltechs to resacralize their own lives—and those of their opponents.

French and English Toltechs will understand all this sooner than the most gifted Russians. Romantic individualism, the escape valve of advancing technology, spread westward first and more unhamperedly, despite its debts to Kant and Goethe. French and English Toltechs still possess more traditional defenses than their American counterparts, but they are now being exposed, each year more nakedly, to the new spasms of cultural chaos that follow each improvement in turnover. They are being shoved into a harsh and lonely tundra that only a few of their kind can map with clarity of thought.

The Russians are still living in the old ideological tundra, and cannot imagine the new post-pragmatic one. The natural human preference for goods over ideas suggests that the Russian "thaw" will get warmer and warmer.

Incidentally, to interrupt our description of the Russians, each year the German cult of deliberate egotism—shouting, bullying, woman-despising and intentional rudeness, ("Crossing a tennis court at the net while a game is being played")—all these echoes of Wotanic fury become more obviously stupid next to the new need for getting along with others, the first rule of success in the other-directed technological society. Refugees from Hitler soon discovered this, after 1933, in the feminized United States, if they wanted to get ahead. Will stay-at-home Germans learn the dulcet lessons of turnover, or will a rebellious old *furor teutonicus* break out again in some new bloody absurdity? At present it looks as if the Germans will try to mend their manners. The more understanding of their historical situation they get from abroad (why they are as they are and what dilemmas lie ahead of them) the easier their self-therapy will be. If it ever takes place. But let us return to the Russians.

Russian artists are having a hard time of it. Soviet ideologues seek desperately to hold on to power that must be repressive whenever original thought emerges. Enlightened Americans will hope that the pro-intellectual "westernizers" among Russians will slowly win a chance, under a less fearful and less dogmatic communism, and possibly with the unintentional aid of Russian technologists, to restore Russia to her former position in the arts. The more understanding that Americans give all the Russians, Aztech as well as Toltech, the sooner this will take place.

Austerity was once essential to the Russian Revolution, both to make it succeed and to give it a mystique, to make it sacred. (The same was true of our own pioneer "Winning of the West.") Now austerity, though still necessary to individual clarity, is doomed by new machines and the hunger of people for cars and panties. The Soviet Union, despite its ideological differences, is already closer in spirit to the United States than it is to China, because its people want what Americans have, even if the price is the gifted individual's alienation from society. Austerity will nevertheless go slowly, at troika speed, no doubt, in a once-theocratic state, where everyone "belongs," but it seems sure to go. When the Soviet Union becomes as rich and as modernly miserable as the United States, then individual Russians will be permitted to go to hell in their own way. Until then they will merely hanker for the chance.

At the end of the lecture Timmy (Trofimov) asked for an appointment to see me the next day in my office. Nellie Rankin left by herself, looking very sad indeed, and wearing blue jeans and an old sweater, but at the door the plump Butch (Lopakhin) caught up with her. He greeted her with a friendly smile, and did not look disturbed when she went on without so much as looking at him. He kept on right after her.

THE NEW RULING CLASS

16

The next day, when I arrived at my office on time, Trofimov-O'Toole (or Timmy, which fits him much better) was already there. No one paid any attention to him. He was one more seedy student, and no more picturesque because his run-down condition, if examined closely, could be seen to surpass that of the others. Unlike his girl friend, he had not dressed up for the occasion. Nor was he playing Beat. He looked as if he would be happier in bed, asleep in the same rumpled and spotted gray slacks, the same grayish shirt, the same greasy red tie that was knotted in a loose hangman's noose, the same grimy raincoat. He lacked any capacity to command respect, as Nellie had with a loud ringing voice and an overcultivated accent. She could stimulate extraversion; he could not. Instead, he seemed to wish to be overlooked, and he was.

"I want to make up that exam," he told me. At the end of the preceding semester he had presented a letter from a doctor to the authorities, and obtained their permission to defer an examination until a serious condition of his eyes had improved. He had needed only a few more credits for his degree, and then had found a reason that exempted him from getting them.

"Are you ready for it?" I asked.

"Yes," he said, and I gave my permission, but I had misgivings when he left the office. I thought he would never show up for it. His habit of avoiding graduation was so old, I feared, that he would never overcome it. How healthy his bloodshot, pale-blue eyes were, behind his extra-thick glasses, I did not know, but I was not given much reason for hope by his past record or by his sweetheart's complaints. He looked sick to me, much too pallid, too thin-chested, too heedless of his relations with others to be able to take such a decisive step as qualifying himself for even a mediocre job. He had no stock courtesies, no small talk, no regular habits of bathing or nail-cleaning.

To my delight he appeared for the examination, and wrote the best set of answers that I had ever, at that time, received from any student in that course. Whether my question concerned Tolstoy or Beckett, Durkheim or Veblen, Horney or Sullivan, Whitehead or Wittgenstein, Spengler or Giedion, he had obviously read them in their own words, and not merely taken down my description of their thought. He had looked up the Greek origin of a French sociological term, and he knew by heart the lines in which Yeats had first enunciated his theory of masks. More important, he had ideas of his own on all the questions asked, and ideas that might easily be worked up into essays that would make a place for him in the literary world. If only he would go on with the zeal that had suddenly taken hold of him!

Soon I heard from the Dean's office that he was on the list of those to be graduated at the end of the semester, and please to send in his marks early.

Meanwhile the lectures went on, and he was always there.

It is not necessary to compare any more nations. We have been looking at the United States, France, England, and the Soviet Union with but one aim: to discover their historical connection with the new technicization of human beings. In this sense the United States is the oldest nation on earth, and Russia one of the youngest. They are all great powers. They show that national strength is achieved according to national ability to make individual citizens power-minded. Nations become strong not only through natural resources, but through the incentive they give their people to work for a common strength. In recent years, fear of punishment has yielded noticeably, as an incentive, to hope of gain. Russians sleep more soundly; Yugoslavs rise early so that they may hold two jobs and pay a withholding tax that is almost fifty percent; Americans work none the less hard because they do not have to worry about their police. Money is the most efficient taskmaster of all.

Hope of gain became the prime motivation as soon as the incredible productivity of the new machines triumphed over age-old misgivings. It is only since World War II that men have really belived that their traditional poverty is on the way out and they can, in some measure, control their economic destinies.

Past acceptance of poverty may prove, incidentally, to have been the principal source of religious fatalism, and may also have played an important part in the genesis of philosophy and art. It is only when men have renounced the pleasures of wealth that they can become truly contemplative. So long as hope of power of any kind distracts them, they cannot expose themselves nakedly to the impact of reality; they will want instead to shape it to their own interests.

In all probability this means that art and philosophy, as they have been handed on to us from an impoverished past, cannot expect to have much meaning, in a rich present, except as decorative defenses against unpleasant accusations of excessive materialism. You who come to classrooms to study them are most likely wasting your time. You should go to a shop, lined with books or pictures or records, that will build your defenses faster and cheaper. You are more up-to-date than those who still seek to make philosophy or art the center of their lives. You are also more apt to be trivial, more subject to external influence, than your ancestors who, perhaps only because they were poor, believed that they could give their lives meaning. Now meaning must be sought *against* the new proliferation of wealth and knowledge.

It is still difficult for have-not nations to believe that a mind-changing millennium has arrived, but merely because they are not yet in a position to see what it has already done and cannot reasonably be expected to refrain from doing in the future.

I would have enjoyed making further national comparisons, drawn from personal experience, that would have included industrially advanced countries in Western Europe,

industrially backward countries in the Balkans, the Near East
and Latin America. But they would only have reinforced the
conclusions reached among the great powers.

Italy, however, deserves a quick glance because she is
right now in the very middle of the drama we have been watch-
ing. Her better films, most of which come to New York, have
presented it with a brilliance that we used to expect only of
good social novels. It is the drama of changeover from ancient
folkways to modern "progress." A remarkably high number of
Italian films have had the same basic plot. A worker in an industrialized northern city, usually Milan, goes to the still-archaic
South, usually Naples or Sicily, and gets some rude instruction
in the persistence of ancient folkways from slothful and violent
southerners. Even when this plot is not used, it appears in essence in the mind of the film maker as soon as he shoots a scene
in the South. Instantly he is a modern anthropologist, taking
down the fascinating behavior patterns of primitives who are
sure to be superseded in time by his own more enlightened kind
of intelligence.

In Italy, where the technological society is just beginning to arrive, thanks to the Marshall Plan (its principal advance agent), social documentation excites the imagination of
film makers, who have been privileged to receive a great new
story, at the same time vividly concrete and vividly abstract
(or portentous) along with a great new medium for reporting it.
They do not have to cope with the nostalgia for Victorian leisureliness that prejudices most Anglo-Saxon readers against the
more angular and more intellectual modern novel. Instead, they
can count on the candy-store, soda fountain receptivity that prevails in the darkness of a movie house, an atmosphere that
prejudices the audience in favor of their product, if only they
know how to do their job. What is more, they now have in Italy
an audience that is dying, after hundreds of years of poverty and
censorship, to be told, with laughs or tears, what is happening
to it.

The conditions that produce the new Italian titans
have been described by the journalist Luigi Barzini as part of a
historic difference between the North of that country and the
South:

In Naples and in Milan . . . wholesale fruit and vegetable merchants . . . belong more or less to the same class of people. They have roughly the same education. . . . They probably know each other and nod when they meet. They consider themselves colleagues in a vague way. Here all similarities cease.

The Neapolitan usually tours the countryside with his henchmen, bullying and protecting peasants in his well-defined sector, and forcing them to sell their products only to him at the price he fixes. He defends his territory and his vassal farmers from the encroachment of competitors. He carries a gun. He shoots straight. He can kill a man if necessary. He can command killers. As everybody knows that he can enforce his will and defend his power by killing his opponents, he never, or almost never, has the need to shoot. . . .

The Milanese is an entirely different kind of man. . . . He carries no gun, is followed by no henchmen, rarely sees the farmers he buys from, almost never tours the countryside. He sits in a modern office, surrounded by dictating machines, graphs on the wall, brisk secretaries. His business is carried on by telephone, with brokers and buyers in Germany, France or Switzerland, by the carload or the trainload, peaches from Verona, apricots from Naples, oranges from Sicily, grapes from Apulia, potatoes or cabbages from Tuscany. . . . He naturally makes a lot of money, in good years one hundred or one thousand times more than his Neapolitan colleagues. But the Neapolitan does not mind. He is not unhappy about it. He wants other things than money, rarer and more satisfactory things. He wants to be well-known (his sinister nickname must be recognized in the whole province); to be feared (policemen, at times, must forget they saw him go by); to be powerful (politicians must beg for his help at election time). He also wants to be loved (he will redress wrongs and protect unimportant people asking for his aid).

Similar, sometimes equally striking differences exist between the North and South of the United States, and in corresponding parts of France, Yugoslavia and other countries. But modern Italy is still so close to antiquity, at least in its *Mezzogiorno*, that Barzini has been able to report a dramatic clash between ancient folkways, dating back to the mobster Procrustes, and the Stenorette millennium.

The clash lacks suspense, but it is still dramatic. We know which city will prevail; the cooler abstractions and shrewder self-alienations of the Milanese will win far more power (with paper, not muscle) than the earth-bound, myth-bound Neapolitans. The only triumph of Naples (or Sicily) appears on bloodstained film screens, in stories of southern madness that charm the chlorinated, fluorinated clerks of Turin and Chicago (or at least the more literate among them), who would never otherwise see the old phallic brutality and charm of the overlord, except in the ironic poses of Vittorio de Sica, Alberto Sordi and Sophia Loren. The rituals of the South feed us a substitute for the folklore that was taken from us by the source of our greater wealth.

For the same reason novels about the American South (or West) have generally more appeal than novels about the American North. They do more to revive our sense of connection with the past, with the earthy, bloody past that has been all but washed away.

In the banks of Zurich, the ultimate scorekeepers of our time, Milan was certain to defeat Naples, as certainly as a century earlier a cold, scrivener-on-stool New York had defeated a hot, Zouave-pantalooned New Orleans. The more sentimental kind of Toltech (sure to be washed away himself) usually laments this passing of "the good old days" with tears that are really shed for his own inability to understand the world he has inherited or make a place for himself in it.

The characteristic literary mind of our time cannot or will not consider the new ruling class (more Northern, of course, than Southern) that has been created by the new conditions of power. The custodians of the word prefer to deride, or when possible quite disregard, the custodians of authority. (This is still impossible in Russia, but it happens every day in the United States.) Their motivation is obvious: the new ruling class cannot be denounced in the old black and white terminology, and to find new shades of grey that might fit them would be mind-cracking work, not to mention the surrender of assumptions of superiority it would require. They are not "robber barons" of open public-be-damned infamy. They are not anti-socialist hirers of scabs. They are not shameless exploiters of their fellow-man. They are not anti-intellectual or anti-aesthetic philistines. No, they collect art, read books, encourage unions, increase the minimum wage law, boost unemployment insurance, fight for civil rights, support the UN, make automobiles more safe (all this over the protest of the less forward-looking in their own ranks, to be sure) and in a word do as much as the public will let them to help it. If they slip up somewhere along the line—as John F. Kennedy did about McCarthy or J. William Fulbright does about the Negroes—it is only because they have to be re-elected by a constituency that is not quite ready to be as enlightened as they are.

The new ruling class *has* to be enlightened. It would not keep its power long if it were not. Times are changing too fast. When a radio commercial runs, "Who cares? General Electric cares!" everyone in the know recognizes that this particular corporation, after some price-fixing scandals, has found the right approach, the right style in which to educate the public in the new ethos of selfless public service. "Sure, we need a profit," it is saying, "but only in order to do more for *you*."

What has happened? One by one, each of the once-unpopular slogans of the avant-garde—economic, political, aesthetic, philosophic, religious—has been taken over by the new ruling class. They have found that to be enlightened, as much as the public permits, is the surest way to succeed. (Besides, it makes them feel better.) The farthest-out objectives of Toltechs have been appropriated by intelligent Aztechs, who have found by much experience that only the best-sounding objectives will look good in print and lead to reelection and bigger dividends. Though slow to catch on, the public will finally not be content with less than an ideal—that is, an ideal-appearing—world. And it must be given words that will create this myth of inevitable progress toward the light, or else it will not respond in a way that helps business.

One more ancient religious goal has been politicalized. Our chairmen of the board, while still thinking of themselves as "nice guys," have been turned into Grand Inquisitors who must give the people the illusion they want, along with enough to eat, or else everything will come to a halt. Here and there a crabbed corporation or a reactionary senator may continue in power, but only because some Tobacco Road in the public's mind has not yet been mopped up. The major trend is toward avant-garde ideals that can be made to work by the masters of the art of the possible.

Anything less would make the best educated, and ultimately the most influential members of the public feel uneasy. They might have to think of mopping up, not the Tobacco Road in somebody else's mind, but the Fifth Avenue in their own minds. They might have to stop thinking that progress can be safely social. They might have to look at their own disregarded lives. They might have to ask themselves some harsh questions. The most pervasive myth of all, the one that sells more candidates, more goods, more magazines, more newspapers, more programs than all the others put together, would be open to doubt.

We are witnessing a repetition, with a significant difference, of what the original Aztecs did to the original Toltecs. They took over their power, their high civilization, their beautiful creations, and then mimicked word for word their philosophy and their beliefs. The new Aztechs are not, however, cutting out the hearts of the Toltechs to make the sun rise. They are merely attempting to make their ideas work. It is a more humane procedure, and it has a laudable objective, to bring peace on earth to men of goodwill through increased productivity. (Its very laudability rankles in the minds of some Toltechs, who mistrust the enemy even when he comes bearing jobs.) Can the Aztechs bring it off?

Can they sustain their avowed belief that despite a decline in craftsmanship and really alarming rise in psychiatric disorder, men have not jeopardized their rapport with nature or themselves, and the same Promethean courage that led to technological advances will also lead in time to commonsense solutions of the problems they created? Or must the new ruling class, all optimists, yield to the logic of the pessimists who say that men have been irremediably injured by their new control of nature, their "godalmightiness," and nothing can prevent a worldwide catastrophe that may well depopulate the earth.

In favor of the avant-gardized Aztechs is their willingness to take on responsibilities such as past rulers neither imagined nor had to face. The unsuspected complexity of the post-atomic world has been an overwhelming experience for those professionally exposed to it, as memoirs every day reveal; but leaders have been obliged to cope with it, as best they could, either by delegating authority to staffs (naturally the preferred method) or by their own readiness to accept the burdens of eminence. In most cases they have developed a prodigious capacity to abstract essentials from deskfuls of dull but important documents. By comparison with the leaders of 1914 or even 1939, their zeal, their intelligence, their speed are truly impressive. They have had to take into account many new factors, emotions, minorities, small nations, side-effects, fresh scientific discoveries, that never troubled those who preceded them. They have become high-wire performers, brilliant but expendable; nervous, well-paid, warmly applauded, too remote to be real, and subject to sudden fall and total oblivion. (How pathetic the bronze plaques on the buildings they open!) And their skill can be extraordinary, while it lasts.

Statesmen are as gladly forgotten as the bricklayers and cement-mixers who build the buildings they dedicate. Too much is going on. Everyday we have to clear our heads of names, in order to exist ourselves. Everyday our new art moves farther away from the past, and imagines a day (which can never arrive) when we will live a hundred percent in the present.

Not in favor of the avant-gardized Aztechs is their lack of substance as human beings. So much of their energy is devoted to winning the approval of others that they are drained of personal authenticity. (Congenital smilers win all the prizes, and leave authenticity to those who have to fight for it, usually with a frown.) The sharpest questions they ask themselves are those they think the public, their public, will ask them. At heart they are cowards who would not dream of sticking to any lost cause because it was a good one. Their occasional "courage" is for display purposes only; it comes from secret polls that favor it as something that will pay off fairly soon. No one will ever hear of them "out-frowning false Fortune's frown." Fortune to them is the sole arbiter. She designates her favorites on the front page of their morning newspaper, the oftener the better, and her decisions are final.

Merely to stay in office, they have long since had to drop all values of intimate validity, and pass instead to skillful simulation of them. They become *actors*. They give the public, *their* public, images it will accept. If they happen to have chil-

dren, wanted or unwanted, loved or unloved, it is easy for them
to appear as warmhearted fathers. A smiling image is presented
as often as possible to the public, which fills in the emotions
that are supposed to go with it. Soon the public, at least some
of it, will begin to believe that anyone who is such a good father
will also make wise and responsible decisions. His sharp deals
with an odious political boss will be overlooked. The Boy Scout
immaturity in his voice will not be heard. He is accepted as a
wise and responsible leader. The story is familiar enough, but
its effect on the man himself has not been considered. It turns
him into the worst kind of opportunist, to use no harsher word,
and puts decision-making at the mercy of film tricks. It is not
surprising that film stars run for office and get elected. They
know that emotion, especially sentimental emotion, wins the
assent of a public that has no way of getting even slightly acquainted with the leaders it "democratically" elects.

This kind of demagogy, even when it is used for enlightened causes, does *not* win the assent of thoughtful, honest
citizens, who are therefore tempted to "secede," as far as that is
possible, from a situation they see no way of getting under rational control. If they are no longer young, they lose interest
when they see what the masters of mass emotion "get away
with." If they are young, they sometimes try to become masters
of mass emotion themselves, since that is the road to success,
and not only in politics but in business. Products and services
must now be sold, more often than not, by similar encroach-
ments on some public's failure to think. If young people cannot,
for one reason or another, become masters of mass emotion, they
sometimes take courses like this one (read books like this one)
to see more clearly what is being done to them and by whom.

No intelligent student can be favorably impressed by
our new ruling class. In the poetic language of Yeats, they think
"in the mind alone" and not "in a marrowbone." In the more
direct language of the Angry Young Men, they are "phonys."
In the novelistic language of D. H. Lawrence, who gave the
Angries and the Beats their cue, they do not live out of their
solar plexus, which "knows," but out of an "idealized mental
consciousness" which is always false. In the medical language of
Dr. Simeons, they abuse the cortex in their control of other

men's diencephalons and represent a bad turn in man's evolution. In the sociological language of Max Weber, they seem to give an unwholesome twist to the Protestant ethic. In the psychological language of Binswanger, who adapts the philosophical language of Heidegger, they carry the "mind-body split" still farther towards pathology.

In their own language, they have shut out so many aspects of contemporary experience that they cannot be relied upon to ask the right questions of advisers or computers. Therefore they cannot accurately *plan*.

One well-known American instance of this failure was our government's repeated misinterpretation of the Cuban people after Fidel Castro came into power. We chose to imagine our own mental states as also existing among the Cubans, rather than try to see them as they saw themselves. (The new ruling class has to be enlightened, but only in terms of the public that keeps it in power. Consideration of other publics, though essential to intelligent decisions, is beyond its capacity.) Our misinterpretation of the Cubans led to seriously misguided actions, which we now forget temporarily because the Soviet has been persuaded to remove its missiles from the Caribbean.

Another manifest failure of the avant-gardized Aztech mind has been American involvement in Viet Nam. "The idea, that Communist or Viet Minh rule under Ho Chi Minh might be better for the Vietnamese than any alternative political system, has never been really examined in the United States because it is unthinkable. Although it is often admitted that a good portion of the Vietnamese population seemed to have this idea (Eisenhower thought it might be 80 percent), it has never been seriously suggested that this view is worthy of any respect by Americans." So writes Robert Scheer, in what seems an impartial step-by-step account of "How the United States Got Involved in Viet Nam." If computers entered into our decision to send large forces to Viet Nam, as they are reported to have done, they were not fed the important fact that four out of five Vietnamese have voted for the Viet Cong in every free election held to date.

But Cuba and Viet Nam will be seen as minor examples of the proneness to error of our new ruling class, once it is appreciated that our problem is people, and how to make them truly intelligent (which would imply openness to others). The new technical conditions of success, the new public postures required of those who achieve leadership, rule out the possibility of effective intelligence. To get a hearing from a public of any size, not to mention a "mandate," a leader must become so expert in deceiving others, as well as himself, that he soon lacks any personal validity worth discussion. The principle of *vox populi, vox dei* has been extended to the point of perfect surrender before any expediency at all. Thoughtful planning has been replaced by helpless drift. The national disasters that we have already witnessed are trifles compared with those, as anyone familiar with the hazards of drift is already aware, that are sure to come.

And it is only a small minority among us, used to seeing clearly on a small scale before they will venture to think in large abstractions, who can perceive the imminence of these great disasters. But the technical conditions of *their* talent, their age-old mistrust of the merely intellectual, their earthy, truth-loving preference for "the things themselves," make them unable to speak a language that would be understood by any public of any size. They have not been able to master the new "democratic" hypocrisies. They cannot promulgate the myth of inevitable progress through education. They cannot use concepts to shield themselves from reality. Like the captive Trojan princess, they are condemned to speak the truth and to be disbelieved. They know what happened to her, and they "secede."

They cannot think there is a genuine rôle for them in such a society. They expect to reach no audience that is not composed of a few others who feel exactly the same despair as their own. They refuse to "conquer" their opponents slowly by force of example. They refuse to see the "big" public as a beautiful woman who will give them her fullest love if only they will subdue their own emotions and study hers.

There is no big public any more, they say, and no man speaks for man. Communication has come to an end. Now it is every man for himself. Our new ruling class is as blind as the people who follow it. They will all be sunk some day without trace. The only hope of decent survival is to have nothing to do with them.

It is too bad, of course, that they have managed to get hold of almost all the money. There are ways, however, to wheedle some of it away from them. We must find how to do it, and then make a clean break, get clear of them forever. Poverty was all right in the old days, but not now.

Timmy paid me a compliment on the lecture, which surprised me, until I realized that now that he was working for his degree, I might expect him to be more agreeable. Apples would be polished.

TERROR AND PLAYING IT COOL

17

Lopakhin-Leicester, or Butch, who had been an apple-polisher from the start, now became less so as the day of his graduation approached. I am afraid my lectures made him take a new view of me when it became clear that he would soon no longer need my help in some possible dispute with authority, educational or military. My subject was the complex everyday dialogue between men of action and men of thought, or the lack of it, and in the course of my lectures I made certain statements that got under his skin. Now he began to feel free to let me have his candid opinion of those statements, and with only partial concealment of his emotions. Once in class I had mentioned that "Feel Free" was the motto of an institution I admired, and he was taking me at my word.

When I made the statement, "No intelligent student can be favorably impressed with our new ruling class," he objected to this, as well as to my statement that the new ruling class lacked "substance as human beings." He objected not by coming up to my desk and speaking to me, but by writing a letter on elegant engraved stationery which bore only his name and was sent from an excellent Park Avenue address where he had, as he later explained, "taken an office." Actually, he had merely rented desk space, and did not have to pay for it because he did some work for the real tenant of the office. He had learned fast how to make the best possible impression. His letter was beautifully typed on an electric machine by a first-class stenographer.

After a tactful beginning he wrote: "Is it not dangerous

to tell students that they should not admire those who are charged with the responsibility of directing the society in which they live? Must not there always be leaders and led? You yourself have said so, and I admired you for it. Would it not be wiser to tell students that they must appreciate the serious-ness of our leaders, especially the leaders of the business com-munity? I firmly believe there is no more dedicated group of men anywhere in the world. I am also sadly aware of the fact that our students are only too glad to misunderstand them. With all due respect, I suggest that it is an error to compound the confusion of our students, who should be made to realize what excellent leadership we have, especially in the business commu-nity. We need a common purpose, and we can only get it from our leaders."

It was apparent, of course, that this was a mild and doubtless toned-down version of what he really felt and thought. When he appeared for the next lecture I walked to his seat in the front row and thanked him for his letter, and said I would be glad to discuss it with him. He said he would see me after class. I noticed that he kept turning his head to see who was entering the room. Perhaps he was looking for Nellie Rankin. If he was, he must have been disappointed. She did not come. Nor had she come the last time.

The lecture continued the theme to which he had ob-jected. Among other things it said:

It has become customary to explain the behavior of students with the atom bomb. It hangs over them, and therefore they breed like rabbits or ask the Dean for free contraceptives, frug all the time or will not frug at all, read every book they can find or refuse to open any, shave their heads Zen-style or let their hair grow longer than Paganini's or McCartney's. Some authorities say they do not see the point of going on. Others that they love life more than anyone else ever did. If all these contra-dictions add up to little, it cannot be denied that students do live in a world which has, for the first time, the power to destroy them fast. They are born into terror.

The threat of destruction is something we all have to live with from now on. But we have to live with another terror that is more intimate, more real and finally, I think, more important. It cannot make its way into general discussion. It will never get the headlines the bomb got. Students, however, especially students like you—who live in New York, the center of the true under-the-skin revolution of our time, and must try to cope with it—will recognize the reality of a new terror, greater than that of the bomb. That is, unless you have completely indurated your skins.

Our greatest terror is that we may not be able to live good lives. We are not savages. We have been conditioned for centuries, even when we come from what used to be called "humble stock," and frequently all the more so because our parents were denied an economic or an educational opportunity to seek the highest self-fulfillment. We have been conditioned by an old accumulation of ethical obligations that stays in our minds even when we break sharply with the sexual or social tabus of our ancestors. We are more moved by moral fears than we care to admit, and we are afraid that the new conditions of life, as we experience them from day to day, make virtue, if not impossible, at least extremely difficult.

Women fear this, customarily, less than men or not at all. The traditional task of raising of families frees them from the guilt that acquiescence to technicization induces in men who are sufficiently imaginative to understand what is happening to them. The jobs that women hold, moreover, are usually of a kind that can be regarded by them as socially useful and therefore not subject to moral concern. As a result, the wives of executives or highly placed professionals rarely understand the sense of meaninglessness that frequently assails their husbands. By instinct they know how to palliate it or divert attention from it with traditional feminine cunning (parties, trips, more children or, when necessary, acceptance of their mate's promiscuity) but they can only understand it when they feel it themselves, and a most exceptional portion of sensibility is required for that. Usually mates do not discuss their deepest problems. (This does not help our theater, which must dramatize our most intimate conflicts or turn into expense account entertainment—exactly what has happened to it.)

Virtue becomes more complex and more demanding according to one's gifts. The same law holds that we have noticed everywhere else in our examination of the new society: of those to whom much is given, overmuch is expected. They must meet the demands of their group and of their own self-criticism, an excessive moral burden which usually puts them into a crippling double bind. They would prosper more surely if they were free of the demands of conscience.. (Psychoanalysis therefore helps them when it attacks their obsessive superegos.) And they have the intelligence to perceive that the new prosperity, which they naturally wish to enjoy, excludes virtue as an impediment to good technology. Turnover requires that every human weakness be exploited.

The word "virtue" has unpleasantly priggish associations for many of us. But because it suggests a Victorian schoolmaster with a birch in his hand is not sufficient reason to censor it from our vocabulary. We want to be virtuous. We want to be heroes, openly recognized as such. Even the dirtiest beatnik wants to end up with his face on a nice clean postage stamp. That is why we censor "virtue," and prefer to cling to our grievance against our grandfathers' abuse of it. It reminds us of the clear and admirable self-fulfillment that we shall almost certainly never achieve.

Most of us still insist there is nothing in the new prosperity that excludes virtue. They refuse to notice its effect—a standing joke among realistic businessmen, journalists and other day-to-day observers—upon the use of words. It is a sorry self-deception. When truthfulness goes there is no virtue. Our positive thinkers also refuse to ask themselves the questions that now must be asked by any adult who wishes to be healthy. When they are teachers, and they abound in the teaching profession, they confuse students who want to see their lives clearly.

The chief source of terror today is not military. Men and women feel they have come close to having fuller and more interesting lives than their ancestors ever had. The new supernatural has made this possible. They enjoy more power and more freedom than anyone else who bore their name. But the new supernatural has also taken away as much as it gave. It has behaved as Yahveh did to Job. The modern Job, however, has a harder time. He has to realize that Yahveh is an invention, but man's inventiveness is not. It surrounds him everywhere with its comforting embrace. It is the sign of wonder that children worship first. It will end by making him meaningless, unless he can give meaning to it. But this requires that he be stronger than it, and truth is his only weapon.

Most of us fear that we can never attain such strength, and so we fall into extreme anxiety. It is hard to realize that our only fault lay in trying to improve our condition. We had a reasonable desire, we realized it with suffering and sacrifice, and now we are punished for it. Our fate does not feel just. We are not ready to understand the capricious ability of reason to turn without warning into wild and horrid unreason. Such things can happen only somewhere else to someone else.

Not in the land with a Great Seal that shows the Eye of God over a pyramid marked 1776 and the self-flattering motto (in Latin) "He smiles on our new beginnings," printed on every dollar bill. An institution that started out with so much collective hope cannot generate so many private misgivings. The literature that reports them must be all wrong. So benign a beginning could not reverse into malignant mischance.

Nevertheless each failure to live in a state of genuine hope leads further into terror. Our original expectations are as much part of us as our testicles or our ovaries. If we are reminded in any way of anyone who has a better life than ours, who seems to be fulfilling his expectations (and every success story is trying to make us believe this, and employs every trick of a dirty trade to put over unlikely heroes), we *hate* him. We sink still deeper into terror, "the sickness unto death," the psychologically unforgivable sin.

Our true state of mind cannot be revealed to anyone. It is hidden by a censorship that makes the sexual censorship of the Victorians, as revealed by Freud, seem paper-thin. Our pursuit of power, which can only be won by a smiling air of triumph, rules out any disclosure of our innermost fears. On the contrary, at this point we redouble our affirmations, in the desperate hope that they will exorcise our terror.

In my experience, the most affirmative students are the worst. They are so busily engaged in maintaining an attitude that is without basis in fact, that they cannot open their minds and learn. Their best hope is to hurry into the business world, where a hopeful mask may be of use to them as salesmen, in case it is accompanied by a shrewd sense of reality. Usually, however, such students become disillusioned with business, and cannot adjust themselves to the dictates of money. They have forgotten that no one, even the most saintly, can afford to forget money.

A rigid censorship of one's terror leads today to "playing it cool." We pretend our terror does not exist. We become compulsively cool. Above all, as a visiting Harvard student told me, we do not want to "lose our cool." It is too valuable to us, it protects us against the fears that we are not yet ready to bring out into the open.

Most students, quite naturally, want to feel cool. Too big and too difficult a world has been served up to them in their classes, and they want time in which to consider it with appropriate detachment. The young people conditioned by World War I were called the Lost Generation. The young people of World War II were called the Mislaid Generation. Now the millennium has produced the Cool Generation.

There is much to be said for playing it cool. It is better than the glandular affirmations of the positive thinkers. It is also better than the canny negativism of the Beats. It recognizes a real situation and deals with it with psychosomatic wisdom. It puts off big questions until one is ready for them, if one ever is. It takes an excessive strain off the cortex. It promotes enjoyment of the rest of the body. It encourages wider perspectives than those of overcautious relatives and teachers. It allows time to find one's special aptitudes, in contrast to those desired of one by parents (who nearly always want their children to vindicate them).

It is a mere temporizing device. Sooner or later we must face our most uncool passions if we want to achieve authenticity. If ever there was a need to play for time, there is a need of it now. Coolness can be instinctive wisdom. It may degenerate easily into its opposite; it may end up as nothing better than a new kind of mackintosh for the mind; but in its initial action it seems in most cases to be intelligent.

What brought it into being? Many things, the most

important of which, I think, was the corruption of the avant-garde. So long as the avant-garde meant what its name and unpopularity said it was, youth had clear leadership to follow. When the avant-garde declined into its present position, as a petted prop to an all-consuming consumer economy and a further aid to turnover, youth needed time to get its bearings, time that was best bought by playing it cool. The terror that followed the corruption of the avant-garde had to be held off, while eager young minds could look for their own resources in a time of educational bereavement.

To understand this and many other developments in the younger generation, it is necessary to review quickly the history of the avant-garde. When it began in France in the 19th century, so far as its origins can be traced with assurance, its members believed in it not only as a way of life but as the sure wave of the future. It was easier for artists (and scientists too, so long as they had a hard time) to find a sustaining faith when they and their friends believed that a new work of art must necessarily speak a language that not many others could be expected to understand right off, but in time the rest of the world would catch up with their vision, share it, and appreciate it. The great mass of mankind was only waiting for spiritual pioneers to lead them into a new consciousness that nonintellectuals would also soon enough comprehend and assimilate. (Such was the conviction not only of social revolutionaries but of Impressionists.) The advance-guard naturally moved ahead of the regular army, but after a while, of course, the army would catch up, and all would share in a great victory. Humanity would *go forward.*

Faith, in the sacredness of the avant-garde, sustained artists (and others) for a long time. They quarreled inevitably about its composition—who belonged to it and who did not—but they never questioned its value as a bringer of light to a world that needed it. Nor did they ever imagine that it would some day sustain their deadliest foes. To question it would have been like questioning art itself. In youth they eagerly identified themselves with it, and sometimes, if they were still able to startle the solid citizens, in old age too. It meant being like a child, able to see what the Emperor really had on, and to announce it without fear. Everyone desires such freedom, and artists put to shame anyone who renounces it. (This was before "freedom" had become an exploitable cliché, the secret weapon of museum curators and fashion magazines.)

The advance-guard was necessary because a new industrial civilization had produced a new mass of people (quite unlike their anonymous ancestors, the creators of ballads, embroidery, folk music, folk pictures and folk dances) who had been alienated from the healthy popular styles of the past, people who actually preferred bad or dubious art to good—*kitsch* sunsets over Turner, Gounod over Bizet, Puccini over Verdi, Waldteufel over Wagner, Sardou over Chekhov, Bernhardt over Duse. The people must be led back to real taste by genuine artists who knew better. And in thought the people would be purged of oversimplification. The people need not perish; they would be saved by a true vision. Art would play the part formerly played by religion.

The new vision delighted in finding opportunities to correct the false gentility of those whom an expanding industry had made rich and finicky. The prime target of the artist was always a stuffy bourgeoisie, from whose gold and brocade parlors he had joyfully ripped himself. In the United States one of the most outspoken leaders of a poor but still unterrified avant-garde was Alfred Stieglitz, who said, "Everything is relative except relatives, and they are absolute," to his mother and used his share of his father's earnings to help other artists, specifically John Marin, and Arthur Dove, to tell their less indulgent fathers to "go to hell." He was also able to help Georgia O'Keeffe, Mareden Hartley, Paul Strand and other good artists. The new marketplace, which favors collectors and galleries over artists, has not permitted anyone to succeed him.

The avant-garde was then engaged in breaking up a too, too solid order that threatened it with suffocation. It had the unerring accuracy of rebellious youth, and its target was always a tyrannical and befuddled father. In literature it shocked him with words that he used daily, but had not seen in print for centuries. In painting it made him see mountains and mandolins as cones and cubes. In music it gave him ballets that caused his more correct children to riot. In sculpture it showed him women ready for love. In architecture it changed all his ideas about stonework with steel and glass. (Then he merely recoiled; he did not yet see what a boon this was to be, and the other innovations as well, to his own investments.)

He was sick, and the avant-garde was healthy. If he would only relax and let himself enjoy life, the avant-garde would make him well. He served the day, but artists had faith. In time he would surely learn to appreciate them. Meanwhile he paid them no mind, or ridiculed them. And somehow they managed to keep going, with or without his support.

Now that they have long since succeeded and been taken over by shrewd students of their commercial worth, we can be sentimental about them (there is much money still in nostalgia for *La Belle Époque, Art Nouveau,* African Masks, Cubism or anything else that helps interior decoration) or we can try to see them with a clarity that may be useful here and now. The avant-garde was a by-product of the technological revolution, whose early days created a vigorous response (symbolized by the Crystal Palace, the Brooklyn Bridge and the Tour Eiffel) to established ways of doing things. Out of a complex struggle grew avant-garde faith, which was in essence a faith in the ability of alert minds to see more clearly and act more decisively than those weighed down with greed or custom. The later stages of the technological revolution, however, have all but destroyed that faith by *assimilating* it. This is especially observable in the United States, but it is spreading elsewhere, and is already found every day in Western Europe, as a glance at the art magazines will reveal. Business has found money in the avant-garde, not only because its products can be sold at a profit, but because its faith can be used, for a while at least, to give business a dignity it sorely craves (and pays publicists to achieve in print), as well as a moral justification. Every article of present-day commercial faith was once an unpopular avant-garde idea that the bourgeoisie specifically rejected—from the idea of collective bargaining to the idea of tall buildings set back expensively from the street and surrounded by trees and flowers. Men of power have retained their power by appropriating the intellectual products of those who rebelled against their predecessors.

The faith of the advance guard, created by lonely Toltechs, became too valuable an Aztech property to be left in their hands. It could be used to create an atmosphere of hope in a society which lacked spiritual impetus. A mere whiff of it made the selling of cars and clothes easier. It had chic. It also provided a glow of religious fervor that helped fund raising for scientific institutions and universities. It added imaginative ideas, now loosely called "Keynesian," that helped governments to keep things going. The faith of the avant-garde, which was doing so badly "money-wise" in 1914, that its future millionaires were still "starving," became five decades later an unlisted security on the New York Stock Exchange that helped to sustain all the others. It radiated hope in a place that might have been too dull, too crass, too stupid to survive without it. It provided a shot in the arm for the new "Romans," a shot of antibodies that had been taken from the sacrificial bodies of a few despised "Greeks."

It is now being used by the Romans—used up. Rulers who could not create a faith of their own have already almost exploited a borrowed faith out of existence. The little magazines of the advance-guard are systematically combed for ideas by picture magazines and newsmagazines with a large circulation. New orchestral effects find their way from concert halls into musicals, as much as the bigger audience will bear. New painting styles are copied by the "rag business," or used by fashion magazines to give it glamour. The story of the Toltecs and the Aztecs has been repeated centuries later by their technicized successors. The hard-won faith of craftsmen has been put to work by cruder conquerors, who are as barren of real faith and real ideas as the Aztec king Moctezuma, who collapsed soon under pressure.

No Toltech believes anymore that the great mass of mankind is only waiting for spiritual leaders to guide them into a new consciousness. Avant-garde faith is now a dead letter. The vanguard no longer expects the regular army to catch up with it, except commercially. It knows that its discoveries will be exploited to the limit, and therefore tries to make them too "far out" to be of any use. The regular army knows well that symbolic victories can be sold for real money. But the mental receptivity that made the symbolic victories possible, the reverence for life, the sense of the sacred, the respect for matter

—such "intangibles" have no meaning for the marketplace mind save as they contribute to a saleable commodity. To the Toltech they are the most valuable things of all, even if they get no bids.

Can we overlook this situation as quickly as possible? Most of us will. Especially if we have a touch of the Toltech tarbrush on us, a touch that would become especially painful if we tried to outfrown false fortune's frown, went against our peer group, ignored adverse publicity. Most of us will try to pretend that we are as bleached as our society wants us to be. Minorities among us, however, unable to achieve a really good bleach-job, will secede openly from a society that now seems to them destruction itself, will burn their draft cards and go to prison as conscientious objectors. (Some will go to happenings as heroes.) Still other minorites will view the scene with serenity as soon as they have found a good enough vein in the left forearm to take a hypodermic syringe. More serious minorities will seek a more serious detachment with the *Gita* or the more hopeful psychologists and sociologists.

Opportunistic artists will try to pretend that the avantgarde lives on, with as much vigor and faith as ever. It is possible for them to carry out, and appear to succeed in, this pretension because they do not listen to anyone who disagrees with them. They need only the vocal support of a few others like themselves to obtain impressive publicity, and they are temperamentally suited to the ephemeral attitudes that rapid economic turnover demands. They employ the attention-getting devices of precocious infants. Their favorite adage is, "Why should I think about posterity? What did posterity ever do for me?" A spoofing cynicism marks their style, along with the threat, "You're a square if you don't go along with me." Yet they demand the prestige that was won for art by more history-minded predecessors.

Their opportunism is a natural enough response. They do have talents; and they are under constant pressure from their families and their dealers to cash in on them. Unephemeral art can only be created by men who are in harmony with past, present and future. We produce few such men today, and the ease with which real money can be earned by the abuse of symbolic talents reduces their numbers every year. So we get sham vigor and sham faith in ever-increasing amounts from the beneficiary-victims of the new prosperity. Although hundreds of names come to mind, there is no point in singling out any of them for attack. They need sympathy and understanding instead, even when they abuse their talents most. They have been estranged from what might have made them happy.

Good students will be troubled by this account of what has happened to a faith in the advance-guard that might have sustained them during their college years. When it discourages them too much they will disbelieve it. The reason all students are worried is that they are not as sure as they once were that the knowledge they are acquiring can lead to happiness. Their faith in progress has been disturbed. They still find this faith in the books and pictures and buildings and music they love. But now everything is confused, and they do not know where they are. They have to pick their way carefully among the genuine and the pseudogenuine, which can look so much alike. They need a guide as much as Dante did, when he entered the Inferno, and no Virgil appears to help them.

They feel at home in the past, but the present dismays them. The present is their Inferno.

They forget that Dante created his Virgil. He read Virgil and then by an act of imagination he made him into his guide.

Meanwhile our students live in terror and play it cool.

Butch left immediately after the lecture, without coming up to my desk. Timmy approached with compliments, and told me that Nellie Rankin was rehearsing in the Giraudoux play and would open in it soon in a theatre in the Village. At last her chance had arrived. She was to be the star.

WHAT CAN BE DONE
FOR THIS WOMAN?

18

I went to the opening of Nellie Rankin's play. Someone telephoned my office and left word that a ticket would be waiting for me at the theatre, and Miss Rankin especially hoped that I would be able to come. It was only a single seat because tickets were hard to get.

When I reached the theatre I was ushered to a place next to Timmy. He too had been given a single seat. He was wearing a dark suit and a necktie. The condition of his ears suggested that he had honored the occasion with water. And his spectacles looked less gummy than usual.

He noticed my scrutiny, and hid his hands. *"J'ai les ongles en deuil,"* and explained in apologetic English that he had been reading the play in French and was still thinking in that language. I said that my nails had always been dirty until I married and had to begin to think about such things, to please my wife. He looked as if he doubted it. I said he would change too when he got married. He looked as if I were an enemy who had to be endured. After all, I was over thirty, the age when everyone becomes an enemy of youth.

In the theater, in aisle seats, and chatting with one another, sat some reviewers from magazines and newspapers whom I had either met or had pointed out to me on other first nights. The play had been produced on Broadway some years before and had been an admired fiasco. Now that it was being revived with its original title, *Intermezzo*, in a more modest theatre in the Village, with no gold cupids on the boxes, everyone wondered whether it would do better this time. "Who is Nellie Rankin?" asked a woman behind us. "I never heard of her."

"Well, she'd better be good," said a man. "It's that kind of a show."

"I never heard of her," repeated the woman.

Timmy turned around and spoke to the woman. "She's terrific," he said angrily. "Watch!" And I liked him more than I had ever liked him before. The woman said nothing audible, though she seemed to murmur something to the man with her, something that did not flatter Timmy. I hoped he was going to be proved right.

Soon after the curtain rose, Nellie came on stage as Isabel, a substitute teacher in a provincial French town, who is the embodiment of innocence, "as clear as a mountain brook." She teaches her ten-year-old pupils to recite "A tree is a tall man rooted in the ground. He spreads out his arms and eats through his fingers. In tree language, a murderer is called a wood-chopper, a corpse is called timber, and woodpeckers are fleas." She believes in ghosts, and has a rendezvous with a dead young man by the side of an enchanted lake where he drowned. She wants the dead to come back and "teach us to live not like clods but like spirits!" The action of the play is her slow awakening to life after the ghost is exorcised and a living young man takes his place in her imagination.

I had not realized that Nellie possessed so much theatrical intelligence. After a beautiful first act the play had less magic for me than when I saw it the first time; the author's delightfulness became intrusive; the characters seemed only particles of him; but Isabel, as played by Nellie, severed herself from the enormous charm of Giraudox and made me think of every young girl who must pass from poetry and death into prose and life. Isabel called for reality rather than cuteness, and to my surprise, Nellie had the courage to "throw away" lines that could have gotten laughs and to play instead for the truth of over-prolonged adolescence. She had diagnosed the reason for the play's original failure, and had realized that the drama of a young girl's awakening would last longer in the audience's mind than the most exquisitely droll lines.

After the first act, when we went out into the lobby

and from there into the street, Timmy seemed worried about her reception. "She got more laughs than that in the dress rehearsal," he said. After the second act he said, "I think they like her." At the end of the play she received several curtain calls and shouts of admiration. The woman who sat behind us spoke generously to Timmy, "She's very good! She's very good!" At the back of the orchestra section of the theatre I saw Butch, clapping his hands and shouting. He must have had to buy standing room. I suspect that he disappeared during the intermissions, so as not to be seen by us. He might have had to reveal that he had no seat.

Timmy wanted me to go backstage with him to congratulate Nellie in her dressing room. "She expects you," he said.

I said, "No, I'll write her a letter. Tell her she was wonderful. She made me cry. I've got to go uptown and meet my wife." I did not say that my wife had been annoyed because there was only one seat for the play and she had had to go to a French movie instead.

The next day the newspapers said that the play had dated, but Nellie Rankin was unquestionably one of the most exciting new actresses of the year. Her picture appeared in three of the papers. She would not have to play Mexicans any more.

That evening, of course, she did not appear for my lecture. But Timmy and Butch did—and sat far apart. The lecture was about women.

It is impossible, of course, for any man to understand any woman. Certainly, with the frequent observations of my wife on my own obtuseness ringing in my ears, I cannot pretend to be an exception to the rule. What is said here is said with as much tentativeness, hesitancy and uncertainty as any man could feel.

I am in further difficulties because now I am obliged to suggest a few answers to questions that I raised a long time ago. They are questions on which I cannot "play it cool." This whole course (book) has been a deliberate self-immersion in hot water. I must continue to play the fool and rush in where men of greater intelligence would never dare to tread. The questions were phrased as contrasting statements:

"In domestic problems the optimists believe that although many homes and children have been injured by new forces of dehumanization, men and women are going to find better ways of living together as material conditions improve and they are educated to a better understanding of themselves; and children will be better trained than ever as we learn more about their minds. The pessimists believe that sexual relations have been brutalized to an astonishing degree by the new knowledge. We have found no way to channel humanely the new libido released by labor-saving devices and increased urbanization; children are badly trained, home life is a mess, psychiatry a failure, women worse off than ever . . ."

All women must be concerned with these uncertainties. Most women will dislike seeing them put into plain English, because their very formulation raises doubts. Selective inattention, in the name of blissful ignorance, will soon eliminate them from the mind of almost every member of the female sex, even when she has been formally introduced to a higher education. A few intelligent women will realize, however, that the doubts of the pessimists must be considered before any attention can be given the hopes of the optimists. Perhaps, in a few lives, all will work out for the best, but only if heed is paid the darkest counsels of our best thinkers, who have been quoted here, more than once, to the effect that individual happiness becomes especially precarious when the way to it is taken for granted. Human beings *are* treated quantitatively as mere objects, and they *do* prefer to be treated thus, if it relieves them from asking themselves difficult questions.

Women's spontaneous desire to bring up their children in an atmosphere of hope is a magnificent social asset. All of us count on it, along with their ability to make our houses, our meals, our holidays more attractive and more cheerful. It is the *unconscious* talents of women that we love and respect most. They are natural artists in the enjoyment of life, because the brevity of their attractiveness makes them experts in the appreciation of every moment. As such, in our day-to-day life, they outweigh the thoughts of our most profound thinkers. I myself have written:

"The function of women is entirely different from the

function of an isolated thinker. No matter how profound his thoughts, he finally speaks for himself and a few others like him, rather than for the large-bosomed sorority who are charged with the responsibility of bringing babies into the world and training them to live in it. Such a thinker can no more pretend to inform us authoritatively about the nature of things than the simplest hausfrau. And certainly he will be a poor thinker—an atavistic throwback to patriarchal days—if he forgets that women can only perform their necessary functions in an atmosphere of hope. The atmosphere of hope that they do actually create out of their biologically induced will to believe is as continuous a reality as any of his gloomy insights or dismal laws. Even if the world were blown up on schedule at the exact hour he predicted, we would count on their naïveté to help rebuild it. And we would count on it with the same empirical assurance that permits us to be confident of the movement of the stars, the boiling point of water, the arrival of puberty, the Second Law of Thermodynamics."

Nevertheless, women's hopefulness is most healthy, in the new possibilities opened up by vacuum tubes and jet propulsion, when it is tempered with a sober appreciation of everyone's natural limits. Boundless hope is an attempt to conceal private despair, and a more dangerous drug than heroin because the damage it does to the brain passes unseen and indeed is commonly considered a social asset because it cheers others. Educated women, even those who would prefer to remain as blissfully ignorant as country club matrons, will therefore soon be obliged to reexamine their own preference for a trusting hopefulness. In a few years new wealth has done what the habit of impoverishment did not do; it has made human beings expect happiness to come from the outside, to be rewarded for emptiness, to be given antidotes for boredom. Intelligent women are discovering that typically feminine responses to domestic issues are not sufficient any more; they must be reviewed in the light of masculine thought, and skeptical masculine thought. Even the simplest hausfrau is being pelted with problems of divorce, alcoholism, drugs, sexual deviations, juvenile delinquency, escapism, indifference and apathy that will no longer yield to old-fashioned home remedies. Unexamined hope works least of all for women who have been trained to think.

Hope is still, however, the theme song of all our major publications and networks. The media are dominated by professional optimists (the more credible the more they actually believe for a while in what they are saying) and these men are all expert long-distance seducers of women. Without the craving of women for hope they would not sell nearly as many rust-removers or power-steered vehicles as they do. The need of millions of women to pretend that the world is just as nice today, as it was in the days of an imaginary Old West, has unquestionably kept the American economy on an upcurve ever since V-J Day. Our smelters have accelerated their tempo of achievement in geometric progression during the last two decades because they have been encouraged by the atmosphere of hope that American women demand.

Technicians are men, and men surpass themselves before a gallery of women. Technicians desire appreciation, and women give it best. Why does the carpenter stay late bending wood into a graceful staircase? Why does the biochemist wake up in the middle of the night with a new plan for making an antibiotic water-soluble? For the money alone? No, imagination asks for understanding.

There are no shy gestures of courtship, however, when businesslike word-men take over and seek to impregnate illusionist minds. Innocent gallantry is turned into masterly seduction. Business would fall off sharply if it failed to soften up women. Hitherto undesired goods must be sold by Don Giovanni methods of flattery and aggression, hope and attack. Selling softens and then seizes. What does it seize? More than the simpleton Giovanni got. It seizes women's minds, reduces them to the ranks of consumers, converts them into paying recipients of service.

A few gifted women rebel, but their rebellion rarely comes off. The first count against any gifted woman is the settled conviction among her contemporaries, who believe this to be article one of the democratic faith, that any talent, in either sex, is a ludicrous makeshift for a defect. Does a woman write well or paint well or doctor well or midwife well? It is merely because her eyes are crossed or her spine curved or her ovarian secretions are in undersupply. Still more likely, she came from the wrong side of the tracks and her father slept with her for years. Once again the democratic faith has been twisted by its exploiters—and abuse of environmental factors—to equate normality with every middle-class meanness, to deny the inherency of exceptional vision or exceptional skill, to explain natural superiorities away. The law of compensation has been converted from a humane source of humility and mutual respect into a rancorous leveler. (Of men as well as of women.)

The history of feminine talent in literature suggests a final reliance on tenderness, even when the feminine mind is sharpest. From Lady Murasaki to Colette the best women writers have possessed keen intellects and strong characters as well as a fundamental gentleness of feeling. Gifted women see and feel many things that the most gifted men do not, and most of these things are *soft*, that is, they require empathy and openness to be appreciated. A high degree of civilized receptivity is needed to understand them. In a busy marketplace they go unnoticed. In the technological society they are programmed out of existence. The harassed man in the street finds no reminders in them of his sainted mother, who was always properly at her stove. Stunted conceptualists hoot at them with social science certitude. Psychoanalysts dismiss them as miserable by-products of penis-envy. Bluestockings insist they have become unhistorical, and in their books and talk suggest that women must now scream as stridently as men, if they want to be heard. Traditional feminine softness is not appreciated except as it promotes the sale of dresses, flower seeds, subdivided sunsets and garbage disposal systems. Then it is ardently praised in the very best words that money can buy. Once again symbolic values could not be appreciated until they were converted into cash.

It is slightly more than two centuries since Mirabeau coined the word "civilization" and specifically associated gifted women with its self-restrained and *tender* demands. His invention occurred in a place that believed each of its splendid chateaux had been inspired by an exceptional woman and in a time that believed in the progressive elevation of both sexes. The faith in civilization that the *noblesse-oblige* marquis expressed at the outset of the industrial revolution was not subsequently helped by a sentimental, *arriviste* tendency to take it for granted. Civilization has now been taken for granted so long, by those who preferred to ignore the disciplined softness it requires, that we all fear it is soon going to leave us forever.

Gifted women are among the worst victims of civilization's present decline. Their subtle contributions have long been denied by ideologues and artists with an inferiority complex, or defective masculinity, that can only be appeased by a scornful denigration of all women. As a result of systematic attacks on them, gifted women now live in a reign of terror which wants them to be customers and nothing more. Their distinction has been denied. Their social usefulness is not desired.

A second handicap is imposed upon gifted American women, almost invariably, by their religious background. Whatever their particular church, they have been exposed to a theology which had its origins in Old Testament patriarchalism and was determined to remove every trace of an earlier matriarchy which it detested as abomination. The softer feminine values, such as are praised often in the literature of India, China and Japan, are rarely praised in the Bible, and then only when they support masculine standards of behavior: standards that are consistent, patriotic, firm. They might have weakened the efforts of militant minority sects to maintain themselves by virtue of superior austerity against the overwhelming sensuality of the Near East. (So intense even now that it frequently brings sexual depletion in the twenties.) The softness of woman was feared as a primary assault upon the religion of the prophets. Softness in men was also feared; hence the specific denunciations of sodomy.

And this fear was felt not only in "stiff-necked" Hebraism; it was also Hellenic. Robert Graves has shown, with a playfulness that I do not believe injures his thesis, that the Greek myths reveal a progressive eradication of matriarchal "chaos," as well as a progressive development of masculine order. (With sodomy tolerated.) The tragedies of Aeschylus, Sophocles and Euripides can be read as variations on this theme. By the time Plato arrived all publicizable cultural activities were conducted by males, and the counsel of women had been reduced to the male-reported tribute of Socrates to his revered instructress Diotima.

The weight of Western culture has been anti-feminist,

with but few exceptions, for a very long time. Most contemporary women could not, as they say, care less, since many laws and customs now favor them rather than men, and they are after all the principal spenders of the new prosperity that hard-pressed mates or fathers have put at their disposal. A few women still do not like this situation, which they think reduces their sex to greedy purchasing agents, and it is with these few heretics that I am concerned here.

It is not accidental that several excellent women scholars, under the leadership of Jane Harrison, have directed their attention to prehistory, to the time when matriarchal "chaos" had not yet been replaced by patriarchal order. They have become fascinated with the religious or psychological world that existed before Abraham, before Zeus, before Christ, before Quetzalcoatl. They want to understand the female mythology that preceded the literature of males. They seek glimpses of the earliest known life on earth—as women saw it.

Their motive is like that of the ancient cave-painters of Altamira and Lascaux. They seek fertility—not however of the ancient kind that desired beasts to eat and more and more children to help subdue them. Even when they want children, intelligent women also seek a more modern kind of fertility. They have learned that affluence has one grave disadvantage: it alienates women from themselves, unless they can use it to gain a totally new education. Today the first step toward reliable self-knowledge is to understand one's still close ties to antiquity. Archaic men and women control us more profoundly than we care to believe, in our parvenu ignorance.

Women who seek this kind of insight are bound to be ignored and ridiculed, especially by their own sex. Prehistory is too remote; it soon ceases to be fun. Only a few women can see its relationship to their struggle for fulfillment in a hostile shopping center. They have learned that their famous "emancipation," about which they heard so much in college, actually has been turned into a servitude to mascara and air-conditioners.

It sounded wonderful at first, the emancipation of women that had been dramatized by Ibsen and Shaw and was demonstrated daily in medical schools, law schools and publishers' lists. After centuries of enslavement, women were at last free to take their rightful place in an enlightened *agora* which needed their artistic and scientific talents (Mary Cassatt and Madame Curie), as well as their humanitarian sympathy (Jane Addams and Eleanor Roosevelt). In succeeding years the number of prominently "free" women has steadily grown, but they capture the public imagination less because they are now a familiar part of the international scene. Also we now know that they are subject to the same pressures as their male competitors, and these pressures are of a kind that makes for greater social efficiency and leaves individual human beings in a limbo of tactfully phrased neuterdom. Women, too, are subject to psychic castration.

The limbo in which we make people of both sexes suitable for public service insists upon "nice," congenial and hopeful attitudes as well as clean, well-dressed appearances. No bank, university or wrecking corporation can afford to tolerate garterless stockings or flip tongues. The filthiest, most foul-mouthed MacDougal Street beatnik would soon concede this, if he were to inherit a few shares of corporation stock. He rarely decides on his dirtiness as a matter of principle. The only principle on which we are all united is that organization men should never behave like oddballs. They must not only look right and smell right and talk right; they must think right—which means not only going along with the consensus of opinion, but censoring as early as possible any unfortunate taste for the weird, the uncanny, the acausal, the numinous, the terrifying, the majestic, the poetic. *We all* demand this of our organization men (mail clerks, bank tellers, chairmen of the board), even those of us who are most spirited and most original. Someone else must do the dirty work, the empty work that makes our splendid ontimeness possible and frees a few for less predictable endeavors.

A few gifted women can be free, if they see through the tricks that turned their sex's nominal emancipation into actual servitude to continual novelty and unending things. Also, if they understand the difficult new psychological feat that is now historically demanded of them. And have the courage and ability to perform it. They can defeat the impersonal social forces that seek to turn them into talkative nonentities, helpless victims of instinct, if they learn how to unite effortless "feminine" talents with "masculine" cognitions that require more work.

In the language of Jung, the first psychologist to consider this problem, they have to confront the relatively unknown and undeveloped gifts that lie dormant in female minds, that for a very long time have been more perceptive and more skilful in matters of feeling than in matters of thought. In the language of Simeons they have to harmonize age-old diencephalic understanding with new cortical knowledge. Jung says that so abrupt a break with past patterns will inevitably create some awkwardness. He also says that it can be a healthy awkwardness that will lead a few women into a state of awareness that enables them to satisfy both their ancient and their modern demands for a full life. (In the Notes will be found an interesting statement by Jung's wife on some of the difficulties that face a woman who sets herself such an admirably untraditional and lonely task.)

Some exceptional women can free themselves from the internal demons that seek to prevent a fusion of thought and feeling. But even after so heroic a victory they will still find themselves confronted with a social situation that demands further and equally arduous effort. One more instance of the most successful psychotherapy being unable to cope with the millennium. It is a situation that one of my students, whom I will describe later, called "the death of love." She made me realize that love requires leisureliness, and leisureliness is a prime victim of technicization.

Love is not hard to come by because people are getting more selfish. The insistence upon the need to love, which we find in every prophet of every religion, means that it was always difficult for people, including the prophets, to love one another. Selfishness is a constant, somewhat like the amount of excrement that has to be disposed of every day. But our new mechanical skills, which were meant to give us more time for love, turn out to work the other way. They absorb the time and energy that might have been free for the contemplation and enjoyment of others. They also give us the illusion that we have at last escaped the shadow of egotism. We are not as ready to appreciate our fellowman as our harder-pressed forefathers. We can *get* so much more.

In theory, Americans should not have to be reminded of this. Especially educated Americans who have, of course, read their most famous poet, who spoke too often of love. He also wrote, "I loafe and invite my soul." Their social reliability requires that they never really loaf or invite their souls. This must be why their holiday clothes become gayer each season, and they spend so much time on cruises. A calculating mind is not lost on the laziest island in the Caribbean. They figure as they frug.

It was one of my students, a married woman who intruded less upon my consciousness than Timmy or Nellie or Butch, who used the expression "the death of love." Or did I use it first, and did she merely repeat it? I do not know, but I associate it with her. In the cruel style of the Lonelyhearts columns, let us call her Mrs. Troubled. She had some problems, and she confided some, though not all of them, to me.

To her the death of love meant a new kind of *Liebestod*, and it moved her more profoundly than the scene in *Tristan und Isolde,* which she had admired greatly in her college days. The death of love, she said, is real, not fictitious; she sees it wherever she looks. It is in her own family, in her children, in her husband, perhaps also in herself. She is troubled. All the "values" she was taught to cherish are in jeopardy, if they have not already vanished. Once she had faith, and now she has only doubts.

Her faith was broad. She believed in the agony of Jesus on the cross, and she also believed in the heroism of those who resisted Christianity when it became an oppression. She admired the courage of Socrates in his cell, and she also admired the teacher who taught her to mistrust every word of Plato. She enjoyed the rich sonorities of a Rasoumovsky quartet, and she also enjoyed the dissonances played on the piano by the head of the music department when he showed her that Beethoven's romanticism had to be replaced by something more athletic. She was stirred by Cezanne's solidity, and she was also stirred when Picasso broke it up. She shuddered when the innocence of Tolstoy's Natasha was threatened by the hateful Anatole, and she almost wept when the beautiful Robert de Saint-Loup turned out to like boys, not girls.

Her sympathies were broad. Her heart went out to Arthaud when he "died" for a while of electrotherapy, to a young Brooklyn gangster when the brutality of his life made him vomit with disgust, to an organization man who actually believed that he had nothing to worry about in the future, to beatniks who believed that sex would make them happy, to retarded children who had to be set apart from others, to Negro maids who got only ten dollars for a whole week of housework, to the Communist who was tortured by paratroopers in Algeria, to the Jews who went silently to death in Auschwitz, to girls who were hunted down like animals in slave labor camps, to animals who were slaughtered in Chicago, to drug addicts, to writers who could not sell their manuscripts, to the victims of the police, to girls who had babies without husbands.

She liked to go to good restaurants. She was glad she had had love affairs before she got married; she did not want any more afterwards. She enjoyed keeping house for her husband, and saw to it that his guests ate as good food and drank as good liquor and wine as they could get anywhere else. She went to Europe almost every year; her husband's job required it; and she learned much there about food and what to serve with it. She enjoyed doing over her house without the aid of a decorator, and having it photographed by magazines.

Lately the doctor has been telling her to take some hormones, but on the whole she surprises him by her excellent health. She has never had to go to a psychiatrist, but she is thinking about it now. (Or was when I saw her the last time.) She has talked briefly with three, of different schools, and they have all disappointed her. They do not seem to understand what is troubling her. She does not have any of the problems that they were looking for. They listened to her with sympathetic faces, but she felt their faces really wanted to smirk. No one could have real sympathy on tap for anyone who came along. Or so she thought.

When she told a friend that her life seemed meaningless the friend recommended a book by a theologian which dealt specifically with meaninglessness. The book was all right as ideas, very interesting; but it did not speak from experience. The author had not felt what he wrote about. He had merely chosen a subject that was sure to interest people who had passed a certain age.

She is not going, she told me, to take an overdose of sleeping pills. Her husband needs her, and so do her children. She does not believe they love her, and she is beginning to wonder if she loves them. Perhaps she too is a victim of the horrible selfishness that she now sees everywhere. She feels herself surrounded by smirking faces and empty hearts. She knows that she should return good for evil, and give love where she does not get it; but it is hard, and she knows she cannot do it spontaneously, without effort. And what is worse than forced love?

Of course it is possible, she said to me, that the most spontaneous love *was* forced at one time. If she didn't *make* herself overlook her husband's spinelessness, which he got, of course, from his mother, where would their marriage be? There would be nothing but daily quarrels, because he is only getting twenty-five thousand a year and if he spoke up to his boss he would be getting fifty. Or more. She has trained herself not to mention it; he stays out all night when she does.

One of the psychiatrists suggested that she felt she had been treated unjustly, and perhaps he was right. Perhaps she should have gone back to him. He may have had something there. Even if he turned out to be a phony. Sometimes she feels *she* is an awful phony. The interior decorating, the wonderful dinners, the choice of wines, the French that she speaks to UN diplomats, the dislike of sex, the disappointment in her children. Sometimes she believes there is something wrong with everything she has done. Her sympathy with the downtrodden—that seems phony too. And her good education—what does she read now? And love—of course! it *had* to die! Why expect anything else?

What can be done for this woman? (Or the many others like her?) Nothing. She has to do it all herself. If she gets around to it.

There is little likelihood she will. She resists the psychological reeducation that can be so helpful to women of her class. She also resists the multi-disciplinary reeducation that the millennium now demands of everyone who prefers to stay out of its enticing limbo. It would be uncharitable to expect more of her than occasional self-reproaches and occasional good resolutions. When she took time to think about her life, she felt dissatisfied with it; but after a few hours it seemed all right again. Consciousness evaporates fast, unless it is constantly replenished by the lonely suffering that any worthwhile work of art or science will require.

The few women who already understand that they must conduct their own reeducation themselves will be acquainted with loneliness and suffering. They will get the authority from them. They will also learn that the death of love is not a new social disease but a self-inflicted wound that society merely keeps raw. We can live a life of love, if we want to.

After the lecture Butch left at once, but Timmy came up to my desk. He said nothing about the lecture; Mrs. Troubled, an earlier student whom he had never met, meant little to him. But he had news of Nellie. "It's just as well you didn't go backstage with me. She was mobbed. I didn't get a chance to see her for over an hour."

THE GRIEVANCES OF
WEALTH

19

It was in an "English chophouse" that Butch introduced me to his friend, whom he called "the computer boss." The
name of his friend was Dr. Novomesky (or something close to
that). He was large, blond, rather woodenly handsome, and
about forty-five years old. He had been born in Prague, taken
degrees in mathematics and philosophy, and defected to West
Germany and later to the United States in the 1950's. To my
surprise he did not attack American culture in the manner to
which I had grown accustomed in my travels, during my conver-
sations with European intellectuals. He was almost embarrass-
ingly pro-American, and not out of a desire to be polite to me
but out of what was only too clearly a genuine conviction. He
spoke English with an accent that sounded more like New York
than Oxford and had remarkably few echoes of Prague.

"Where else would you be able to get such a choice of
restaurants?" he asked while Butch was reading the wine list
and ordering two of the best bottles of claret in the house. And
instantly answered himself, "Nowhere! New York has everything. Americans have everything, but they do not appreciate
what they have," he continued rather accusingly. I assumed, from
a look that passed between them, either then or later, that he
had heard from Butch some of the ideas I had expressed in my
lectures, and had decided to set me straight if I were overcritical
of my own country.

It is unfortunate that I cannot tarry here for a fuller
portrait of Dr. Novomesky. He was an interesting man, who
flew his own plane and had driven in automobile races, and he

was also well-read or knew where to find what he did not know, but to report him at the length he deserves would throw this incidental account of certain students out of kilter. Here he can only serve as accessory to a curious exchange that took place between Butch and myself.

Dr. Novomesky was modest in his claims for what computers could do. (Both then and later when he showed me some computers in New Jersey.) He said that they could help physicians to diagnose diseases; help psychiatrists to observe significant patterns in their patients' revelations; help philosophers to get a clearer understanding of the structure of the mind and the "thinking" potential of machines; help fliers to travel faster and more safely; help city planners to assemble the many facts they had to understand if they were to make our cities better places to live in; help medical research, physics, chemistry and other scientific work in many ways—"but as for the *big* questions, the eternal questions which I understand you are continually bringing up in your lectures, no, computers cannot help us with those, and really I do not believe they should be expected to."

This did not satisfy Butch, who seemed to want to make me withdraw certain "derogatory" remarks he said I had made about computers. (Actually I had been critical of the people who over-relied on them.) He challenged me to give him or Dr. Novomesky the hardest questions I could think of. He was sure that when these were programmed correctly the answers would amaze me. Computers had helped him with his investments. They were going to change the face of the future. Despite his obvious admiration for Butch's understanding of the stock market, through which he had made some money, Dr. Novomesky seemed embarrassed by the youngster's enthusiasm for the machines. I laughed and changed the subject by asking Dr. Novomesky some questions about the danger of racing cars.

But Butch repeated his challenge after my next lecture, and a week or so later I sat down at my typewriter and wrote three questions. After my next class I gave the three questions to him and thereafter became so busy that I forgot them. Some months later the questions were returned to me with answers. Since both questions and answers seemed to have been typed on the same electric typewriter by the same first-class stenographer who had copied Butch's letter to me, I did not know whether the questions had been submitted to Dr. Novomesky. I was inclined to suspect that if they were, he had merely indicated how they would have to be programmed, if they could be, and that Butch himself, perhaps without much aid from a computer, had provided the greater part of the answers himself. I therefore regard them as his answers, rather than any machine's. (He must however have discussed the questions with Dr. Novomesky, whose touch does not seem absent from the answers.) At any rate, here are the questions, the answers, and the interpretations that I put upon them.

First Question: How would the computer evaluate the following statement? "Let us suppose that certain individuals resolve that they will consistently oppose to power the force of example; to authority, exhortation; to insult, friendly reasoning; to trickery, simple honor. Let us suppose they refuse all the advantages of present-day society and accept only the duties and obligations that bind them to other men. Let us suppose they devote themselves to orienting education, the press and public opinion toward the principles outlined here. Then I say that such men would be acting not as Utopians but as honest realists. They would be preparing the future and at the same time knocking down a few of the walls that imprison us today. If realism be the art of taking into account both the present and the future, of gaining the most while sacrificing the least, then who can fail to see the positively dazzling realism of such behavior?"

Answer: The statement is by Albert Camus (France, 1913–1960) and appeared originally in the French newspaper *Combat* in 1945. (Dr. Novomesky must have supplied this information. I cannot imagine Butch knowing it or digging it up.) The computer regards the statement as useful because it provides men with an ideal of ethical behavior. The ideal is practical. It should be called to people's attention because it might help to encourage them to work harder, to discourage absenteeism, reduce exorbitant wage demands and increase productions. (This part of the answer seems to have come straight from Butch's heart.)

Interpretation: Such "idealism" is psychologically Utopian. It takes for granted a selflessness that few people ever achieve and then only when they are aware of their own continuing capacity for the worst selfishness. It is either naive or the self-hypnotized demagogy of an intellectual. It will appeal to those who are only too willing to confer upon themselves the most difficult austerity ever attributed in the past to a few spiritual heroes. Actually, every priesthood, religious or secular, demands such selflessness *in theory* from each of its members, and realistically never expects to get it. The statement by Camus may be excused historically, as part of the afterglow of the *Résistance,* but as a counsel to people who must live with the realities of our own day, two decades later, it should be recognized as "sincere" but not altogether honest.

Second Question: How would the computer evaluate the following statement? "What is needed is a common purpose, as large and overriding as that which has, since the seventeenth century, drawn forth the energies of the scientist, the inventor, the capitalist, the engineer, and the bureaucrat—and for a while enlisted the support of all men. What is this new purpose? Nothing less than the next transformation of man. This will call, I believe, for a unified though highly diverse culture, which will enable men and women to be at home, as full-fledged citizens, in every part of the planet, in a generous, loving give-and-take with all other cultures; likewise at home with every part of their own selves on all their historic layers and thus capable of drawing into the service of their common purpose, energies that, if allowed to expand by themselves, as technics now does, would be disruptive and dangerous. . . . Here is a creative potentiality that is almost without limit, provided that the arts of love keep pace with the arts of power, and man loves himself and all other living creatures more than he loves the machine on which he has all too intently concentrated."

Answer: The statement is by Lewis Mumford (American, 1895–19—) and first appeared in an article called "The Forces of Life" (1965). The computer finds the statement useful, more useful even than the statement by Camus. It shows more awareness of the new problems of cybernation, and correctly calls upon man to become equal to them by transforming himself.

Interpretation: The statement is more misleading than that by Camus. Camus recognized the need for "certain individuals" to take upon themselves an arduous psychological task. The Mumford statement calls for what Lancelot Law Whyte has described as "the next transformation of man" in a book of that title, and requires that this come about through a much more complex culture than man has previously been called upon to achieve, a culture that finally depends on love. Love is exactly the quantity that cannot be assumed to come "next." As used here, the word is an after-dinner belch of affluence. French intellectual demagogy has been replaced by American intellectual demagogy, which likes to assume that society is going to do with ease what the most disciplined man finds all but impossible.

Third Question: What can students who find the technological society antipathetic and ubiquitous do to ease its pressures on them?

Answer: There is no such thing as a technological society. Many people live more rationally because they have better technological means at their disposal, but that does not warrant the use of a dubious journalistic phrase to describe the society in which they live. Intelligent students will heed the following unqualified response of the computer: "Cooperation with technology means success; failure to cooperate with technology means failure."

Interpretation: Really intelligent students have heard this before, and some have already found ways to prove it false. They have performed acts of dissent which have won them more success (more fame and more money) than if they had merely given their assent. Opposition to some of technology's side effects has already made a lucrative business of selling unadulterated bread, houses in the country and responsible television. And the list is growing. The phrase " technological society" is no more dubious or journalistic than "capitalist society" or "communist society," and now it is becoming more useful than either of them.

Students will need temporary relief from the pressures of technology according to the complexity of their talents. If they can turn their hand to making good bread or good journalism, their awkward age will be shorter than if they must try to write a good novel or paint a good picture. When the pressure becomes insupportable they can—and usually do—look for someone close at hand, by blood or marriage or sympathy, to look after them for a while. Like new businesses, they need long-term credit. Honest talent is perhaps more helpless than ever before, because the new technology increases its dependence daily on the misuse of words. Reparation is attempted through foundations, which are by-products of advanced technology and sometimes attempt to correct its errors.

So ended a weird episode. Sometimes I almost doubt it ever took place. I sent my interpretations to Butch, but got no reply from him. By that time his graduation seemed near at hand, and I suppose he did not want to jeopardize it with any display of resentment. He merely smiled amiably at me when he appeared for my next-to-last lecture.

The last time we met we were discussing what can or cannot be done for Mrs. Troubled. I think the most important fact about her present unhappiness—and the unhappiness of many other people like her—is that she feels a deep, unacknowledged grievance. She has had more than her share of the advantages of the new prosperity, and occasionally she reminds herself to be grateful for them, but she also has a strong sense of deprivation. At present this sense of deprivation means more to her than anything else. She would gladly live in a walk-up, she told me, if she could get rid of her sense of injustice.

It affects her most acutely as the conviction that she is not *really* needed by her husband. She runs his house for him, she looks after his health and that of his children, she gives him sound advice on important matters of business when he asks it, she is frequently congratulated by him on her good judgment, her good management, her good looks, her taste, her tact, her expert handling of the business associates on whom he must make a good impression. She still attracts him as a woman. She knows he depends heavily on her. And yet it is a long time since he paid any attention to her when she spoke seriously. She tries to tell him that he is not as interesting as he used to be, that he says the same things over and over again, and sees no one except people who are apt to be useful to him in business. She tells him that she is drying up too, but he does not listen. Or he shrugs his shoulders and says, "What do you expect? We're in a hard game, honey, but eight more years and we'll get out of it."

She feels she could have taught him so much that now he will never know because his mind is closed. But what seems to her "much" always turns out to be "little" when she tries to mention it. She knows no way to put feminine values into words he will understand. Flowers mean almost nothing to him, and he never really looks at their children. He is unaware of their beauty, their pathos. He gets annoyed if they fail to help her clear the breakfast table, or if their grades are only fair, or if they say, "She did good" instead of "She did well." He does not know how to relax and enjoy them, and when she mentions it he says, "Honey, if I relaxed, the kids would have to go to public school." He thinks faster than she does, but most of his thinking, she feels, is all wrong. He has already had to have part of his throat cut out, at Memorial Hospital, and talks huskily, and if he keeps on the way he is going, he may lose his whole voice box. The doctor has warned him.

There is so much she could have learned from him too. When she met him, she thought it would take a lifetime to speak French, Italian, Spanish and German as well as he did. Now she can get along in five languages, but he has failed to learn hers. No ideologist has prepared him.

What can be done for Mrs. Troubled? She feels a grievance because she is not living as simply and as quietly as her sister, who is married to a real estate man in New Mexico and never seems to worry about anything except the difficulty of getting a clear title to land in a place where property has been divided up into fractional parts by the Spanish-Americans for hundreds of years. Mrs. Troubled has had newer problems thrust upon her, and just enough education to realize that she will have to start all over again if she is to begin to understand them. For all her oddities, Mrs. Troubled is a bit like each of us assembled here to think about the new opportunities that have been put under our noses and then snatched away.

Mrs. Troubled suffers from the new grievances of wealth. And so do all of us. Even those who had to get scholarships. Even those who could not afford the subway fare to ride here—and walked. The millennium has been thrust upon us, like a winning ticket in the Irish Sweepstakes, and we don't know what to do with it. If we are crude, we merely put the money in the bank—or take off on a cruise. If we are not crude, we are subject to a sense of grievance. Self-pity is a *rich* emotion. (Much as Durkheim has shown that the impulse to suicide begins with deliverance from dire want.)

Mrs. Troubled's grievance is no more rational than that of a baby who has been pampered from birth but still feels he has not received enough love. It is just as real. And it is shared by many of us, including some of our apparently untroubled statesmen, businessmen, scholars, scientists, philosophers, religionists, and artists. This becomes apparent when we take a closer look at some of the underlying emotions, seldom admitted in public, of our most distinguished citizens.

First of all, our statesmen. They have been made powerful by our new wealth (in trained, eager young men as well as in lasers and rockets) and they have also had their hands tied by it. They are by no means always free to follow the course that their best intelligence would dictate to them. They have to get embroiled in costly mistakes—for example in the Near East, in the Caribbean and in Southeast Asia—because the voters who gave them their power cannot see the intricate problems of foreign affairs with dispassionate clarity. The farsighted technician that resides in every good statesman is continually being forced by public ignorance or special-interest cupidity into errors for which he knows he alone will be blamed by history.

No American President, for instance, can afford to be the first to lead his country into its first publicly acknowledged military defeat, even though a nominal defeat in one area might lead to much more important victories in the future. Presidents therefore frequently feel a grievance against the self-assured people who put them into the White House and then oblige them to act more stupidly than they wish to. Their sense of grievance appears now and then during an irritable moment in a press conference or a private interview when the questioner strikes too close to home. The public ignorance that causes the presidential sense of injustice is hopefully expected, according to our favorite mythology, to be corrected in time by "education," but since the required education would have to be emotional, sensory and spiritual as well as intellectual, and lead to genuine wisdom, a more reasonable expectation would be that this situation, of which every close observer is aware, will lead instead to ever more serious mistakes. We can only hope that our enemies' mistakes will be still worse. Meanwhile it is a safe prediction that presidential tempers will get shorter, while the public raincoats its mind more contentedly. In time a thoroughgoing catastrophe may teach us the need to devise a new political system which divides the presidency, somewhat after the manner of Greek masks, or constitutional monarchies, into a smiler who holds popular emotions and a stoneface who gets the dirty work done. By that time we would have learned that education is not Santa Claus.

It does not seem possible that our businessmen should feel a grievance against the quasi-socialist windfall that has redoubled the vigor of capitalism, and made them richer than ever before; yet they do. It is a grievance that must be kept still more secret, however, than that of Presidents. To express it would be bad for business. It originates in the fact that businessmen are by no means the soulless monsters that they are thought in once-Marxist, now-general opinion to be. They are not always happy when they must devote themselves solely to making money. Frequently they desire to be completely ethical. They do not enjoy the new twist to technical progress that requires them to use language a little less than accurately if they are to prosper. Oversimplifications that originated with envious intellectuals have made us deny businessmen their common portion of humanity. Nearly all literature presents them as monsters or buffoons. Their own over-pragmatic contempt of intellect and their own neglect of intellectual skills have not helped their case. In the circumstances they feel a golden grievance that is difficult to make others understand and must never be revealed. (Their wives would do well to regard this as one of the chief sources of their frequent emotional outbursts. They also do not like being considered, by their children, as "rather inconsequential" beasts of burden.)

Our scholars resent the anti-intellectual slights they

incur daily in a business-dominated press. (Unless of course they
are English or French, when they get attention that American
scholars do not.) They do not like being treated at social gather-
ings (except the few where they are in the majority) as natural
inferiors who must be tolerated as pedantic bores. Hence they
cling self-injuriously to their own kind. Our new wealth and
the need to spread it more equitably have lately improved their
economic status; our new problems have also increased their
social utility; and it looks as if their prestige will grow with
popular recognition of the need for them to keep the ship of
state afloat. *Amour-propre* and money finally mean less to them,
however, when they are truly able, than an opportunity to
develop their talents; and the new intoxications of power have
robbed nearly all scholarly pursuits of the sense of leisurely
play, of true freedom of mind, that led to the most original
discoveries of the past and the most cooperative teamwork. The
fun went out of nuclear physics, for instance, the fun that had
begun in the international fraternity which thought itself sealed
off from the rest of the world at Goettingen—the fun went out
the minute the bomb was dropped. A more responsible, a less
playful era began.

The position of other scholars is not greatly different.
Their privileged playground has been condemned by popular
demand to merge with the rest of an ugly metropolis. Imme-
morial elms must accommodate themselves to the iron pipes of
jungle gyms. Scholars receive more money and less freedom.
Usually they seem to feel aggrieved by the vulgarization that
has accompanied their new wealth. In becoming good citizens
they may lose the boyish independence that led to freshness of
thought. They fear that the mind which has to consider every
angle will see nothing with much originality. And they do not
like having to be policed by ever more numerous hordes of
administrators. (Coe College, Iowa, has more administrators
than Cambridge University.) The romantic liberty of scholarship
is over. Ideas that once would have explained *everything* now
have to be modestly dovetailed with a million prosaic facts.
(Interdiscipline is a mug's game.) Society seems to be *rehabil-
itating* its scholars, as if they were juvenile delinquents. They
live under the rule of wardens, usually called Deans.

Religionists—the serious ones—feel a grievance against

the new prosperity because it has meant larger congregations, larger contributions and less conviction. Wealth, as they very well know, has never led to faith. Historically it has dissolved it.

Artists have clung to their freedom more than any other group, but they too are now threatened by a new tyranny of public opinion which withholds a livelihood when it is not amused. New taxes mean that there are fewer small patrimonies on which they can keep body and soul together. On the other hand, there are more tempting commissions which require, along with the higher cost of living, a full indoctrination in the marketplace. Not all of them are equipped for it. And the art mart quickly becomes more sordid than any other, because it deals in sacred objects, things of beauty. Few faces are so full of grievance as those of artists who not long ago believed they could escape, by the sheer excellence of their work, the compromise and shabby surrender they disliked so much in their neighbors.

Mrs. Troubled, then, has much company in her sense of injustice. Men of state, men of affairs, scholars, priests, teachers, artists are her companions in secret complaint. They enjoy the millennium, but it deeply distresses them.

Can she arrange to receive its blessings but not its curses? Can they? Is modern freedom possible? (Modern salvation, modern *satori,* modern enlightenment?)

Yes, it is possible. But not often.

Butch left without a word as soon as the lecture was over. In a few weeks he received his degree and wrote me a letter. It was obvious that he did not wish to antagonize me, I might still be useful to him later. He expressed his gratitude to me (more than most students do), but he also managed to insert with great dexterity a phrase that regretted the trend of certain of my later lectures which had proved a disappointment to him after the promise of the first ones. It was as close as he dared come to a parting shot.

He is now in his third year in law school. The last I heard from him he had just bought a small apartment house. The announcement came on his impeccable letterhead. It invited me to a housewarming party. I didn't have time to go to the party.

THE DEATH OF CHAOS

20

Timmy kept me informed about the events which followed Nellie Rankin's success as the star of *Intermezzo*. Her name was put on the marquee of the theatre, and the ads played up her performance rather than the script by a famous French author. When she wasn't shooting a movie in Philadelphia she was appearing on television shows. She was kept too busy, he explained, to be able to write me and thank me for my letter and my flowers. She had asked him to do that for her.

Every night he called for her after the show and escorted her to an apartment, full of Tiffany glass and pictures by Burne-Jones, Redon and Moreau—all originals, of course—that had been lent her by a relative of the producer's who was away in Europe. So she couldn't very well ask for a raise. The new apartment was near Beekman Place, and she didn't miss the garbage cans and tricycles of the lower Village at all. A less important member of the cast was taking over her old apartment. She was selling her Mexican furniture. She would no longer need it. "I'd better buy French things now," she said.

Even offstage her accent was now slightly French rather than slightly British, and it came a lot easier to her. Every interview had to mention that her mother was French and had once scrubbed the floors of a church in the Gaspé country.

Timmy's biggest news, he said, was that he was writing a play for Nellie and would work full-time on it as soon as he received his degree. It would dramatize his story of the theft of a Chardin from the Louvre, only the thief would be a girl, not a man.

Timmy made no mention of Butch. I surmised that he had heard less of Butch's intrusion into Nellie's life than I had. The crisis that had threatened to halt her theatrical career appeared to have passed. How, I still do not know.

Except when she had matinées, Nellie was commuting every day to Philadelphia, where she was playing an important secondary part in a film being shot there in a warehouse. It was to be her début as a movie actress. Her agent believed it would lead to still better parts for her. She had to work extra-hard on Sundays, when she was supposed to be resting. Her forehead had been cut slightly when something had fallen off a wall in the warehouse while she was in the midst of a scene. On her agent's advice she was going to sue for damages, unless the management gave her star billing.

"What a rat race!" Timmy said. "But she's up to it. She used to get exhausted and catch colds. Now she gets five hours sleep a night and never felt better in her life. The telephone never stops ringing. Mostly it's photographers for magazines. How she gets along with all those people I don't know. She calls them all 'dearest.' They horrify me. I hate them!"

Both he and Butch were present at my last lecture. After a summation of the points of fact on which exam-takers might be questioned a week later (the leading ideas of Marx, Durkheim, Weber and other sociologists; of Freud, Jung, Adler and other psychologists; of Spengler, Toynbee, Giedion and other historians; of Kierkegaard, Nietzsche, Heidegger and other philosophers; of Baudelaire, Rilke, Yeats and other poets; and which of them seemed useful, and which did not, in the new times that were upon us)—after this summation, the lecture, which lasted twice the usual fifty minutes and was addressed to adults who took no notes as well as to degree-seekers who did, properly began. It began with a story from the Chinese.

Fuss, the god of the Southern Ocean, and Fret, the god of the Northern Ocean, happened once to meet in the realm of Chaos, the god of the Center. Chaos treated them very handsomely and they discussed together what they could do to repay his kindness. They had noticed that, whereas everyone else has seven apertures, for sight, hearing, eating, breathing and so on, Chaos had none. So they decided to make the experiment of boring holes in him. Every day they bored a hole, and on the seventh day Chaos died.

It is a story from the very oldest times, which so often tell us more about the very newest times than anything in between. Hence our growing interest in shamans, Toltecs or whoever it was that started the civilization we now fear we are going to lose. Every one of us is in the position of Chaos, and we have already fallen into the well-meaning hands of Fuss and Fret. The holes were bored into us before we knew what was going on. It was all for our own good, of course. Chaos must be destroyed. It is the traditional enemy of education, the modern Carthage, and our teachers and parents are and must be Catos.

Some of us can stand off Fuss and Fret. Such people recognize the need of education, but they also know that if they lose their portion of Chaos they lose their daimon also. Why did Justice Holmes go to burlesque shows in his old age? To stand off the Fuss and Fret of Boston. A mere whiff of the powdered bottoms of Billy Watson's Beef Trust, and he was able to write better dissenting opinions. But now burlesque has become a dreary routine of the new Fuss and Fret, the new be-free-be-sexy formulas of New York, which the intelligent recognize as merely another way of getting them to work harder than ever and feel more depleted. The wheels of industry are turned not by steam or electricity or nuclear fission; but by the promise of orgasm, with a bit of mayhem thrown in. What freed Justice Holmes does not free us. Fuss and Fret have reversed their strategy. Bottoms will no doubt retain their eternal fascination, but bright students will perceive the folly of regarding any particle of flesh with the excessive naiveté of the former puritan. Early marriage is fine for obstetricians and dairies; it is not fine for young talent. Only hell-raisers really learn anything. The good die young, mentally, of self-admiration.

Everyone, including those nearest and dearest to us, *especially* those nearest and dearest to us, will feel relieved when there is no more danger that we are going to behave unpredictably, under the influence of Chaos. Everything will go along more smoothly, and we ourselves will be happier, they are convinced, when Chaos is under tight technical control.

Am I using the word "Chaos" here as a synonym for the psychological term "the unconscious"? I do not think so. I think it comes closer to the moment-to-moment flow of events which can be apprehended now and then by a well-developed sense of wonder but is usually shut out by an urgent desire for order. Chaos is the nature of things. It does not appear only in dreams or slips of the tongue and the like; it appears all the time everywhere. The importance of apprehending it as often as possible is suggested by the literary definition of man as a "poet perpetually conspiring against himself." (Lawrence Durrell) Our greatest defeats go unrecorded.

We reveal more of ourselves by the various kinds of art we create—our sonatas, our meals, our children, our living rooms, our talk—than by our most significant dreams. The historical expression we give our fate is infinitely richer than any repression or any archetype, no matter how important it may be (and is) to understand the repressions and archetypes that have affected our fate. Hence good novels make better reading than the best case histories, and real criticism, which now must pull together the many levels of a life or a work, reflects a fullness of experience that will never be found in clinical "literature." Real criticism, like a good novel, is necessarily rare, and it significantly lacks the organized response sure to be given specialist works that help fellow-specialists to exclude Chaos.

If I have favored French and English education over that of Russia, it is because I think they have allowed people to find for themselves a better balance of Chaos and order. Also because I think our own educational system, which once encouraged students to find individual fulfillment in the French and English manner, has swung over to the cryptoideologies, or disguised authoritarianism, that competitive technology requires. American troops nearly always prefer being stationed in Germany, where they receive at least lip service, to being stationed in France, where they are sometimes openly ridiculed. Our belief in "freedom," which implies a readiness to be opposed and ridiculed, as part of the nature of things, has been put under a strain that it is only human to resent.

Actually, only a few people ever really want freedom, which always ends up by being that monstrous surprise, freedom to be reminded by others of little facts which do not quite jibe with one's idealized image of oneself. As a nation we are drifting into a new kind of authoritarianism, because as individuals we do not care to take a good look at ourselves. Our political dangers originate in our demands for well-paved, well-marked roads, fast telephone service, frozen foods that retain the vitamins—our demands, in short, for efficiency. (I demand it too.) To achieve all this, it is necessary that people overtrim the wick of life in them, renounce their original portion of Chaos.

Most people are only too glad to do this; most Americans, at least. Most Mexicans are not quite ready for it. We call those who are not quite ready for it childish, and await impatiently the day when they will "grow up."

What about those who recognize the need for order but do not want it to be taken over by the forces of death? What about those who do not want to be systematically self-defeating poets?

They cannot stay out of the rat race. If they are honest, they have to admit they are in it, one way or another, long before they can think of how to get out of it. The largest inheritance is no protection against it. The most Beat pretension of immunity to it will not work forever. The first step toward getting out of it is confessing freely how deep we are in.

Nearly all higher education is opposed to admitting there is a rat race and we are already in it. When such things are admitted, riots break out.

Nearly all higher education consists of giving students a battery of concepts—ideologies and cryptoideologies—with which to hold Chaos at bay.

We need concepts. As much as we need a well-organized food supply. We would be helpless without them. Our experience must also be organized, or we would drown in it. But we need not use concepts to *shut out* Chaos. If we fail to be hospitable to concepts and Chaos at the same time, we fail to meet the demands of our new society and weakly surrender to it, either through intellectual inadequacy (excess of Chaos) or through intellectual safe-playing (excess of conceptualism). Your IQ's suggest there is more likelihood that you will choose the latter.

What is more, a general exploitation of the pragmatic faith has meant that you stand a better chance of paying your way if you surrender, as quickly as possible, to some narrow, ready-made concept, such as any business and most professions will be glad to provide, and close your mind to everything else. The intellectual freedom, the resolution of opposites announced by William James in his formulation of pragmatism (1906), cannot be found in it today. To expect it to be there still would be like expecting a dollar to buy what it bought in 1906.

The names of our leading ideologies are well-known. They include our religions in their political aspects, as well as Communism, Capitalism, Socialism and several others. The name of our leading cryptoideology is not as well-known as the fact of its existence. By its very nature it dislikes being given a name, unless the name is "idealistic" and flattering. I think, as I have already suggested, that it should be called Salvation by Checkbook. That indicates the behavior that is forced upon most of us by our new wealth. Even when we don't personally happen to have any of it, our new wealth is the chief historical fact of our time. It determines most of our significant actions. Few of us are so crude as to believe that money alone can "save" us, but many of us believe that it can be used, after its acquisition and enjoyment, in good works that will constitute a decidedly realistic form of salvation. That, in fact, is the utilitarian faith that has already won general acceptance in the United States and looks as if it will spread to other nations as they free themselves from tighter attitudes that were created by aeons of poverty.

Mrs. Troubled believed in Salvation by Checkbook. At first she found the phrase repugnant as a description of her faith, but later she was honest enough to accept it and laugh about it. "Of course you have to have money to do good in this world," she said. (It was an inaccurate statement which I let pass.) "I've helped a lot of people, but only because of what my father left me and my husband gives me to run the house. All right, I believe in trying to help others. It's not enough, I know, but it's all I can do."

She was especially happy about the help she was able to give young artists by buying their work. "Art is the only free thing we have left," she was fond of saying. "I believe in it. I wish I were creative myself, but I'm not. So I do what I can."

She looked startled when I said that I admired her generosity, but she was mistaken about one thing. Art is not free.

She thought I was making a bad joke when I said it.

Since a belief in the freedom of art seems to be inculcated in everyone who attends our better colleges, I had better explain why Mrs. Troubled and a great many others are mistaken about a very important matter. My explanation may further elucidate the cultural determinism that I call the millennium. On the surface it appears to offer liberation; in reality it does nothing of the kind.

Those of us who grew up on the masterpieces of early twentieth century art—the sculpture of Brancusi, the novels of Joyce, Lawrence, Proust, Kafka, the paintings of Picasso and Matisse, the music of Stravinsky and Schoenberg, and other triumphs of the avant-garde—what was it that we admired most in them? If their value to us can be summed up in a single word, I think that word would be "freedom." We were excited by the freedom that had been won by these artists, as well as by more traditional ones like Yeats, Mann, Valéry and Rilke, from the same unimaginative confinements that we had observed at first hand in the calculations of our own relatives and our own neighbors. A less fearful world had been made available to us. Dull repetitions need not be our daily bread. Art had broken loose from crabbed restraint. In our enthusiasm we believed the more sluggish folkways that had depressed us were sure to be dissolved in time by the brilliant innovations of the vanguard.

Sometimes our hope took political form, as well as aesthetic, and we believed a general revolution was at hand. It was not until later that we learned, with shock and pain, that a longing for beauty and a longing for power can be easily confused in a time of many undefined aspirations and many unprincipled propagandists. As Americans, charmed with our own youthful innocence and convinced we had forever transcended the suffering and sinfulness of a played-out Old World, we preferred to confer purity of motive on strangers who seemed to come with letters of introduction from artists whom actually they were even then killing or forcing into exile. We longed to believe in a revolution that worked. After a glorious moment or two on the barricades (we didn't know exactly what barricades were, but they went with revolutions) we would be freed forever from bourgeois boredom and vindicated in the eyes of our relatives and classmates. *Everyone* would go to our plays or our concerts, and what is more, they would understand them and like them.

In the early 1930's a young poet said to a columnist of the Daily Worker, "I'm going back home to New Mexico for the summer, Mike. You don't think the revolution will break out while I'm gone, do you? I'd hate like hell to miss it!"

Less naive American artists, however, had been studying, usually in Paris, the methods of the European vanguard which they admired, and discovered that one of its most effective weapons was called in French *"épater le bourgeois,"* which I translate as "middlebrowbeating."

Middlebrowbeating was a cunning technique which aided some of the most daring, most unaccepted and later most solid artistic careers of the early twentieth century. Its theory ran something like this: the enemy of the artist is not the untutored lowbrow but the half-tutored middlebrow, who knows just enough to be really ignorant, but controls most money and most honors. The best way to deal with him is *never* to talk his language. Shock him. Don't reason, don't expound. Bowl him over. Get him to denounce you in his press. Make *him* come to *you.* Make him creep back for another peep at the enigma you have ingeniously constructed. Only by playing upon his appetite for mystery will you gain the magic that has always protected the artist, whether medicine man or storyteller, against arrogant rulers.

Middlebrowbeating, in one form or another, was used by all of the prominent innovators of early twentieth century art. Now, however, it is a period piece, employed only by epigoni who hope they can still get a rise out of the reader by telling him exactly what they did in bed with so and so. Since there are still so many readers who have not caught up with the nineteenth century, let alone the twentieth, the device works in the more remote parts of Utah and Brownsville. It also sustains more than one Department of English, and Art and Music. To those who live in our own day, however (not many, it must be admitted), middlebrowbeating is as dated as the burlesque shows which kept Justice Holmes in a state of endocrinal dissent from the accepted opinions of Boston. If we need liberation now, it is from the advance-guard academy of New York, which in the name of a freedom that was won at least fifty years ago has become as rigid as the bean-eaters ever were. Middlebrowbeating is now one more *concept,* one more defense mechanism against the newer forms of Chaos. Old highbrows and young hucksters, in museums and magazines, keep a dead avant-garde alive in much the same way that Mary Baker Eddy was driven through the streets of her town in her carriage long after she had actually passed away. Meanwhile the real problem of the real avant-garde, how to establish a dialogue with the middlebrows, which would begin with a frank recognition of the bourgeois within oneself, is avoided with hoots.

An interesting biographical fact united the original artists who developed middlebrowbeating so long ago. They all came of age well before World War I broke out. They reached their artistic maturity in the tranquil period between 1890 and 1914, when peace was so long established that it encouraged youthful energies to flow into expressions of dissent from traditional ways of looking at things. In a time of peace Chaos seems to sit for his portrait. Cultural disintegration was an open secret, but as yet there had been none of the overt calamities that along with still worse effects, such as killing millions of people, have unsettled subsequent artistic styles. Artists could aestheticize their day-to-day experience directly, without having to face the many new problems—political, economic, military, social, psychological, philosophical and religious—that now drain off Mississippis of collective libido. Artists could achieve the lasting fascination that can only be achieved by singleminded concentration on highly professional effects. The masterpieces of the early twentieth century "breaking up" lacked the breadth of their best predecessors—they have been called "art art" that had been so "dehumanized" that it could only be appreciated by fellow professionals—but they played skillfully on the snobbishness of the bourgeoisie whom they attacked, and they burned their way into the consciousness of their natural enemies.

Now the problems of genuine artists are different. They do not live in a time of breaking up; they live among broken pieces. They fear there can be no reassembling of man himself. Therefore they must restudy the nature of man, and begin with a closer look at themselves, not as gifted professionals who can disassociate themselves at will from their own kind, but as humble members of a group that has shaped them more than they were previously willing to admit. It is an agonizing experience for talent, but it may lead in time to a rewon communion of souls, or if you prefer secular terminology, a revitalized collective. If new social forces are to be prevented from destroying all of us, they must be grasped and tamed by an especially gifted few. If technological autonomy is not to make all discussion academic, those with the sensibility of artists must develop the strength of character that distinguished their shaman ancestors. The self-congratulatory truncations of "art art" avoid the great loneliness that now must be faced.

It is not likely we shall soon see a fusion of sensibility and character. Though required of the heroes of the past, the two seem now to be mutually exclusive. If the demands of efficiency leave little time for love, they leave the artist even less time to ripen slowly, to integrate the many many kinds of new knowledge that have been put at his command, to pull together a wildly pluralistic world, to live his way into his material, to allow others to be entirely different from himself and to enjoy them all the more for it. He has been put in touch with a more exciting world than any of his predecessors knew, and simultaneously denied the easygoing poverty that for centuries made it possible for his tribe to mature in its own rhythm. As soon as he comes of age, he is asked to make a living in a market of rising costs and lowered standards, or to subsist as a sponge, without self-respect. He must make good young, moreover, if he is to satisfy popular mythology and qualify for charitable support. At the very time when artists need more aging than ever to catch up with the world they must understand and interpret, they are confronted with cares that would disturb a certified public accountant. If they fail somewhere along the line, they can hardly be blamed. Yet their work receives on the whole more censorious criticism than that of anyone else, including Presidents. It is not surprising that they dodge into hospitable cliques and refuse to listen to anyone else.

Their central dilemma is created by the shortness of time: whether to try to make a splash when still young or to retire humbly from the scene of combat and develop their gifts in comparative solitude. The first alternative leads them invariably to jettison history and to suffer the fate of the historyless, that is, to be forgotten soon, even when apparently most successful. (Any kind of Pop or Mom Art will do as an example.) They have over-adapted themselves to the millennium. The second alternative usually leads to over-receptivity to the fascinations of the new knowledge, to slow submergence in the academy.

The dilemma is whether to be a flash in the pan or a bore. The comments of reviewers suggest that an artistic genera-tion usually lasts five years, as opposed to the fifteen-year aver-age that seems to prevail in professional football. Obviously, the rougher sport is art. Few of those who retire into solitude ever emerge with anything worth listening to. They have rejected the authority that comes only with suffering. If new spiritual leadership is to be given our society, it can come only from those who take on society's new burdens and complexities. Those who make themselves fully vulnerable to the technological society may perhaps in time hope to understand it or interpret it. They will have to have strong minds and strong personalities to hold up under the strain.

It was when I mentioned time to Mrs. Troubled that she understood at last what I had meant when I said that art was no longer free. (Or at least she seemed to.) She knew already there was not enough time for the young artists she admired to pick up the old manysided culture that came so easily to an earlier generation of artists. (Her uncle had belonged to it; he made the Grand Tour and painted like Sargent.) If the new artists stopped to think about the culture (a word which made them laugh) they would never get anything done. They had to *produce*. One of them said he hadn't read a book in eleven years, and that by Dale Carnegie in a magazine digest. But his pictures sold right along. A New York museum was offering him a retrospective; two books had been written *about* him; and now he was going with the best dealer of all. If he had stopped to think about anything else but painting, he said, he wouldn't have gotten anywhere. His first wife had given him *problems*. His second wife gave him no *problems*.

None of this made Mrs. Troubled feel less respect for this artist or the others. She began, as she said, to "understand what they were up against." She thought her husband was up against something similar. "They're not free to be themselves. They're driven. That's it! They're driven." It was the closest she could come to saying what she meant.

This time I could agree with her. Once artists were subject to a discipline they had taken over from earlier priest-hoods, along with some of their prestige. It was the discipline imposed upon them by their belief that art had a *sacred* function. Now the old self-imposed disciplines of art are melting away before the new group-imposed disciplines of money. Art, like nearly everything else, has been desacralized.

The desacralization of art cannot, however, be mentioned. Billions of dollars would melt away. The value of pictures in museums and private collections would be drastically lowered, if they were regarded for a single moment as merely clever manipulations of symbols rather than as genuine victories of spirit over matter.

When the value of art—a word which means here literature, music and the other arts—rests not upon genuine love and living faith, but upon the words of plausible publicists, it is bound to come down in price. And in esteem. Devaluation follows desacralization, as the night the day, but for the time being art will hold its own in the market, for the simple reason that few of those who buy it really look at it. It is not regarded with the same scrutiny that cuts everything else down to size. Its value is temporarily sustained by the *mystique* of seeming "wholly other." It appears to give meaning and dignity to the overstuffed void.

When the skill of publicists overextends itself and a general devaluation of art takes place (it seems unthinkable now but cannot be avoided), the chief beneficiaries will be artists. Their deepest love will be restored to them, in place of a pumped-up public esteem. Too often they have aided the desacralization of their art, because their sense of the sacred was too narrow, too ignorant, too personal. They used symbols; they did not believe in them. After art's devaluation, they may believe in them again. They may be forced into the symbolic life of love and community. They may cease painting concepts and begin painting Chaos again. He is always waiting to be noticed. And when he is, there can be a recovery of the sacred.

Respect for Chaos can only be felt by those who accept in full the tragedy of displacement. They have gotten used to being homeless; indeed, their homelessness is the source of their search for meaning. If they felt "rooted" in a community, as their ancestors did, they would surely suspend their most valuable activity, which is to open themselves up to a wholly new world as well as the one that never changes. Fear of rootlessness leads to building booms, architects' blueprints, handshaking bankers, the smell of fresh plaster, the sense of new hope. All of this is better than living in slums, however fast the new housing developments are turned back into slums, with girls raped in elevators and rats once more under the bed. But acceptance of rootlessness, of the new state of mind into which all of us are born today, is still better. From acceptance of rootlessness, with all its tragic implications, might come human beings worthy of the new dwellings that are being prepared for them—today in lands that are rich, tomorrow in lands that are poor.

Acceptance of modern rootlessness requires courage. (Willingness to admit what everyone else is trying to conceal.) It also requires a trained ability to think, to distinguish clearly between what is good for large numbers of people who demand one sustaining mythology or another and what is good for a small number of people who must try to live with things as they are.

These few will not be impressed with the rewarmed debate about the death of God. It was an interesting discussion when Nietzsche first used the phrase in an entirely different age and amid conditions that bear little resemblance to those that exist. today. God is indeed dead in all who do not realize that the spirit moves very fast where it listeth. His remains stink, except in academic nostrils, when theological issues are raised out of the context that has put everyone's faith under a more confusing trial than has ever existed before. It is presumptuous or over-shrewd to talk of God's ability to survive morally when it is *one's own* ability to survive morally that is in question. Theologians who are not on intimate terms with themselves (which means seeing themselves quite coldly as objects) and have no familiarity with their most immediate everyday surroundings (which means throwing away seminary-born concepts and look-ing straight at Chaos)—such theologians merely play for head-lines, or reveal their own confusion, when they project their own spiritual death upon God. If there is a God, why must we bore Him?

The theologians I have known seemed like near-sighted children when seen in the same room as artists, or thinkers who wrote like artists. The theologians had no first-hand knowledge of nature. They had not been there. And some of them wanted to go there very much. Sometimes they thought naively that it meant sleeping with a harlot the night before preaching a sermon on the woman taken in adultery. They had a larger view than artists, whose neglect of intellect often makes them petty and provincial. But they lacked something more important. Their scholarly discipline, that is, their fear of life, made them unable to learn from experience. Both they and the artists had known loneliness, but all of them had seized any opportunity thereafter that offered a chance to escape it. They were willing to diffuse their talents if only they could prevent a return of an original sense of homelessness.

We are all born with a perception of the sacred which we can develop or neglect. Most of us, including our artists, prefer to neglect it.

What can students learn from the present predicament of artists? Almost everything they need to know. Artists drama-tize the condition of man better than anyone else, because they love so much, enjoy so much, believe so much—and dry up so vividly when they run out of faith. When *they* go bad we know everyone is in danger.

Faith is always hard to sustain. In the best of weather, in the best of health it can give out. Historically it has flourished in times of trial and given out in times of prosperity. Now we live in a millennium which promises no end to prosperity or desire for prosperity. How to find faith in spite of it; that is all we have to learn.

After my lecture Timmy said he liked it better than my book about the Remnant. It didn't allow anyone to have the illusion that he belonged to the Remnant, when as a matter of fact almost nobody did. And it was more specific about the problems we actually faced.

Early the next morning Nellie telephoned me. She apologized for waking me up, but Timmy was in jail. Would I come and try to help her get him out?

He had been caught taking a dollar tip from their table in a restaurant where they had eaten a meal together after her show. The waiter had been "laying for him," she said, because he had done it before. The waiter, an excitable Armenian, refused to let her pay back the dollar, so that Timmy could go free. Instead, the waiter had called the cops.

When I reached the police station Nellie whispered irritably that Timmy had done it to avoid getting his degree. The waiter, white-haired, stoop-shouldered, flat-footed, exhausted, was being told by a sergeant, in a dirty windowless room where there was no chair for anyone, that charges against Timmy would mean that both of them would have to appear in court. Finally the waiter accepted a dollar and rode home in a taxicab with Nellie and Timmy. He was teaching an Armenian song to Nellie, and Timmy was saying, "It's wonderful!" The streets were almost empty. Sleepy-eyed men trudged toward subway shells. The sun was coming up, gilt on grey.

Timmy took his final exams and received his degree. That summer and that fall, instead of looking for a job, he worked on a play for Nellie. "It had a clever idea and wonderful dialogue," Nellie told me accusingly in the lobby of the psychiatric ward where he was taken after a leap of despair, onto subway tracks. "But it's too complicated, too subtle. It's *chaotic*. He listened to you more than he did to me. You're to blame for all this. He wouldn't have jumped under the subway train if it hadn't been for you."

He was released from the ward when another patient attacked him with a knife and he fought for his life. "I wonder if that was a stunt," he told me later in his favorite bar on Charles Street, amid signs that informed us how to say "Cheers!" in a dozen languages, "just to see if I wanted to live. Well, I do, and by God they're going to listen to me some day! Including *Miss* Nellie Rankin!" He was not seeing her any more, he told me.

What he is doing now I cannot say. He called me once again from the same cheerful bar, and sounded hopeful about something or other, not at all like his old tearful self, but I could not go there to hear the latest report on how he still manages to keep out of the chromium maze. I was too busy. I had to work on this book. Sometimes I wonder if turnover hasn't taken me over too.

BIBLIOGRAPHY

Other authors and titles are to be found in the Notes and the Index. The poetry, fiction and drama that are emphasized in the text will be found there, not here.

ADLER, ALFRED, *Social Interest*, translated by John Linton and Richard Vaughan. New York: Capricorn Books, 1965. (If an American paperback is available, as in this case, use it. The same rule applies to the whole bibliography.)

BARRETT, WILLIAM, *Irrational Man*. Garden City: Anchor Books, 1958.

BENOIT, HUBERT, *The Supreme Doctrine*, translator unnamed. New York: Pantheon Books, 1955.

CAMPBELL, JOSEPH, *The Masks of God: Primitive Mythology*. New York: Viking Press, 1959.

CASSIRER, ERNST, *Language and Myth*, translated by Susanne K. Langer. New York: Harper & Bros., 1946.

CHUANG-TSE, ET AL., *Three Ways of Thought in Ancient China*, translated by Arthur Waley. London: George Allen & Unwin, 1939.

DUBOS, RENÉ, *Mirage of Health*. Garden City: Anchor Books, 1959.

DURKHEIM, EMILE, *The Division of Labor in Society*, translated by George Simpson. Glencoe, Illinois: Free Press, 1947.

ELIADE, MIRCEA, *The Sacred and the Profane*, translated by Willard R. Trask. New York: Torchbooks, 1961.

ELLUL, JACQUES, *The Technological Society*, translated by John Wilkinson. New York: Alfred A. Knopf, 1964.

FREUD, SIGMUND, *Civilization and Its Discontents*, translated by Joan Riviere. Garden City: Anchor Books, 1958.

GIEDION, SIEGFRIED, *Mechanization Takes Command*. New York: Oxford University Press, 1948.

HARRISON, JANE, *Themis*. Cleveland: Meridian Books, 1965.

HEISENBERG, WERNER, *Physics and Philosophy*. New York: Torchbooks, 1958.

HUIZINGA, JOHAN, *Homo Ludens*, translator unnamed. Boston: Beacon Press, 1955.

HUXLEY, ALDOUS, *Literature and Science*. New York: Harper & Row, 1963.

JAMES, WILLIAM, *Pragmatism*. New York: Meridian Books, 1955.

JUNG, C. G., *Psychological Types*, translated by H. G. Baynes. New York: Pantheon Books, 1964.

KEYNES, JOHN MAYNARD, *The General Theory of Employment, Interest, and Money*. New York: Harbinger Books, 1965.

KIERKEGAARD, SØREN, *The Present Age*, translated by A. Dru. New York: Torchbooks, 1962.

LAWRENCE, D. H., *Apocalypse*. New York: Compass Books, 1965.

MARX, KARL, and ENGELS, FRIEDRICH, *Basic Writings on Politics and Philosophy*, edited by Lewis S. Feuer. New York: Anchor Books, 1959.

MAY, ROLLO, ANGEL, ERNEST AND ELLENBERGER, HENRI, editors, *Existence*. New York: Basic Books, 1958.

NIETZSCHE, FRIEDRICH, *Thus Spake Zarathustra*, translated by Walter Kaufmann. New York: Compass Books, 1966.

ORTEGA Y GASSET, JOSÉ, *On Love*, translated by Toby Talbot. Cleveland: Meridian Books, 1957.

OTTO, RUDOLF, *The Idea of the Holy*, translated by John W. Harvey. New York: Galaxy Book, 1958.

PLATO, *The Collected Dialogues*, edited by Edith Hamilton and Huntington Cairns. New York: Bollingen Series, Pantheon Books, 1961.

SÉJOURNÉ, LAURETTE, *Burning Water*, translator unnamed. New York: Grove Press, 1960.

SIMEONS, A. T. W., *Man's Presumptuous Brain*. New York: Dutton Paperback, 1962.

SPINOZA, BENEDICT, *Works*, translated by W. H. White. New York: Modern Library, 1935.

STENDHAL, *On Love*, translated by H.B.V., under the direction of C. K. Scott-Moncrieff. Garden City: Anchor Books, 1957.

WATTS, ALAN W., *Psychotherapy East and West*. New York: Pantheon Books, 1961.

WEBER, MAX, *The Protestant Ethic and the Spirit of Capitalism*, translated by R. H. Tawney. New York: Scribner paperback, 1960.

WHITEHEAD, ALFRED NORTH, *Science and the Modern World*. New York: Mentor Books, 1948.

WIENER, NORBERT, *The Human Use of Human Beings: Cybernetics and Society*. Garden City: Anchor Books, 1954.

YEATS, WILLIAM BUTLER, *A Vision*. New York: Macmillan paperback, 1964.

NOTES

NOTICE
Page viii, the scholars met in a symposium on technology and society at the Center for the Study of Democratic Institutions in December, 1965, at Santa Barbara, California.

Chapter 1. OVERTURE: UNOFFICIAL AMERICAN AID TO FRANCE
Page 10. Julien Benda, *La Trahison des Clercs*, translated from the French as *The Treason of the Intellectuals*, Boston, Beacon Press, out of print.

Page 10. McLuhan, *Understanding Media*, New York, McGraw-Hill paperback, 1965.

Page 12. Sullivan, *The Interpersonal Theory of Psychiatry*, New York, W.W. Norton & Co., 1953.

Page 13. McLuhan, *ibid.*, reversal of a less popular attitude toward the media in McLuhan, *The Mechanical Bride*, New York, Vanguard Press, 1951, out of print.

Page 14. Stein, *Capitals, Capitals*, which appeared in 1925 in This Quarter and was later set to music by Virgil Thomson. I heard the music and remembered the line.

Page 14. "Masculine protest" appears in Adler, *op. cit.*

Page 16. For elaboration of the point about shamans see Campbell, *op. cit.*, and Mircea Eliade, *Shamanism*, translated from the French by Willard R. Trask, New York, Bollingen Series, Pantheon Books, 1964.

Chapter 2. ON FINDING ANCIENT ENEMIES IN A MODERN BED
Page 18. Chekhov, *The Cherry Orchard*, translated from the Russian by Tyrone Guthrie and L. Kipnis, Minneapolis, University of Minnesota paperback, 1965.

Page 22. The subway writing was observed by a student of mine, name forgotten.

Page 24. Nietzsche, *The Birth of Tragedy*, translated from the German by Clifton P. Fadiman, New York, Modern Library, undated. William James, *op. cit.*; Carl Spitteler, *Prometheus And Epimetheus*, translated from the German by J. F. Muirhead, London, Jarrold's, 1931; Jung, *op. cit.*; Freud, *Basic Works*, translated from the German by A. A. Brill, New York, Modern Library, undated; Lawrence, *Phoenix*, New York, Viking Press, 1938; William Sheldon, *The Varieties of Temperament*, New York, Harper & Bros., 1954; Karen Horney, *Our Inner Conflicts*, W.W. Norton, 1945; David Riesman with Nathan Glazer and Reuel Denny, *The Lonely Crowd*, Garden City, Anchor Books, 1950.

Page 24. Bernardino de Sahagún, *Historia General de las Cosas de Nueva España*, Mexico City, 1946, quoted by Séjourné, *op. cit.*

Page 25. Séjourné, *op. cit.*

Page 28. The shaman's statement is quoted in Campbell, *op. cit.*, from H. Ostermann, *The Alaskan Eskimos*, Copenhagen, 1952.

Page 31. "Knowledge is power," Francis Bacon, *Meditationes Sacrae*, 1597.

Page 31. "Quiet desperation," Henry David Thoreau, *Walden*, 1954.

Page 31. "Robot" appeared in Karel Ĉapek, *R.U.R.*, 1923.

Page 31. Helena Curtis, *The Viruses*, Garden City, Natural History Press, 1965.

Page 32. The Mandaeans are discussed in Hans Jonas, *The Gnostic Religion*, Boston, Beacon paperback, 1963. For treatment of Gnostic parallels in modern science, see Wiener, *op. cit.* "What Is Alienation? The Career of a Concept," by Lewis S. Feuer, appears in *Sociology on Trial*, edited by Maurice Stein and Arthur Vidich, Englewood Cliffs, New Jersey, Prentice-Hall paperback, 1963.

Page 33. "Hoarse crying in the wilderness," chronic throat complaint of prophets; Isaiah, xl, 3, Matthew, iii, 3; Mark, i, 3; Luke, iii, 4; John, i, 23.

Page 33. "If you can't lick 'em, jine 'em." American political folklore.

Page 34. Ninth Symphony of Ludwig van Beethoven ends with "Ode to Joy" by J. C. F. von Schiller, which salutes multitudes with numerical enthusiasm no longer felt in times of population explosion.

34. Marx predicted the rule of proletarians, *op. cit.*, and Veblen the rule of engineers in *The Engineers and the Price System*, New York, Harbinger Books, 1963.

<h2 style="text-align:center">Chapter 3. FEAR OF THE MARKETPLACE</h2>

Page 37. "Desacralized" appears in Eliade, *op. cit.*

Page 39. Edgar Z. Friedenberg in *The New York Times Magazine*, January 16, 1966. See also his *Coming of Age in America*, New York, Random House, 1965.

Page 41. "The ever normal cookie jar" appears in an article of the same name by W. H. Ferry.

Page 43. Spinoza, *op. cit.*

Page 45. "Soothe as they inform" comes from an article in *The New Yorker* by A. J. Liebling, date and title forgotten.

Page 46. The lines from Dante appear in *Inferno*, Canto III, lines 34–39.

Page 48. José Ortega y Gasset, *The Revolt of the Masses*, translator unnamed, New York, Mentor Books, 1950.

Page 49. Kierkegaard, *op. cit.*

Page 49. For "mind-body split" see Ludwig Binswanger in *Existence*, listed in Bibliography. See also *Existential Psychology*, edited by Rollo May, with essays by Gordon Allport, Herman Feifel, Abraham H. Maslow, Carl R. Rogers, New York, Random House, 1961. For discussion of Descartes see Barrett, *op. cit.* See also Weber, *op. cit.*

Page 51. Baldwin's essay appeared in *Notes of a Native Son,* Boston, Beacon paperback, 1957.

Page 51. Einstein's statement appeared in *Einstein and Peace,* edited by Otto Nathan and Heinz Norton, New York, Simon & Schuster, 1960.

Chapter 4. THE OVERSTUFFED VOID

Page 53. Freud, *Collected Papers,* Vol. 5, London, Hogarth Press, 1949.

Page 53. Otto Rank, *Beyond Psychology,* New York, Dover Books, 1941.

Chapter 5. AZTEC INTO AZTECH

Page 62. Stendhal, *The Red and the Black,* translated by C. K. Scott-Moncrieff, New York, Modern Library, undated.

Page 63. Ellul, *op. cit.*

Page 63. Séjourné, *op. cit.*

Page 64–65. Sahagún, *op. cit.*

Page 66. "The Disease Called Politics," by Theodore Roszak, appears in *Seeds of Liberation,* edited by Paul Goodman, New York, George Braziller Inc., 1965.

Page 66. "Business is no good," appears in *The Letters of D. H. Lawrence,* edited by Aldous Huxley, New York, Viking Press, 1933. The letter is addressed to E. M. Forster.

Page 67. Rainer Maria Rilke, *Letters to a Young Poet,* translated by M. D. Herter Norton, New York, W.W. Norton & Co., 1934. My phrase, however, comes from my retranslation of a French translation.

Page 68. The book by Snow was published by the Cambridge University Press in 1959; the article by Leavis, later published as a book, first appeared in *The Spectator,* London, March 9, 1962.

Page 68–69. Huxley, *The Perennial Philosophy,* New York, Harper & Bros., 1942.

Page 70. Huizinga, *op. cit.*

Chapter 6. HEALTH (PARTICIPATION)

Page 73. Paz, *The Labyrinth of Solitude,* translated from the Spanish by Lysander Kemp, New York, Grove Press, 1961.

Page 76. Rahv, *Image and Idea,* New York, New Directions, 1949.

Page 78. Keynes, *op. cit.,* which raises the question: why does not the New York Stock Exchange erect a monument to him near that which honors George Washington, in front of the Sub-Treasury Building, on Wall Street, and of about the same size? Were not his services to the financial community of at least the same size?

Page 78. "Sullen art" comes from Dylan Thomas, *Collected Poems,* New York, New Directions, 1953.

Chapter 7. SICKNESS (WITHDRAWAL)

Page 83. Gerald Sykes, *The Hidden Remnant,* New York, Harper & Bros., 1962.

Page 86. *Axël*, see *Cruel Tales* by Villiers de L'Isle Adam, translated from the French by Robert Baldrick, New York, Oxford University Press, 1963.

Page 86. Ortega's remark appears in *Notes on the Novel*. See his *Dehumanization of Art*, below.

Page 86. Engels' Law is described by John Wilkinson in his Translator's Introduction to Ellul, *ibid*. It was originally described by Engels in *Anti-Dühring*, New York, International Publishers paperback, 1966.

Page 87. Baudelaire, *Flowers of Evil*, bilingual edition, edited by Marthiel and Jackson Mathews, New York, New Directions, 1955.

Page 88. Sheldon, *op. cit.*

Page 88. D. H. Lawrence, *Women in Love*, New York, Modern Library, undated.

Page 89. William Hazlitt, *Selected Essays*, London, Hogarth Press, 1933.

Page 90. "Travel light" appears in E. M. Forster, *A Passage to India*, New York, Harcourt, Brace & Co., 1924.

Page 91. "The double bind" is from Gregory Bateson, *et al.*, in *Behavioral Science*, October, 1956, and is described by Watts, *op. cit.*

Page 92. The first quotation is from George Herbert Mead. See *The Social Psychology of George Herbert Mead*, edited by A. Strauss, Chicago, Phoenix, 1956.

Page 92. (Second Quotation) Benoit, *op. cit.*

Chapter 8. THE RAINCOAT MIND

Page 94. Whitehead, *op. cit.*

Page 95. Matthew Arnold expressed this idea, in almost the same words, both in *Essays in Criticism*, First Series, 1865, and in *Literature and Dogma*, 1873.

Page 99. The quotation is from Lawrence Lipton in *The Arts in a Democratic Society*, Santa Barbara, The Center for the Study of Democratic Institutions, 1966.

Page 102. The visiting novelist was Stuart Cloete, in conversation with the author.

Page 103. Arthur Schlesinger, Jr., in a book that he edited with Morton M. White, *Paths of American Thought*, Boston, Houghton Mifflin Co., 1963.

Chapter 9. AGAINST THE WEATHER

Page 106 to 109. The quotations are successively from Antonin Artaud, *Lettres de Rodez*, Paris, 1948; Chandler Brossard, *The Bold Saboteurs*, New York, Farrar, Straus & Young, 1953; answer to a questionnaire by *Time*, date and title forgotten; Henry Miller, *A Henry Miller Reader*, edited by Lawrence Durrell, New York, New Directions, 1959; another answer to the *Time* questionnaire; Jack Kerouac, *On the Road*, New York, Viking Press, 1957; another answer to the *Time* questionnaire; Alan Harrington, *Life in the Crystal Palace*, New York, Alfred A. Knopf, 1959; quotation from an adolescent in Jules Henry, *Culture Against Man*, New York, Random House, 1963; tape recording by Corinna Fales, student, during interview with unnamed Negro woman in Newark, New Jersey, 1965; Henri Alleg, *The Question*, translated by John

Calder, New York, George Braziller Inc., 1958; Gustav Herling, *A World Apart*, translated from the Polish by Joseph Marek, with an introduction by Bertrand Russell, New York, Roy Publishers, 1952; Siegfried Giedion, *op. cit.;* Giedion, *op. cit.;* Edward Dahlberg, *Because I Was Flesh*, New York, New Directions, 1963; Brossard, *op. cit.;* William Burroughs, *The Naked Lunch*, New York, Grove Press, 1959; *Tibet and the Chinese People's Republic*, International Committee of Jurists, Geneva, 1960; Harrington, *op. cit.*

Page 110. The story about Flaubert is told by Thomas Mann, *Past Masters*, translated from the German by H. T. Lowe-Porter, New York, Alfred A. Knopf, 1934.

Pages 110-111. The quotations are from *Identity and Anxiety,* edited by Maurice R. Stein, Arthur J. Vidich and David Manning White, Glencoe, Illinois, Free Press, 1960, and includes successive passages from the following authors: Erik H. Erikson; William Earle; Lawrence Kubie; Joseph Bensman and Bernard Rosenberg; Kurt Riezler; I. A. Richards; and Martin Buber.

Pages 111-113. The quotations are from Pablo Picasso, *Statements*, Paris, 1923; Igor Stravinsky, *Poetics of Music*, Cambridge, Mass., Harvard University Press, 1947; William Butler Yeats, *Per Amica Silentia Lunae*, New York, Macmillan, 1918; Lawrence, *op. cit.;* James Joyce, *A Portrait of the Artist as a Young Man*, New York, Viking Press, 1916; Fernand Leger, *Fernand Leger*, Paris, Gouthiers-Seghers, 1956; George Santayana, *The Life of Reason*, New York, Charles Scribners' Sons, 1954; Ludwig Binswanger, *op. cit.;* Jean Cocteau, *Le secret professionel*, Paris, 1924; Simone Weil, *Waiting for God*, translated from the French by Emma Craufurd, New York, G. P. Putnam's Sons, 1951; D. H. Lawrence, *ibid*. The Picasso, Stravinsky, Yeats, Leger, Cocteau and Weil statements are to be found in *The Twentieth Century: The Breaking Up*, edited by Robert Phelps, New York, George Braziller, 1965.

Chapter 10. SACRED, REMOVAL OF THE

Page 120. Eliade, *op. cit.*

Chapter 11. OTHER STUDENTS, OTHER QUESTIONS

Page 125. Sheldon, *Varieties of Delinquent Youth*, New York, Harper & Bros., 1950.

Page 130. Otto, *op. cit.*

Page 131. "Primary" and "antithetical" are important words in Yeats' *A Vision*. See Bibliography.

Chapter 12. SALVATION BY CHECKBOOK (USA)

Page 136-137. Weber, *op. cit.*

Page 139-140. Simeons, *op. cit.*

Page 141. Lawrence, *Studies in Classic American Literature*, New York, Viking Press, 1964.

Page 142. Lawrence, *The Plumed Serpent*, with an introduction by Richard Aldington, London, William Heinemann Ltd., 1959.

Page 142. The references to parties and girls are to be found in David Riesman, *Abundance for What?*, Garden City, Doubleday & Co., 1964.

Page 144. Trofimov's quotation comes from John Donne, *Devotions* (XVII), 1624.

Chapter 13. SALVATION BY ART (FRANCE)

Page 147. The information about Ellul's passage from Marxism to Neo-Calvinism was provided the author by Professor Chaim Perelman, Professor of Philosophy, Free University of Brussels. The interpretation is the author's.

Page 151. Ellul, *op. cit.*

Page 152. Edmund Husserl, *Ideas*, translated from the German by W. D. Boyce-Gibbs, London, G. Allen & Unwin, 1931. See also Barrett, *op. cit.*

Page 152. Jean-Paul Sartre, *Nausea*, translated from the French by Lloyd Alexander, Norfolk, Connecticut, New Directions, 1949.

Page 153. Sartre, *Being and Nothingness*, translated from the French by Hazel E. Barnes, New York, Philosophical Library, 1956.

Page 155. D. H. Lawrence, "How Beastly the Bourgeois Is," in *Selected Poems*, with an introduction by Kenneth Rexroth, New York, New Directions, 1947.

Page 158. Franz Kafka, *The Castle*, translated from the German by Edwin and Willa Muir, New York, Alfred A. Knopf, 1930.

Page 158. Albert Camus, *The Stranger*, translated by Stuart Gilbert, New York, Alfred A. Knopf, 1946.

Page 159. A. Marcel Proust, *Remembrance of Things Past*, translated by C. K. Scott-Moncrieff, New York, Random House, 1927.

Page 159. André Gide, *Corydon*, translated from the French by Hugh Gibb, New York, Farrar, Straus & Co., 1950.

Page 159. Jean Genet, *The Thief's Journal*, translated from the French by Bernard Frechtman, New York, Grove Press, 1964.

Chapter 14. SALVATION BY TEAMWORK (BRITAIN)

Page 162. For "U" and "Non-U" see *Noblesse Oblige*, edited by Nancy Mitford, with essays by Evelyn Waugh, Christopher Sykes, et al., London, Hamish Hamilton, 1956.

Page 163. John Osborne, "Sex and Failure," article in *The Observer*, London, January 20, 1957.

Page 164. Kingsley Amis, *Lucky Jim*, Garden City, Doubleday & Co., 1953.

Page 165. Walter Allen, review of *Lucky Jim*, *The New Statesman*, London, January 30, 1954.

Page 165. Geoffrey Gorer, "The Perils of Hypergamy," article in *The New Statesman*, London, May 4, 1957.

I am indebted to *The Beat Generation and the Angry Young Men*, edited by Gene Feldman and Max Gartenberg, New York, Citadel Press, 1958, for calling my attention to these pieces.

Page 166. Both quotations are from Robert Wraight, "What Is Art Coming To?" article in *Horizon*, New York, Spring, 1966.

Page 170. Durrell, *The Black Book*, New York, E.P. Dutton & Co., 1960.

Page 170. William Blake, *Songs of Innocence*, 1789.

Page 172. Snow, *op. cit.*

Page 173. Leavis, *op. cit.*

Page 173. Trilling, *Beyond Culture*, New York, Viking Press, 1965.

Page 174. Huxley, *op. cit.*

Page 177. "Systematic doubt" was the description by René Descartes of his method.

Page 178. Arnold Toynbee, *A Study of History*, New York, Oxford University Press paperback, 1961.

Chapter 15. SALVATION BY IDEOLOGY (SOVIET UNION)

Page 183. Daniel Bell, *The End of Ideology*, Glencoe, Illinois, Free Press, 1959.

Page 185. Robert Frost, "New Hampshire" (1923)—see his *Complete Poems*, New York, Holt, Rinehart & Winston, 1949.

Page 185. Boris Pasternak, *Dr. Zhivago*, translated by Max Hayward and Manya Harari, New York, Pantheon Books, 1960.

Page 186. Yevgeny Yevtushenko, *A Precocious Biography*, New York, E.P. Dutton & Co., 1964.

Peter Viereck, "The Split Personality of Soviet Literature," article in *The Reporter*, New York, March 15, 1963.

Page 187. Peter Viereck, article in *Tri-Quarterly*, edited by Charles Newman, Evanston, Illinois, Northwestern University, Spring, 1965 issue called "Creativity in the Soviet Union."

Page 187. Yevtushenko, *Poetry*, edited and translated from the Russian by George Reavey, New York, October House, 1963.

Page 187. Cassirer, *op. cit.*

Page 188. Koestler, *The Yogi and the Commissar*, New York, Macmillan Co., 1948.

Page 189. Kenneth Keniston, *The Uncommitted*, New York, Harcourt, Brace & World, 1965.

Page 192. For an educator's response to the excesses of "romantic individualism," see Jacques Barzun, *The House of Intellect*, New York, Torchbooks, 1959.

Page 193. The tennis court rudeness was described in a Kenyon Review article that appeared in 1960 while I was lecturing in German universities. Name of author and article forgotten.

Chapter 16. THE NEW RULING CLASS

Page 199. Luigi Barzini, *The Italians*, New York, Atheneum Press, 1964.

Page 200. Yeats, "A Prayer for Old Age," 1934.

Page 205. Scheer's article was published by The Center for the Study of Democratic Institutions, Santa Barbara, 1965.

Chapter 17. TERROR AND PLAYING IT COOL

Page 208. "Feel Free" is the motto of the same Center.

Page 213. In accordance with the snob-hastened obsolescence of slang that has been mentioned elsewhere in this book, the word "cool" has already, before this goes to press, been replaced by such words as "tough" and "boss." Such protean maneuvers only mean a terror of definition and reality.

Page 215. Herbert J. Seligmann, *Alfred Stieglitz Talking*, New Haven, Yale University Library, 1966.

Chapter 18. WHAT CAN BE DONE FOR THIS WOMAN?

Page 220. To avoid possible identification of "Nellie Rankin," she appears here in an imaginary production of a play by Giraudoux. Actually she appeared in a production of a play by another French author.

Pages 223–224. Sykes, *op. cit.*

Page 226. Mirabeau, *L'Ami des Hommes ou la Traité de la Population*, See also Lucien Febvre, *Civilisation, Le Mot et l'Idee*, 1757. Paris, Centre International de Synthèse, 1930.

Page 227. Robert Graves, *The Greek Myths*, New York, George Braziller Inc., 1959.

Page 228. Jane Harrison, *op. cit.*

Page 228. See also Siegfried Giedion, *The Beginnings of Art*, Volume I of *The Eternal Present*, translated by Ralph Manheim, Bollingen Series, Pantheon Books, 1962.

Page 230. C. G. Jung, *Two Essays on Analytical Psychology*, translated by R. F. C. Hull, New York, Bollingen Series, Pantheon Books, 1953.

Page 230. Simeons, *op. cit.*

Page 230. Emma Jung, "On the Nature of the Animus," paper published by the Analytical Psychology Club, New York, undated, from which the following is quoted:

"From time to time we hear it said that there was no necessity for woman to occupy herself with spiritual or intellectual matters, that this is only an idiotic aping of man, or a competitive instinct betraying megalomania. If this is indeed true in many cases, nonetheless this explanation of the matter is inadequate. Neither arrogance nor presumption drives us to the audacity of wanting to be like God—that is, like man. We are not like Eve of old, lured by the beauty of the fruit of the tree of knowledge, nor does the snake encourage us to enjoy it. No, there has come to us a command, a necessity that compels us to bite into this apple, whether we think it good to eat or not. What we have to face is that the paradise of naturalness and unconsciousness, in which many of us would only too gladly tarry, is gone forever." The rest of her paper is a detailed examination of this theme, too long and too intricate for quotation here.

Page 230. In connection with the discovery that technicization means less time for love, for taking a genuine interest in other persons, the student may wish to consider two books about love that were written by men who did not suffer from a lack of leisure and therefore could treat their subject with some of the imaginative attention it deserves. The books are both called *On Love;* both are listed in the Bibliography, and their authors are Stendhal and Ortega y Gasset.

Chapter 19. THE GRIEVANCES OF WEALTH

Page 235. For the comments of a man who works daily with a large group of computers, see Hasan Ozbekhan, *Technology and Man's Future*, a paper published by the System Development Corporation, Santa Monica, California, 1966, from which the following is quoted: "Technology . . . cannot dictate outcomes. What does dictate those outcomes is moral choice, and it is precisely with a moral choice of an extremely practical kind that we are confronted to-day. Whether we shall be able to face up to it, define it and act on it depends on our capacity to change our ethic and infuse it with new values. This involves difficult emotional and intellectual adjustments. Only such adjustments, however, can free us from our traditional politics of means and lead us to the higher levels of a politics of ends."

Page 243. "Rather inconsequential" comes from Keniston, *ibid*.

Page 244. The information about Coe College and Cambridge University was received by the author in conversation with the then C. P. Snow.

Chapter 20. THE DEATH OF CHAOS

Page 247. The quotation is from Chuang-tse, *op. cit.*

Page 249. Durrell, Clea, New York, E. P. Dutton & Co., 1960.

Page 250. For treatment of "the forces of death," see Norman O. Brown, *Life Against Death*, Middletown, Connecticut, Wesleyan University Press, 1959. See also Weber, *op. cit.*

Page 253. The story was told the author by Mike Gold.

Page 254. *The Breaking Up* is the subtitle of Phelps, *ibid*.

Page 254. "Art art" is a phrase used by Ortega y Gasset in *The Dehumanization of Art*, translated from the Spanish by Helen Weyl, Princeton, Princeton University Press, 1948.

Page 257. "Wholly other" appears in Otto, *op. cit.* In his German it is called the *"ganz andere."* To George Brantl I am indebted for the information that in medieval Latin it was wittily described as *"totaliter aliter."*

Page 258. Nietzsche, *op. cit.*, Bibliography.

Page 258. The discussion of Chaos and homelessness would not be understood by anyone who failed to appreciate that those who do accept homelessness and face Chaos are inevitably penalized, and penalized heavily, for their courage. They assume not only the legal obligations that all citizens must assume; they also take on additional obligations that are moral, aesthetic and philosophic, perhaps also religious. They freely impose upon themselves, or have imposed upon them by their talents, *extra* disciplines that other men— men of affairs and men of state, as well as prudent artists and scientists— most carefully avoid. The dealer who sells a painting has only to meet the demands of the law. The man who paints it may also take on burdens that nearly all of his contemporaries would now prefer to forget.

INDEX

Abraham, 228
Abundance for What? 142n
Addams, Jane, 229
Adler, Alfred, 14, 115, 247
Aeschylus, 227
Africa, 104
Algeria, 13, 51, 232
Alleg, Henri, 107
Allen, Walter, 165
Allport, Gordon W., 49n
Altamira, 227
Americans, 1, 58, 138, 148, 176
Amis, Kingsley, 164
Arnold, Matthew, 95
Artaud, Antonin, 106
Art Nouveau, 216
Asia, 41, 97, 104
Associated Press, 97
Auschwitz, 187
Avant-garde, 15f, 156, 214 *et seq.*, 253
  et seq.
Axël, 86
Aztecs, 5, 23, 62 *et seq.*

Bacon, Francis, 31
Baldwin, James, 51, 172
Barrett, William, 49n
Barzini, Luigi, 199
Barzun, Jacques, 192n
Basic Works of Sigmund Freud, 24
Bateson, Geoffrey, 91n
Baudelaire, Charles, 79, 87, 247
*Beat Generation, The & The Angry
  Young Men*, 165n
Beatles, 163, 177
Beauvoir, Simone de, 136
Because I Was Flesh, 108
Beckett, Samuel, 115, 196
Beethoven, Ludwig van, 34, 37, 187, 231
Beginnings of Art, The, 228n

Bell, Daniel, 183
Benda, Julien, 10
Benedictines, 4
Benoit, Hubert, 92, 115
Bensman, J., 111
Berdyaev, Nicolas, 115
Bergson, Henri, 38
Bernhardt, Sarah, 215
Beyond Culture, 173
Beyond Psychology, 53n
Bible, 32n, 144, 189, 227
Binswanger, Ludwig, 49, 112, 115, 205
Birth of Tragedy, The, 24
Bizet, Georges, 215
Black Book, The, 170
Blake, William, 170
Bohr, Nils, 38
Bold Saboteurs, The, 106
Bonn, University of, 190
Boris Godunov, 188
Brancusi, Constantine, 252
Brantl, George, 257n
Brave New World, 2
Britain, 74, 162f, 196
Bronowski, Jacob, 73
Bronx, 86
Brooklyn Bridge, 66, 216
Brossard, Chandler, 106, 109
Brothers Karamazov, The, 188
Brown, Norman O., 250n
Brownsville, 254
Brussels, Free University of, 147n
Buber, Martin, 111
Buchanan, James, 27
Buddha, 47
Buffet, Bernard, 184
Burgundy, 150
Burroughs, William, 108, 172

California, 60, 147

California, University of, at Berkeley, 36, 127
Calvin, Jean, 32, 45
Campbell, Joseph, 16, 28
Cambridge University, 249
Camus, Albert, 115, 158, 237
Capek, Karel, 31
Capitals, Capitals, 14n
Caribbean, 7
Cartier-Bresson, Henri, 136
Cassirer, Ernst, 115, 189
Cassatt, Mary, 229
Castle, The, 158
Castro, Fidel, 7, 205
Catholic Church, 74
CBS, 40
Center for the Study of Democratic Institutions, 205n, 208
Cézanne, Paul, 231
Chase Manhattan Bank, 79
Chase, Salmon P., 74, 79
Chekhov, Anton P., 18, 87, 126, 215
Cherry Orchard, The, 18, 87
China, 78, 104, 118, 190, 227
Christ, 32, 37, 47, 129, 188, 227
Christianity, 56, 61, 94, 129, 231
Chrysler Motors Corp., 186
Chuang-tse, 24f
Churchill, Winston, 169
Churriguera, 145
Clea, 249
Cloete, Stuart, 102
Coe College, 244
Cocteau, Jean, 112
Coleridge, S. T., 74
Colette, 226
Coming of Age in America, 39n
Communists, 9, 138, 251
Computers, 93, 235
Copernicus, 94
Cortés, Hernán, 26, 62, 105
Corydon, 159
Coventry, 171
Crystal Palace, 216
Cuba, 7, 27, 78, 205
Cubism, 216
Cuernavaca, 25
Culture Against Man, 107n
Cumberland Gap, 122
Curie, Madame, 229
Curtis, Helena, 32

Dada, 157
Dahlberg, Edward, 108
Daily Worker, The, 253
Dante, 46, 219
Darwin, Charles, 27

Dehumanization of Art, The, 254n
Democracy in America, 153
Denny, Reuel, 24n
Descartes, René, 49, 177
Detroit, 171
Dewey, John, 115, 133
Dickens, Charles, 163, 169
Diotima, 227
Disneyland, 188
Dnieperstroy, 76
Donne, John, 144
Dostoevsky, F. M., 37, 115, 184, 188
Dove, Arthur, 215
Dublin, 38
Dubos, René, 20
Dubuffet, Jean, 184
Duhamel, Georges, 136
Du Pont, 50
Durkheim, 115, 196, 247
Durrell, Lawrence, 170, 249
Duse, Eleanora, 215

Earle, William, 111
East Hampton, New York, 85
Edison, Thomas A., 133
Education Sentimentale, 110
Eiffel Tower, 66, 216
Einstein, Albert, 51
Eisenhower, Dwight D., 205
Eliade, Mircea, 16, 37, 118 *et seq.*
Eliot, T. S., 77, 115, 192
Elizabeth I, 175
Elizabeth II, 175
Elizabethans, 15
Ellul, Jacques, 2 *et seq.,* 63, 147, 161
Engels, Friedrich, 86, 124f
Engineers and the Price System, 34n
"Equal in Paris," 51
Erikson, Erik H., 110
Essays in Criticism, 95n
Eternal Present, The, 228n
End of Ideology, The, 183n
Eton, 171
Euripides, 227
Existentialism, 56, 112, 153
Existential Psychology, 49n

Fales, Corinna, 107n
Fascism, 9
Feifel, Herman, 49n
Feldman, Gene, 165n
Ferry, W. H., 41
Feuer, Lewis S., 32n
Fielding, Henry, 163
Flaubert, Gustave, 38, 110, 125
Flowers of Evil, 79n
Ford, Henry, 122, 153

Ford Motor Co., 186
Forster, E. M., 66n, 90n
France, 2 *et seq.*, 145 *et seq.*
Franklin, Benjamin, 11, 136, 155
Frazer, James G., 115, 120
Freud, Sigmund, 12, 24, 53, 115, 184, 212, 247
Freudianism, 56
Friedenberg, Edgar Z., 39
Fromm, Erich, 115
Frost, Robert, 79, 185
Fulbright, J. William, 201

Galileo, 94, 186
Gartenberg, Max, 165n
Gaulle, de, Charles, 153
General Electric Co., 201
General Motors Corp., 62, 186
Genet, Jean, 159, 172
George III, 168
Georgia, 86
Germany, 104, 188f, 249
Gide, André, 159
Giedion, Siegfried, 108, 115, 228n, 247
Gilbert, W. S., 169
Giraudoux, Jean, 220n
Glazer, Nathan, 24n
Gnosticism, 32
Gnostic Religion, The, 32
Goethe, J. W. von, 193
Gold, Mike, 253n
Golden Bough, The, 120
Goodman, Paul, 66n
Gorer, Geoffrey, 165
Gorki, Arshile, 67
Gounod, Charles, 215
Graves, Robert, 227
Greek Myths, The, 227
Griboyedov, A. S., 85
Guggenheim Museum, 187
Gutenberg, Johann, 127, 189

Hamlet, 33, 35
Harlan, James, 75
Harrington, Alan, 107
Harrison, Jane, 228
Hartley, Marsden, 215
Harvard College, 59
Haw Haw, Lord, 163, 177
Hazlitt, William, 89
Heidegger, Martin, 115, 158, 247
Hemingway, Ernest, 77
Henry VIII, 162
Henry, Jules, 107n
Herling, Gustav, 108
Hidden Remnant, The, 83n, 140
Hitler, Adolf, 46, 80, 167, 182, 193

Ho Chi Minh, 205
Holbein, Hans, 162
Holmes, Justice Oliver W., 248, 254
Homo Ludens, 70n
Homosexuality, 158f
Horney, Karen, 24, 115, 196
House of Intellect, The, 192n
Huizinga, Johan, 70n
Husserl, Edmund, 152
Huxley, Aldous, 68, 69, 174
Hyde Park, 79

Ibsen, Henrik, 228
Idea of the Holy, The, 130
Ideas, 152n
Identity and Anxiety, 110–111
Idiot, The, 37
Image and Idea, 76n
India, 74, 170, 227
Inferno, 46, 219
Interpersonal Theory of Psychiatry, The, 12n
Italians, The, 199
Itzcoliuqui, 26

James, Henry, 76, 94
James, William, 6, 24, 62, 94, 131
Japan, 74, 227
Jefferson, Thomas, 4
Jews, 140
Job, 211
Johnson, Lyndon B., 97
Johnson, Samuel, 62
Jonas, Hans, 32
Joplin, Missouri, 78
Joyce, James, 37–8, 112, 113, 115, 252
Judaism, 61
Jung, C. G., 24, 115, 131, 184, 230, 247
Jung, Emma, 230

Kafka, Franz, 115, 158, 252
Kant, Immanuel, 193
Keniston, Kenneth, 189, 243
Kennedy, John F., 79, 201
Kenyon Review, 132
Kerouac, Jack, 107
Kerr, Clark, 36, 121
Keynes, John Maynard, 78, 97, 100
Kierkegaard, Sören, 32, 49, 115, 247
Kipling, Rudyard, 163
Koestler, Arthur, 188
Koran, 187
Kubie, Lawrence, 111

Labyrinth of Solitude, The, 73n
Lao-tse, 47
Lascaux, 227

Latin America, 104, 145
Law, William, 69
Lawrence, D. H., 26, 50, 66, 89, 113, 141f, 142, 155, 204, 252
Leaves of Grass, 75
Leavis, F. R., 68, 77, 173f
Léger, Fernand, 112
Lenin, Nikolai, 182
Letters to a Young Poet, 67
Liebling, A. J., 45n
Life Against Death, 250n
Life in the Crystal Palace, 107n
Life of Reason, The, 112
Lincoln, Abraham, 78, 86
Lipton, Lawrence, 99
Literature and Dogma, 95n
Lonely Crowd, The, 24n
Loren, Sophia, 200
Los Angeles, 73
Lucky Jim, 164
Luddites, 33
Luther, Martin, 189

McCarthy, Joseph, 201
McCarthy, Mary, 147
MacDougal Street, 92
McLuhan, Marshall, 10, 13, 115
Machiavelli, Niccolo, 58
Mad, 40
Malraux, André, 153
Mandaeans, 32
Mann, Thomas, 110, 252
Marin, John, 215
Marx, Karl, 32, 34, 115, 123, 124f, 247
Marxism, 56, 102
Maslow, Abraham H., 49n
Matisse, Henri, 126, 252
May, Rollo, 49n
Mayakovsky, Vladimir, 76
Mead, George Herbert, 83, 92
Mechanical Bride, The, 12n
Melville, Herman, 184
Meyerhold, Vsevolod, 187
Mexico, 5, 25 *et seq.,* 63 *et seq.*
Mies van der Rohe, 70
Milan, 199
Miller, Henry, 107
Milton, John, 74
Mirabeau, Victor, Marquis de, 226
Misfortune of Being Clever, The, 85
Mitford, Nancy, 162n
Moctezuma, 64, 67, 217
Moldau, 31
Morris, William, 74
Moscow, 187
Mumford, Lewis, 238
Murasaki, Lady, 226

Mussolini, Benito, 46, 182
Mussorgsky, Modeste, 188
Myshkin, Prince, 37

Nahuatl, 24
Naked Lunch, The, 108n
Naples, 199
Napoleon, 171
Nausea, 152
Nazism, 9, 188
Negroes, 43, 62, 88, 104, 134, 201
New Jersey, 236
Newman, Charles, 187n
New Mexico, 241, 253
New Orleans, 147
Newsweek, 40
New York, 22, 26, 45, 60, 235
New Yorker, The, 45n
Nietzsche, Friedrich, 24, 115, 247, 258
Nimes, 150
Noblesse Oblige, 162n
Northwestern University, 209n
Notes of a Native Son, 51n
Notes on the Novel, 86n

Oaxaca, 145
O'Keeffe, Georgia, 215
On the Road, 107n
Op Art, 42
Ortega y Gasset, José, 48, 86, 230n, 254n
Osborne, John, 163
Ostermann, H., 28n
Otto, Rudolf, 130, 257
Our Inner Conflicts, 24
Ozbekhan, Hasan, 235n

Paris, 8, 160
Partisan Review, 59
Pasternak, Boris, 115, 185
Past Masters, 110
Paz, Octavio, 72
Péguy, Charles, 115
Per Amica Silentia Lunae, 112
Perelman, Chaim, 147n
Perennial Philosophy, The, 69
Phelps, Robert, 113n
Phoenix, 24n
Picasso, Pablo, 111, 113, 231, 252
Pierce, Charles Sanders, 6, 62
Plato, 47, 117, 231
Plumed Serpent, The, 142
Poetics of Music, 111
Pop Art, 156, 256
Portrait of the Artist as a Young Man, A, 112
Pragmatism, 5, 97, 104, 192, 307
Precocious Autobiography, A, 209n

Prokofiev, Serge, 187
Prometheus and Epimetheus, 24n
Proust, Marcel, 159, 252
Puccini, Giacomo, 215
Puerto Ricans, 45, 62

Quebec, 146f
Queequeg, 85
Question, The, 108
Quetzalcoatl, 25, 227

Rahv, Philip, 76
Rank, Otto, 53, 115
Readers Digest, 59
Reavey, George, 186n
Red and the Black, The, 62
Reed, John, 192
Remembrance of Things Past, A, 159, 232
Revolt of the Masses, The, 48
Rexroth, Kenneth, 155n
Richards, I. A., 111
Riesman, David, 24, 142
Riezler, Kurt, 111
Rilke, Rainer Maria, 67, 115, 247, 252
Rio Grande, 25
Robot, 31
Rockefellers, 153
Rogers, Carl R., 49n
Roosevelt, Eleanor, 229
Rosenberg, Bernard, 111
Rossetti, Dante Gabriel, 74
Roszak, Theodore, 66n
Rousseau, Jean-Jacques, 32
R.U.R., 34n
Russell, Bertrand, 106n

Sacre du Printemps, Le, 185
Sahagun, Bernardino de, 25, 64
Santayana, George, 112
St. Lawrence River, 147
Sarah Lawrence College, 86
Sardou, Victorien, 215
Sartre, Jean-Paul, 115, 136, 151f
Scheer, Robert, 205
Schiller, J. C. F. von, 34n
Schlesinger, Arthur, Jr., 103
Schoenberg, Arnold, 252
Scriabine, Alexandre, 185
Seeds of Liberation, 66n
Séjourné, Laurette, 25, 63 *et seq.*
Seligmann, Herbert J., 215n
Shakespeare, William, 30, 37
Shamanism, 16n
Shamans, 16, 23, 27
Shaw, George Bernard, 228
Sheldon, William, 24, 88, 125, 131

Shelley, Percy Bysshe, 101
Sica, Vittorio de, 200
Simeons, A. T. W., 139f, 264
Snow, C. P., 68, 77, 172f, 197, 199B, 244n
Sociology on Trial, 32n
Socrates, 5, 47, 117, 227, 231
Songs of Innocence, 170
Sophocles, 227
Sordi, Alberto, 200
Soviet Union, 55, 58, 67, 75 *et seq.,* 104, 127f, 182 *et seq.,* 196, 249
Spain, 190
Spengler, Oswald, 115, 247
Spinoza, Baruch, 10, 43, 126
Spitteler, Carl, 24, 131
Stalin, 76
Stanislavski, Constantine, 187
State Department, 85, 143
Stein, Gertrude, 14
Stein, Maurice, 110n
Stendhal, 62, 90, 103, 125, 230n
Sterne, Laurence, 74
Stieglitz, Alfred, 215
Strand, Paul, 215
Stranger, The, 158, 179B
Stravinsky, Igor, 37, 112, 113, 252
Studies in Classic American Literature, 141
Study of History, A, 178n
Sullivan, Harry Stack, 12, 115, 196
Sykes, Christopher, 162n
Sykes, Gerald, 83, 223f

Teotihuacan, 63
Theatre, 210
Thief's Journal, The, 159
Thomas, Dylan, 78n
Thomson, Virgil, 14n
Thoreau, Henry David, 31n, 74
Tibet, 108
Time, 50, 106n
Times, The New York, 39n
Tocqueville, Alexis de, 76, 103
Tolstoy, Lvov, 196, 231
Toltecs, 5, 24, 64
Toynbee, Arnold, 115, 178, 247
Treason of the Intellectuals, The, 10n
Trilling, Lionel, 173
Tri-Quarterly, 187n
Tristan and Isolde, 231
Trotsky, Leon, 138
Troubadours, 15
Turgenev, Ivan, 188
Turner, J. M. W., 215
Twentieth Century, The: The Breaking Up, 254n

Two Cultures?, 68n
Two Cultures, The, and the Scientific Revolution, 68n
Two Essays on Analytical Psychology, 230n

Unamuno, Miguel de, 115, 136
Uncommitted, The, 189, 243n
Understanding Media, 10, 12
United States, 1, 51, 68, 95, 102, 132, 141, 190, 196
Utah, 254

Valéry, Paul, 115, 252
Varèse, Edgard, 36
Varieties of Delinquent Youth, 125
Varieties of Temperament, 24
Vassar College, 142, 148
Veblen, Thorstein, 34, 115, 196
Verdi, Giuseppe, 215
Vesalius, Andreas, 94
Victoria, Queen, 27
Viereck, Peter, 187
Viet Nam, 13, 41, 70f, 205
Vidich, Arthur, 111n
Village Voice, The, 60
Villiers de l'Isle Adam, 86
Virgil, 219
Viruses, The, 32n

Wagner, Richard, 215, 231
Waiting for God, 112
Walden, 74
Waldteufel, Emile, 215
Waley, Arthur, 247n
Washington, 75
Waterloo, 162

Watts, Alan, 91n
Waugh, Evelyn, 162n
Weber, Max, 26, 49, 136f, 205, 247, 250n
Weil, Simone, 112
Wellington, Duke of, 162, 171
"West Kentucky Wesleyan," 59
White, David Manning, 111n
Whitehead, Alfred North, 94f, 104, 115, 196
White House, 89, 242
Whitman, Walt, 74f
Wichita, Kansas, 97
Wiener, Norbert, 32n
Wilkinson, John, 86n
Williams, Tennessee, 167
Wittgenstein, Ludwig, 115, 196
Women, 222 *et seq.*
Women in Love, 89
Woolworth, 62
World Apart, A, 108n
Wraight, Robert, 166n

Xenophon, 47

Yannuitlan, 145
Yeats, William Butler, 30, 51, 112, 113, 131, 196, 204, 247, 252
Yevtushenko, Yevgeny, 186
Yogi and the Commissar, The, 188n
Young Men's Hebrew Association, 187
Yugoslavia, 35, 196

Zen, 53, 74
Zeus, 228
Zhivago, Dr., 185
Zurich, 70, 200